Water Transportation
in Canada

Water Transportation in Canada

Robert J. McCalla

Formac Publishing Company Limited
Halifax, 1994

This book has been published with the help of a grant from the Social Science Federation of Canada, using funds provided by the Social Sciences and Humanities Research Council of Canada.

Canadian cataloguing in Publication Data

McCalla, Robert J., 1947–
Water transportation in Canada

Includes bibliographical references.
ISBN 0-88780-247-8 (bound).

1. Shipping — Canada. I. Title.
HE769.M33 1994   387. 00971   C94-950029-1

Formac Publishing Company Limited
5502 Alantic Street
Halifax, Nova Scotia B3H 1G4

Printed and bound in Canada

CONTENTS

List of Figures   **Page**

List of Tables   **Page**

List of Abbreviations

b/d   barrels (of crude oil) per day. A barrel of crude oil is approximately 160 litres, 35.6 gallons (Imperial), 42 gallons (US) or 0.136 tonnes. The unit of measure describes the output of a producing oil well or the refining capacity of an oil refinery.

dwt   deadweight tonnage. The total load in tonnes of cargo, fuel, stores and ballast that a ship can carry. It is the normal unit of measure for the size of bulk carriers and tankers.

grt   gross registered tonnage. The cubic capacity of the permanently enclosed space on a ship measured at 100 cubic feet to a ton. It is the normal unit of measure for the size of passenger ships, ferries and cargo liners (container ships).

LASH   Lighter Aboard Ship. A cargo-carrying system involving the carriage of barges (lighters) aboard a specially built 'mother' ship.

lo - lo   lift on-lift off. A term which refers to both cargo and the ship carrying such cargo. Cargo is lifted on or lifted from the ship by cranes either mounted on the ship or on the dock. The term is used in contrast to ro - ro (see below).

LNG   Liquid Natural Gas.

OBO   Ore - Bulk - Oil carrier. A type of bulk carrier that can carry—on different voyages—ore, other bulk cargoes (such as grain or potash), or oil.

ro - ro   roll on - roll off. A term that refers to both cargo and a type of ship. Cargo rolls on or rolls off the ship on tires. The term is used in contrast to lo - lo (see above). Some ships have the capability to handle both ro - ro and lo - lo cargoes.

teu   twenty-foot equivalent unit. The unit of measure to describe the carrying capacity of a container ship. Most containers are 20 or 40 feet long. A forty-foot container would be two teus.

ULCC   Ultra Large Crude Carrier. The designation given to the very largest crude oil tankers. A common, although not official, standard for ULCC designation is a tanker over 400,000 dwt.

VLCC   Very Large Crude Carrier. The designation given to large crude oil carriers with a commonly accepted carrying capacity of between 200,000 and 400,000 dwt.

INTRODUCTION

SETTING THE SCENE

Although Canada is one of the major deep-sea trading nations of the world, most Canadians do not think of their country as one in which the oceans and inland waterways play a fundamental role. People have a sense of the great Canadian landmass; they do not appreciate that Canada fronts on three oceans and on the largest inland waterway system in the world. If Canadians know anything about their geography, they know that their country is the second largest in the world; few realize that Canada has the longest coastline of any country, as well. Canada, indeed, is a maritime nation.

The transportation industry has tried to overcome the sheer size of the country by providing land and air connections between East and West, North and South. Railroads have been recognized as the transportation mode which opened Canada to agricultural and industrial development and, in fact, enabled this nation to exist at all. Thus many people appreciate trains for sentimental reasons, even if they do not use them. Paved roads are a development of this century and with the universal adoption of the motor car and technological breakthroughs in truck designs, the importance of road transportation is taken for granted. Air transportation is another creation of this century. In the span of less than eighty years Canada has gone from the Silver Dart[1] to regularly

[1] The Silver Dart was the first plane flown in Canada. John McCurdy piloted the flight on the shores of Bras d'Or Lake in Nova Scotia in 1909.

scheduled jet service to every corner of the country. So people know about planes.

But what of ships and ports, of the Welland Canal, the St. Lawrence Seaway, the Mackenzie River? Does the Canadian public know that Thunder Bay is the largest fresh water grain port in the world? That the Great Lakes enable ocean going vessels to penetrate a distance of 4,000 kilometres into the interior of North America— the same distance as that between London, England and the Ukraine in the former Soviet Union? That the Port of Vancouver is the largest dry cargo port on the West coast of all the Americas—North, Central and South? Montreal is the furthest inland port in the Northern Hemisphere regularly serviced year-round by ocean-going vessels, and Halifax has one of the finest natural harbours in the world. The shipping industry (with its attendant infrastructure) is vital to the economy of this country.

Consider these economic facts for 1989:

- water transportation handled more exports by value ($32 billion) than rail ($27 billion) or air ($9 billion)

- water transportation handled $28 billion worth of Canadian exports to deep-sea (i.e., non-USA) destinations out of the total of $36 billion taken by all modes (Statistics Canada 65–202 and 54–205)

- ports under the umbrella of the Canada Ports Corporation (15 ports in all) created over 65,000 direct and induced jobs; in 1990, close to 400,000 Canadian jobs were related to industry whose cargo was shipped via the Canada Ports Corporation system (Canada Ports Corporation, 1991).

Clearly, water transportation is big business in Canada, and it merits geographical analysis.

In its most general sense, geography is the study of the surface of the earth as the home of mankind; but in more specific terms, geography is the study of the location of human activity as it is affected by, and affects, its physical and human environments. Transportation is one such activity, but the geography of transportation separates its subject into two main interests: the activity itself, and the infrastructure supporting that activity.

The geography of water transportation activity includes the study of the trade patterns of goods as they move through ports, in ships and along and across the waterways around the world. Many people have seen an example of this type of analysis in maps of world oil movement that focus attention on the Persian Gulf. Such maps mark the origins and destinations of the world's oil and the pattern of its movement between these places. But what determines which oil goes where? Obviously many factors are involved: economics, politics and the physical distribution of the resource contribute to trade decisions. These factors influence not only the oil trade, however; they also affect all major trades handled in international and coastwise shipping. Grain trade, coal, potash, and the container trades are but a few of the other "activity " interests which are a part of the geography of water transportation.

All of this activity requires a supporting infrastructure of ports, ships and waterways. The aim of geographical analysis is to describe the infrastructure and to attempt to explain the reasons for its location and how it has changed, as well as to record what influence it has had in the location of other human activity. For example, a geographer would be interested in describing the port, its location, and its facilities, where the facilities are located, and how they fit into the larger rural and urban environment of which the port is a part. The function of the port would be examined: Is the port a terminal for incoming cargoes which are consumed in manufacturing processes, such as oil refining and steel making? Or is the port a gateway that facilitates the passage of raw materials to and from an inland hinterland? Is there a demand by other interest groups in the city to have access to the waterfront which is occupied by port facilities? Has this demand generated conflict? What is being done to resolve it?

Similarly, in considering waterways geographers would be interested in their physical characteristics—depth, length, width, adjoining bodies of water—and the influence that these waterways have on trade development. A shortened distance between continents reduces transportation costs, for instance, and has economic ramifications. Waterways can have strategic importance, as well, controlling the passage of ships between inland bodies of water and the open sea, or between oceans. Thus geography has the overall responsibility of describing and understanding the surface of the earth; transportation geography particularly focuses on patterns and effects of transportation activity and infrastructure.

Time is an important factor in the study of transportation geography, too. Changes over time bring about new trade links and new infrastructure. The last thirty years have witnessed a revolution in shipping technology, port development and cargo handling. Gone are the "old" days of small ships owned by individuals and their companies, of stevedoring gangs unloading vessels piece by piece, and congested waterfronts of finger piers, small sheds and narrow roadways. The shipping world today is more often than not characterized by large, specialized vessels under the control of shipping conglomerates or consortiums; by highly mechanized cargo handling at the dock side; and by large deep-water docks with specialized storage areas for the cargoes they handle.

The transport of bulk oil cargo, for example, has been transformed with the development of the mammoth crude carriers of over 250,000 deadweight tonnes (dwt) and even over 500,000 dwt with drafts of over 20 metres. The former has been given the acronym of VLCC (Very Large Crude Carrier); the latter is referred to as ULCC (Ultra Large Crude Carrier).[2] Dry bulk carriers that transport iron ore, coal, and grain have also surpassed the 200,000 dwt threshold. Vessels have been designed to carry either oil and ore, bulk, or ore (OBO ships). The development of these new ships has necessitated changes in ports and waterways which otherwise could not accommodate them. The carriage of general cargo has undergone, perhaps, a greater revolution. Containerization—the development of a standardized box to carry the myriad of commodities referred to as general cargo (shoes, books, clothes, electronic goods, processed food, automobile parts, and thousands of other products) on a standardized ship—has meant that goods move quickly from one continent to another.

These revolutions in ships not only affect the movement of goods on the seas, but they affect the path of the entire transportation infrastructure, from origin to destination. Consequently, inland terminals have been developed to handle more efficiently the cargoes destined for or coming from tidewater ports; railroads have adopted larger hopper cars or specialized container cars and specialized unit trains are the norm today. But it is at the port interface that the effect of the new shipping technology has been most felt. Wholesale changes to existing port facilities or entirely new port facilities have been built away from the original port sites to accommodate the new ships. Changes in the location of the service sector associated with ports

---

[2] Other special names are given to today's vessels, depending on the cargo they carry and how they carry it. There are ro-ro ships and lo-lo ships; there are OBO and LASH ships (see List of Abbreviations for details). There is even a new designation of cargo, referred to as neo-bulk, that contrasts with dry bulk, wet bulk or break bulk. All of this new terminology was unknown in 1960.

have also taken place with movement away from central waterfronts to locations either nearer the new docks or to positions in new central business districts. The latter have been created through urban renewal, which includes changes to old waterfront land. Labour, in turn, has declined in ports because of the switch to capital-intensive ships and cargo handling.

That these changes occurred is due not only to the desire of the shipping industry itself to maximize profits or to increase the quality of service, but also to the great increase in demand for shipping services. Transportation is a "derived demand": its level of operation is determined by the many industries, resource producers and consumers which pay for its use. In and of itself, transportation can do little to increase the overall demand for its services. Individual companies may attract new traffic because of lower rates or increased service, but this new traffic is usually created at the expense of the company that presently handles it. Real increases in transportation demand occur when growth in resource production, industrial output or consumer affluence increases trade. In the past thirty years, world trade has increased enormously because of such growth. Resource production has expanded within established areas, and has been developed in new areas often far removed from the place of consumption. Worldwide industrial expansion has also taken place; much of what the western world consumes originates in the developing nations of Asia, Africa and South America—all of which have established well-designed export processing industries. And finally, there are simply more affluent people now than ever before who increase the demand for goods that are not indigenous to where they live. So trade has expanded and, consequently, the demand for shipping services has grown. These changes are universal and not confined to one country, but in individual countries specific events have occurred since 1960 to bring about further changes in shipping.

THE CANADIAN CONTEXT

In Canada, specific events have occurred since 1960 that have created further changes in shipping. Developments in the resource sector of the economy, for example, have included the search for Arctic resources of oil and gas, lead, zinc and nickel; and thus the increased significance of a Northwest passage has effected fundamental changes in shipping in that area. The expansion of agricultural production, especially wheat and barley, has created a new infrastructure for the movement of products from the Prairies to where they are needed—which may be anywhere in the world. The mining of coal and iron ore for the raw materials needed by Canadian and international industries has required that new railroads, new ports and new ships be created.

Changes have occurred in other sectors as well. Since 1960 the Canadian population has increased from almost 18 million to over 27 million (in 1991). Canadians continue to move from rural areas to the cities, and urbanization has increased the general wealth of people. These demographic changes have increased the demand for food, raw materials, industrial output and services which are supplied via ocean and domestic shipping, in conjunction with the other modes of transportation. In addition, the waterways now service the recreational demands of Canada's increasingly affluent people.

The key components of change in Canadian shipping and port activity will be addressed in Part I of this study, which will show that, between 1960 and 1989,

- waterborne trade has increased substantially, especially in the international sector;

- in international trade there has been a shift away from the USA and the UK as important export nations, to be replaced by nations in Asia. For imports, the USA is still very important, as are European nations;

- the important commodities traded in international waterborne trade are raw materials; coal shows the greatest growth in export goods;

- containerized goods are now a major export and import of Canadian waterborne trade;

- the number of ships using Canadian ports is down, but their tonnage is up;

- the number of ports in Canada has declined.

In order to address these changes in Canadian water transportation, the book is organized into two major sections. Part I begins with a look at the connection between water transportation and the economy, followed by a chapter outlining the activity of the industry, and another on the infrastructure. Part II focuses on particular developments in Canadian ports and shipping: Chapter 4 concerns the rise of containerization and focuses on Saint John and Halifax as rivals for the new trade. Chapter 5 discusses the issue of changing relationships between ports and the cities they occupy as exemplified by waterfront land development in Montreal. An assessment of the St. Lawrence Seaway is provided in Chapter 6. Chapter 7 concerns cruise shipping development at Vancouver, particularly, but also at other Canadian ports. Chapter 8 addresses the sovereignty shipping claims of Canada in the waters of the Canadian Arctic archipelago. The book concludes by summarizing the developments in Canadian water transportation, with an eye to the future.

The Canadian shipping scene is a dynamic one. The industry of the 1990s is very different from that of the 1960s in almost all of its aspects. Although many of the same ports exist now as did 30 years ago, and although ships still carry Canadian raw materials and manu-factured goods to all parts of the world and return with imports, Canadian water transportation has changed drastically in terms of what cargo is carried, where it is taken and what impact it has on the local and national economy. The geography of water transportation in Canada in the 1990s is a changing geography, and this study aims to suggest where the changes might take this maritime nation next.

PART 1

A GEOGRAPHY OF CANADIAN WATER TRANSPORTATION

CHAPTER 1

THE IMPORTANCE OF THE WATER TRADE

THE VALUE OF WATER TRADE

International trade is vital to the well-being of Canada, and much of that trade is accomplished using water transportation. An influential report on deep-sea shipping written in the mid-1980s estimated that one-third of Canadian jobs were directly related to the export of resource and manufactured products. The report stated that "the relationship between shipping services and the export of goods and commodities is symbiotic. They will either flourish or perish together" (Transport Canada, 1985, 1). Figure 1.1 shows the increasing value of Canadian exports and imports since 1960. Canadian merchandise exports transported by all modes have grown from $5 billion in 1960 to $134 billion in 1989 in current dollars. Imports have followed the same growth trend, but in recent years have been measured below export values, giving Canada a favourable balance of trade in merchandise.[1] Export and import values, compared to the Canadian Gross Domestic Product, have been rising, albeit unsteadily, over time (see Figure 1.2). In 1989 exports as a per cent of GDP stood at 20.6, in contrast to 14.6 per cent in 1960; imports were valued at 20.7 per cent of GDP in 1989, compared with 15.3 per cent in 1960. In the mid-1980s, exports as a proportion of the Canadian GDP peaked at close to 25 per cent.

It is possible to chart the changing contribution of water trans-

---

[1] In 1989, the value of imports exceeded exports, though, for the first time since 1975.

Figure 1.1
Value of Canadian Domestic Exports and Imports

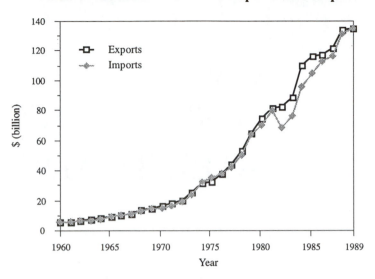

Source: Statistics Canada (65–202 and 65–203)

Figure 1.2
**Canadian Domestic Exports and Imports as a
Per Cent of Canadian GDP**

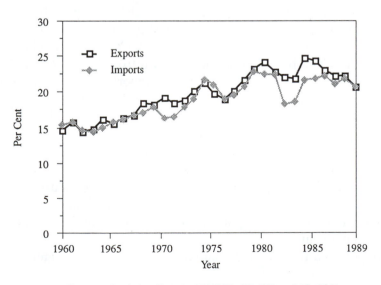

Source: Statistics Canada (65–202, 65–203 and 13–201)

Figure 1.3
Per Cent of Canadian Exports by Value by Mode

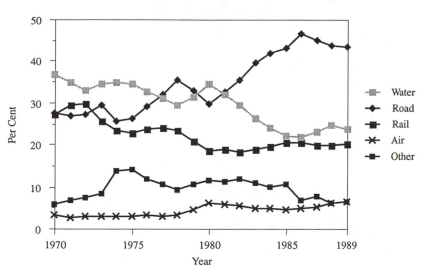

Source: Statistics Canada (65–202)

portation to Canadian exports since 1970 (the first year information on export values by mode was published), but modal split statistics for imports remain unpublished to date. Figure 1.3 shows the proportion of Canadian exports handled by water in terms of value. The water mode is still used to transport a significant percentage of Canadian exports, even though it has lost ground to road transportation in recent years due to increased trans-border trade with the USA. Approximately 24 per cent of all Canadian exports were transported by water in 1989, making it the second most popular mode used behind road (truck) transport at 43 per cent. As Canadian exports have changed from high-bulk, low-value raw and semi-processed materials to low-bulk, high-value manufactured materials, road transport has played a greater role. In monetary terms: the water mode handled $31.7 billion worth of Canadian exports in 1989; road, $58.3 billion; rail, $27.1 billion; air, $8.8 billion; and other (including pipelines), $8.7 billion.

In order to understand fully the water mode's contribution to Canadian trade it is necessary to break down the exports into USA and non-USA (deep-sea) trade. Since 1970 the USA has become more important as a destination for Canadian exports (see Figure 1.4). Slightly less than three-quarters of the value of Canadian exports went to the USA in 1989, while one-quarter went to deep-

Figure 1.4
Canadian Exports by Value per USA and
Deep-Sea Destinations

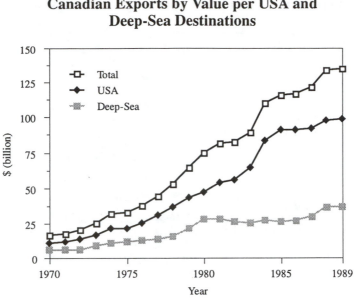

Source: Statistics Canada (65–202)

sea destinations. In 1970 the distribution of exports was less heavily
weighed in the USA's favour.

As one would expect, the water mode is more important in handling exports to non-USA destinations than to the USA; there is relatively little alternative to shipping goods overseas, since air transport
can be prohibitively expensive.

The proportion of Canadian exports to the USA which is handled
by water has been declining slowly but steadily since 1970 (see
Figure 1.5). The total amount of goods exported by water to the USA
is relatively small, and amounted to close to $4 billion in 1989. The
importance of water transport to Canadian deep-sea exports is another story, however. In the deep-sea trade of 1989, water handled
approximately $28 billion of the $36 billion in Canadian exports. In
decreasing importance, air ($5.1 billion), road ($2.6 billion) and rail
($0.4 billion) shared the remaining exports (see Figure 1.6). The fact
that both road and rail are shown to handle deep-sea exports is
explained by the fact that these modes carried the goods outside of
Canada to an American port, where they were then exported either by
water or air to an overseas ultimate destination. So although it has
lost ground somewhat to other modes (especially air), water transportation continues to dominate Canada's deep-sea trade.

Figure 1.5
Per Cent of Canadian Exports to USA
by Value per Mode

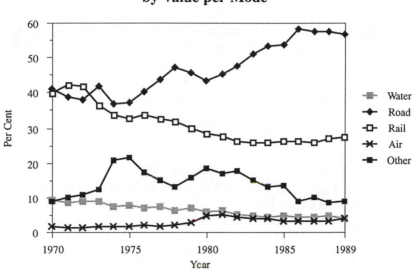

Source: Statistics Canada (65–202)

Figure 1.6
Per Cent of Canadian Deep-Sea Exports to
USA by Value per Mode

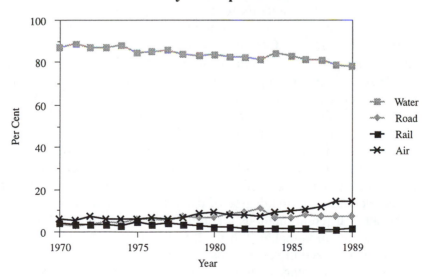

Source: Statistics Canada (65–202)

So what does all this mean? How can we summarize the changing importance of water transportation to the Canadian economy? It can be said that:

- Trade is vital to the Canadian economy and becoming more so. Canadian export and import values relative to the Canadian Gross Domestic Product have been rising over time.

- The water mode has declined in relative importance in terms of export value carried, and is losing ground to road transport, particularly in the USA trade.

- In the deep-sea trade, the water mode continues to carry about 80 per cent of all Canadian exports. In absolute terms the value of exports carried by water to overseas countries has increased from $5 billion in 1970 to $28 billion in 1989 in current dollars.

Thus, in the final analysis, water transportation is essential to Canada. It enables the country to participate in international (especially deep-sea) trade, and it also is vital to domestic transportation (see Chapter 2). A detailed look at the tonnages and commodities traded in international and domestic water transportation follows.

THE TONNAGE OF WATER TRADE

Although it is advantageous to measure the importance of water transportation in value terms, problems are posed by a lack of data. A value breakdown of Canadian imports by the different modes of transport is not available (though export breakdowns have been kept since 1970). There are no published figures on the value of Canadian trade handled by Canadian ports, either; only tonnage figures are available. But this is not unusual. Most countries report their port activities in terms of weight and not value; there is a universal standard for reporting in tonnes, and no such standard exists for reporting in value terms. The latter is subject to different methods of evaluation because the exchange rates of currencies fluctuate; because prices rise and fall, according to the degree of demand and supply of the goods; and because different methods are used by each evaluator. Moreover, inflation or deflation makes it difficult to interpret long-term trends in trade when analyzed in value terms.

There are advantages and disadvantages to reporting trade using either measure. Weight, which is easy to measure in constant units,

Figure 1.7
Canadian Waterborne Trade by Tonnage

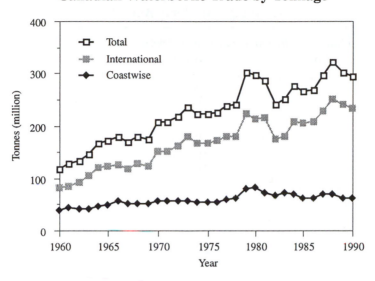

Source: Statistics Canada (54–202, 54–204, 54–205, 54–209 and 54–210)

highlights the importance of raw materials shipped in bulk (such as grain, or iron ore, or crude petroleum); but weight measures tend to de-emphasize the importance of the high value-per-unit weight for break bulk cargoes. Conversely, value, which is not easy to measure and lacks consistency, elevates the status of break bulk goods while the value of the bulk commodities is minimized. Statistically, an accurate study of the growth of Canadian waterborne trade since 1960 must make use of the universal standard: the tonne. Table 1.1 cites key components of change in Canadian shipping and port activity, as measured in tonnes.

Since 1960 waterborne commerce in Canada has been characterized by an expansion and internationalization of foreign trade markets, especially exports, and a relative stagnation of domestic trades. In 1960 the total Canadian waterborne trade was 118.3 million tonnes (see Figure 1.7). This figure includes the international loaded and unloaded cargoes at Canadian ports and the tonnages loaded in the coasting trade; coastwise trade is counted only once, as a "loaded transaction" (to count it again as "unloaded" would distort the actual amounts of cargo transported in coastwise shipping).

In 1990 the total Canadian waterborne trade was 292.7 million tonnes. Although this figure is 2.5 times higher than the 1960 tonnage, the highest Canadian waterborne trade record was set in 1988

Table 1.1:
Important Measures of Change in Canadian
Shipping and Ports Activity

Total cargo tonnes (millions) in waterborne trade

	Coastwise[1]	International	Combined
1960	36.992	81.311	118.303
1989	62.006	239.387	301.393

Important Trading Partners

a. Exports — % of Exports Going to:

	USA	Deep-Sea
1960	48.7	51.3
1989	27.3	72.7

% of Deep-Sea Exports Going to:

	UK	Europe	Asia and Oceania	Other
1960	43.7	28.1	19.1	8.1
1989	9.0	26.8	51.0	13.2

b. Imports — % of Imports Coming from:

	USA	Deep-Sea
1960	55.3	44.7
1989	48.9	51.1

% of Deep-Sea Imports Coming from:

	UK	Europe	Asia and Oceania	Other
1960	7.2	5.9	4.4	82.5
1989	17.6	25.4	8.5	48.5

Important Commodities Traded in International Trade (million tonnes)

a. Exports

	Wheat	Iron Ore	Coal	Containerized
1960	6.247	17.042	0.451	0
1989	12.041	31.968	32.314	6.681

b. Imports

	Crude Petroleum	Coal	Containerized
1960	6.305	9.758	0
1989	18.509	15.289	5.418

Number of vessel movements at Canadian Ports

	Coastwise	International	Combined
1960	238,977	68,173	307,150
1989	57,046	58,787	115,833

.../ cont'd

Table 1.1 (cont'd)

Net Registered Tonnage (million) of Vessels Calling at Canadian Ports

	Coastwise	International	Combined
1960	173.772	152.480	326.252
1989	157.606	363.600	521.206

Number of ports engaged in waterborne trade

	Coastwise Only	International Only	Coastwise and International	Total
1960	63	17	169	249
1989	68	50	120	238

Canada's Largest Port (by cargo tonnes in millions)

	Coastwise	International	Combined
1960	Montreal[2] (7.549)	Montreal[2] (9.811)	Montreal[2](17.360)
1989	Thunder Bay (9.698)	Vancouver (60.530)	Vancouver (63.753)

[1]Loaded tonnes only
[2]Montreal includes Contrecoeur

Source: Statistics Canada (54–202, 54–204 and 54–205)

Figure 1.8
Per Cent of Coastwise and International Tonnages in Waterborne Trade

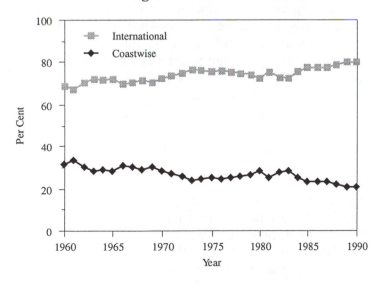

Source: See Figure 1.7

when 320 million tonnes of cargo were moved. The steep trade decline in the early 1980s correlates with the recession of that time. A similar decline has occurred since 1988.

Figure 1.8 shows the international and coastwise components as percentages of total trade. Over the past thirty years the proportion of international trade has gradually increased; in 1990 it comprised almost 80 per cent of the waterborne trade total.

a) International Trade

The international portion can be broken down further into loaded and unloaded cargoes: loaded cargoes can be thought of as exports from Canada, whereas unloaded cargoes are the equivalent of imports. As Figure 1.9 shows, loaded cargoes tend to dominate the international waterborne trade. The increasing dominance of loaded vs. unloaded cargoes should come as no surprise, since we know that exports dominate Canadian international waterborne trade. In 1980, in fact, Canada ranked eighth (equal to the then USSR) among the world seaborne trading nations in terms of international tonnages handled. In exports alone, Canada ranked fifth behind Saudi Arabia, the USA, Australia and the USSR (Couper, 1983, 144–45). Dominant Canadian exports, discussed in Chapter 2, include iron ore, grains, coal and other dry bulk commodities ideally suited to long-haul international shipping.

Another useful differentiation in Canadian international waterborne transportation is that between USA (or trans-border trade) and what can be termed deep-sea shipping, both to and from non-USA destinations and origins. Figure 1.10 shows that the deep-sea trade now dominates that of the USA in Canada's international waterborne trade. This change is highly significant since it shows that much of the increase in Canadian international trade is due to the expansion of new markets overseas, and not to trade with the USA. The last thirty years have witnessed the "internationalization" of Canadian waterborne trade, largely in terms of exported cargoes. Figure 1.11 shows this rise in deep-sea loaded (exported) cargoes.

b) Coastwise Trade

With its four marine areas—the Atlantic coast, the Great Lakes, the Pacific coast and the Arctic—Canada has the longest coastline in the world. Prior to 1983, Statistics Canada reported coastwise shipping statistics for only three areas: the Atlantic coast and St. Lawrence River up to and including Montreal; the Great Lakes and St. Lawrence above Montreal; and the Pacific coast. The Arctic shipping

Figure 1.9
Per Cent Loaded and Unloaded Tonnages in
International Waterborne Trade

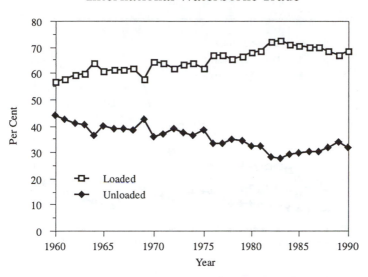

Source: Statistics Canada (54–202, 54–205 and 54–209)

Figure 1.10
Per Cent USA and Deep-Sea Tonnages in
Canadian International Waterborne Trade

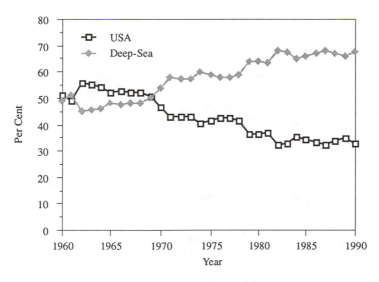

Source: See Figure 1.9

Figure 1.11
Deep-Sea Portion of Canadian International
Waterborne Trade

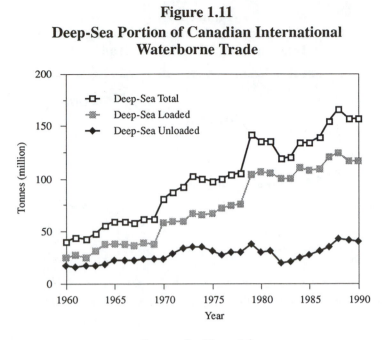

Source: See Figure 1.9

Figure 1.12
Canadian Coastwise Trade Showing Loaded
Tonnages in Each Region

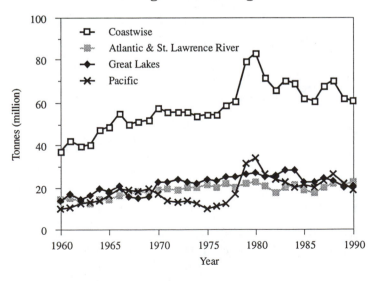

Source: Statistics Canada (54–204, 54–205 and 54–210)

statistics were included in the Atlantic and St. Lawrence River area. Since 1983, coastwise shipping statistics have been published separately for the Atlantic region (Gulf of St. Lawrence, Bay of Fundy and Atlantic Ocean ports) and the St. Lawrence River (from Havre St. Pierre up to and including Montreal).

Figure 1.12 shows the annual tonnage moved in coastwise shipping since 1960. The peak year of the period was 1980 (83 million tonnes); the low was recorded in 1960 (37 million tonnes). In recent years the tonnages have been consistently close to 60 million.

The rise and fall of the coastwise tonnage mainly can be accounted for by activities on the Pacific coast. Cargoes shipped on the Great Lakes and the East coast have increased slightly over this period, with some fall off in the 1980s, but the real fluctuation in domestic shipping has occurred on the Pacific coast: a dramatic rise in the late 1970s has been followed by a persisting decline in annual tonnes traded there. The health of the forest industry and the method of data collection for coastwise shipping are contributing factors. The principal commodities transported by water on the Pacific coast are logs, pulpwood, wood chips and petroleum products (see Chapter 2). If the forest industry is healthy, the movement of logs, pulpwood and wood chips along the coast is great; with a stagnant or declining forest industry, as was the case in the early to mid-1980s, trade obviously suffers. However, Statistics Canada altered the shape of the graph when, in 1979, it expanded the base on which it reports coastwise shipping statistics. Since then the operations of tugs, barges, scows and ferries have been collected on a separate form (Statistics Canada, 54–210, 1979, ix). Since much of the log movement on the Pacific is by tugs towing booms, a great deal of new traffic was recorded and a dramatic rise in Pacific coast coastwise shipping was thus seen in 1979. Of course, the total tonnage in Canadian coasting trade also increased by the same amount.

SUMMARY

In summary, then, Canada's international waterborne trade has grown in weight at a faster rate than its coastwise trade: the former represents close to 80 per cent of Canadian waterborne trade. International loaded cargoes—exports—dominate unloaded cargoes, or imports. The deep-sea trade has taken over that of the USA as the most important component of international waterborne trade. The "internationalization" of Canadian waterborne trade is largely accounted for by growth in non-USA exports, and not in imports. Coastwise shipping has also expanded over time, though not to the same extent as the international portion of the industry; all three regions—the Atlantic and the St. Lawrence River, the Great Lakes, and the Pacific coast—contribute almost equally to the annual tonnages moved in coastwise shipping.

In order to understand more fully the tonnage changes discussed in this chapter, detailed discussions follow on the amount of commodities handled as exports, as imports, and as domestic coastwise trade.

CHAPTER 2
WATER TRANSPORT ACTIVITY

EXPORTS

Canadian waterborne exports are dominated by dry bulk cargoes—especially iron ore, wheat and coal, but also barley, gypsum, potash and similar materials.[1] Since 1960, iron ore, wheat and coal have constituted approximately 50 per cent of all exports handled by water transportation. In recent years (1987 to 1990), the combined proportion of these goods has been slightly less than one half.

Of the three principal dry bulk commodities, iron ore was always the most important by weight until recent years. Up until 1989, in fact, iron ore was the dominant single commodity exported.[2] In 1989 and 1990, iron ore lost its top rank to coal exports. The 1990 loaded tonnages of the three commodities were: iron ore, 29.2 million; wheat, 18.4 million; and coal, 30.9 million. Detailed information about each of the three commodities as well as other important exports follows.

a) Iron Ore

Figure 2.1 shows the iron ore foreign loadings (exports) since 1960. After spectacular growth throughout the 1960s and 1970s, declining

---

[1] Goods handled in containers do not make up a large portion of waterborne exports by weight. Containerized exports have accounted for only between 2.1 and 4.2 per cent of Canadian waterborne annual exports since 1975.

[2] In 1982, however, iron ore exports dropped substantially, corresponding to the weakened worldwide demand for iron and steel products. Iron ore mines in Quebec - Labrador were closed for three to five months during the last part of 1982.

Figure 2.1
International Iron Ore Loadings,
1960–1990

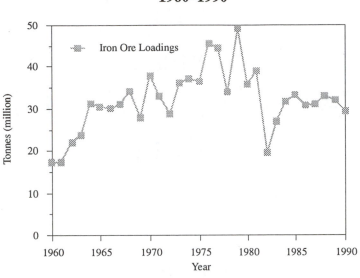

Source: Statistics Canada (54–202, 54–205 and 54–209)

exports were noted in the late 1970s and bottomed in 1982. Since that time there has been slight improvement.

Canadian iron ore exports are determined by growth and decline patterns in the world steel industry, especially in the American sector. Since 1960 world steel production has grown from 379.7 million tons to a peak of 862.6 million tons in 1989 *(Statistical Abstract of the United States, 1990)*. In the early 1980s the industry suffered a severe cutback in production; the world total was only 710.7 tons in 1982 after the earlier high of 824.5 million tons in 1979. In the United States the peak years for steel production were 1973 and 1974, with 150.8 and 145.7 million tons produced respectively. Since that time, however, production has fallen to below the 1960 level of 99.1 million tons, reaching a low, in 1982, of 74.6 million (with some recovery to 99.9 million tons in 1988).

Thus the peaks and troughs in the Canadian iron ore export graph can be accounted for by worldwide and American trends in steel production. However, other export-reducing factors are also at work: strikes in iron ore mining (such as the 1969 and 1972 strikes in the Quebec - Labrador iron ore mines); world competition (Brazil and Australia have each opened large iron ore mines for export of ore to Japan and Europe); and shifts in company policy for iron ore acquisi-

Table 2.1:
Regional Loadings of Iron Ore for Export for Selected Years

1960

	A&SLR[1]	GtLks[2]	Pac[3]	Total
mt[4]	12.4	3.6	1.0	17.0
%	73.0	21.1	5.9	100.0

1970

	A&SLR	GtLks	Pac	Total
mt	32.0	4.1	1.6	37.7
%	84.9	10.9	4.2	100.0

1980

	A&SLR	GtLks	Pac	Total
mt	34.3	0.9	0.6	35.8
%	95.8	2.5	1.7	100.0

1990

	A&SLR	GtLks	Pac	Total
mt	29.1	0.1	<0.1	30.6
%	99.8	0.2	<0.01	100.0

[1] Atlantic and St. Lawrence River ports
[2] Great Lakes ports
[3] Pacific Ocean ports
[4] million tonnes

Source: Statistics Canada (54–202, 54–211 and 54–205)

tion (American steel makers who own iron ore mines in both Canada and northern Michigan and Minnesota particularly affect Canadian trade).

Canadian loading sites for ore have also changed over the years. As Table 2.1 shows, iron ore has been exported from ports in all regions, although the relative importance of these exporting areas has changed. Exports through Sept Iles and Port Cartier, the major iron ore handling ports in the Atlantic and St. Lawrence River area, now dominate the trade. The decline of trade in the Great Lakes region was caused by the closure in 1979 of the Steep Rock mine (near Atikokan); Steep Rock had used Thunder Bay as an export port to serve American markets.

Foreign markets for Canadian iron ore have also changed over

Figure 2.2

Foreign Destinations of Iron Ore Exports for Selected Years

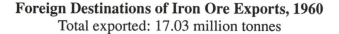

Foreign Destinations of Iron Ore Exports, 1960
Total exported: 17.03 million tonnes

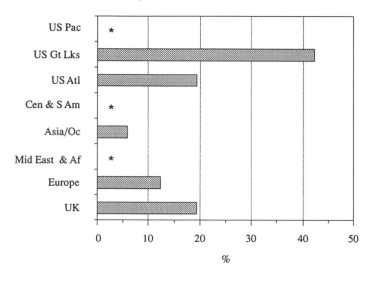

Foreign Destinations of Iron Ore Exports, 1970
Total Exported: 37.69 million tonnes

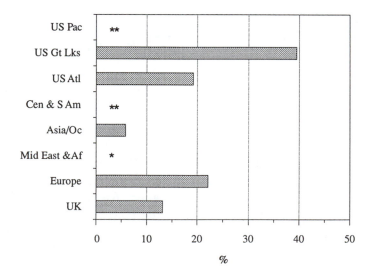

.../cont'd

Figure 2.2 (cont'd)
Foreign Destinations of Iron Ore Exports, 1980
Total exported: 35.83 million tonnes

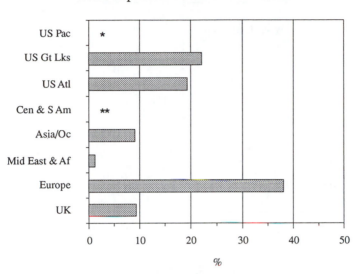

Foreign Destinations of Iron Ore Exports, 1990
Total exported: 29.23 million tonnes

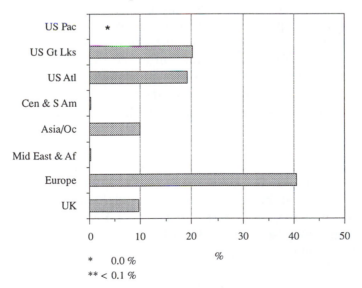

*   0.0 %
** < 0.1 %

Source: Statistics Canada (54–202, 54–205 and 54–209)

Figure 2.3
International Wheat Loadings, 1960–1990

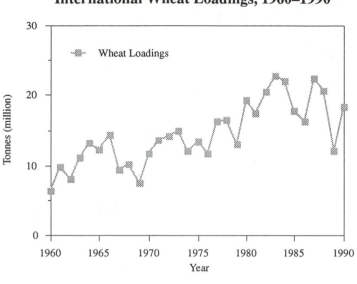

Source: See Figure 2.1

time. In 1960 the United States was the destination of 62 per cent of the exports; 42 per cent was destined for USA Great Lakes steel-making centres alone (see Figure 2.2). Over time the American market has become less important to Canadian trade, while European markets have become more so. Iron ore trade has been "internationalized"; ore is now sent to all populated continents of the world. It is interesting to note that Asia and Oceania, represented primarily by Japan, have increased their share of the market, but at the same time Canadian West coast ports handle almost no iron ore exports. Instead, the eastern ports of Sept Iles and Port Cartier have been sending additional iron ore to Japan to compensate for the decline in Canadian western port loadings.

b) Wheat

Canada's second most important export commodity by water has typically been wheat but, in recent years (since 1984), wheat has fallen to third in export ranking behind iron ore and coal. Figure 2.3 shows that wheat exports have risen steadily from 1960, although there have been many setbacks along the way. Exports peaked at close to 23 million tonnes in 1983 and 1987.

Many factors contribute to the amount of Canadian wheat exported in any one year. Crop yields both at home and overseas will determine how much wheat is available for export on domestic and global scales. Canadian and international government policies for the buying and selling of wheat, and for wheat production subsidies and sales, determine price levels and demand for exports. Canadian transportation systems (including railroads, elevator operators and domestic shipping on the Great Lakes) determine the rate at which the wheat moves from farm to tidewater, and the availability of ocean-going ships affects the time it takes for wheat to reach overseas markets. A strike or bottleneck of any kind in this system will slow down wheat exports or even curtail them altogether.

Major dips in the wheat export graph shown in Figure 2.3 can be explained by a number of factors. The 1967 crop was affected by drought conditions during early growing stages, and even though Canada planted a record wheat acreage, production was down by over 25 per cent (Canadian Wheat Board, 1967–68). In 1974 the Canadian grain crop was down 18 per cent because of cool, wet weather in the spring, which delayed planting (Canadian Wheat Board, 1974–75); the 1975 crop was adversely affected by rain in the harvest period. The 1984–85 crop was affected by severe drought, especially in southern Alberta, southern Saskatchewan and southwestern Manitoba. However, not only poor crop production accounted for these declines in wheat exports. In 1976 and 1985, for example, record crops were experienced in the traditional markets for Canadian wheat (the then USSR, China, India and Pakistan); thus the demand for Canadian wheat declined. One reason for recent decreases in wheat exports is that the fiercely competitive nature of the marketplace has intensified. The USA and the EEC have attempted to increase and/or regain their export market through the use of subsidies which have, in effect, kept down the price of their wheat, and reduced Canadian exports as well.

The fact that Canada has the ability to export over 20 million tonnes of wheat per year demonstrates a remarkable achievement of transportation, given that the great wheat growing areas of Canada are found in the interior provinces of Alberta, Saskatchewan and Manitoba. Getting the wheat to overseas markets involves trucks, trains and finally ships. Principally there are five export points in Canada for Canadian wheat: Thunder Bay at the head of Lake Superior moves wheat directly overseas; the Lower St. Lawrence River ports of Montreal and below are secondary or indirect ports, since grain is trans-shipped from them after completing the voyage from Thunder Bay; the Atlantic coast ports of Saint John and Halifax are also indirect export points, from which grain is trans-shipped after a rail or Lakes - rail journey from Thunder Bay; Churchill on Hudson

Table 2.2:
Regional Loadings of Wheat for Export for Selected Years

1960

	A&SLR[1]	GtLks[2]	Pac[3]	Total
mt[4]	3.3	0.4	2.6	6.3
%	52.4	6.3	41.3	100.0

1970

	A&SLR	GtLks	Pac	Total
mt	7.6	0.1	4.0	11.7
%	65.0	0.9	34.1	100.0

1980

	A&SLR	GtLks	Pac	Total
mt	12.4	0.4	6.5	19.3
%	64.2	2.1	33.7	100.0

1990

	A&SLR	GtLks	Pac	Total
mt	8.0	0.6	9.8	18.4
%	43.5	3.4	53.1	100.0

[1] Atlantic and St. Lawrence River ports
[2] Great Lakes ports
[3] Pacific Ocean ports
[4] million tonnes

Source: See Table 2.1

Bay is a direct export point, as are, finally, the West coast ports of Vancouver and Prince Rupert. Trans-shipment through St. Lawrence River ports has traditionally handled the bulk of the exports but, since 1987, Pacific coast ports have been handling more than 50 per cent of all wheat exports. Table 2.2 shows regional tonnage percentages of exported wheat for selected years.

It should be noted that the Atlantic and St. Lawrence River total includes wheat moved through Churchill. Typically, Churchill has been a minor player in the wheat trade, handling far less than a million tonnes in any year (and, in some years, handling no wheat at all, but only barley). On average, the St. Lawrence River ports of Montreal, Sorel, Trois Rivières, Quebec, Baie Comeau and Port Cartier have handled about 95 per cent of the wheat exported through the Atlantic and St. Lawrence River region between 1982 and 1990; Halifax and

Saint John have handled the remainder. On the Pacific coast, Vancouver's exports have traditionally dominated the wheat trade, but it has lost some of the throughput to Prince Rupert where, in 1985, a new grain elevator was opened. Prior to 1985, Vancouver handled 85 to 90 per cent of wheat exports through the Pacific coast; in recent years, that amount has dropped to around 70 per cent.

The worldwide markets for Canadian grain have remained relatively stable since 1970. In the 1960s, Canada negotiated large wheat sale contracts with the then USSR and China. Consequently, the Asian market grew considerably when, during the same period, the United Kingdom market decreased. Figure 2.4 shows that the UK market for wheat changed from representing one-third of all exports in 1960 to less than 2 per cent in 1990. European destinations for wheat exports have also declined in number. These statistics indicate export percentages for each initial foreign destination of the wheat, and the use of feeder services from Europe to the UK, for example, are not accounted for in the figures. Since 1970 Asia and Oceania, Central and South America, the Middle East and Africa have all expanded their portions of the Canadian wheat export market. The industry has internationalized the Canadian market for wheat, exporting a smaller percentage to the UK and Europe and distributing the available tonnage elsewhere.

c) Coal

Canada is unusual in that, for primarily geographical reasons, it is both a major importer and exporter of coal. Imports are moved across the Great Lakes from the Appalachian region of the United States, and are destined for steel mills and coal-burning power stations in Ontario, whereas exports from mines in British Columbia and Alberta leave Canada's West coast destined principally for Japan. 1981 was a significant year for the Canadian coal trade because then, for the first time, exports exceeded imports and Canada became a net exporter of coal (*Canadian Minerals Yearbook,* 1981, 11.13).

As Figure 2.5 shows, there was rapid growth in the export of coal until the early 1980s, when an international economic lull and a decline in world steel production prevented any further rise in exports. However since that time, exports have reached new heights due to the operation of new mines in northeastern British Columbia and at Hinton, Alberta. New coal-handling port facilities have been built in Prince Rupert, and Roberts Bank has been expanded, as well. The coal handled now is both metallurgical and steaming (the latter is used for thermal generation of electricity).

Figure 2.5 shows the rapid rise in coal loadings in Canada begin-

Figure 2.4
Foreign Destinations of Wheat Exports for Selected Years

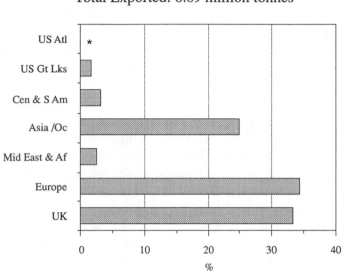

Foreign Destinations of Wheat Exports, 1960
Total Exported: 6.09 million tonnes

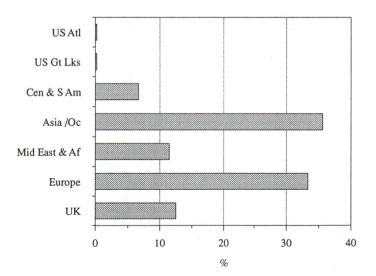

Foreign Destinations of Wheat Exports, 1970
Total exported: 11.67 million tonnes

.../ cont'd

Figure 2.4 (cont'd)
Foreign Destinations of Wheat Exports, 1980
Total exported: 19.23 million tonnes

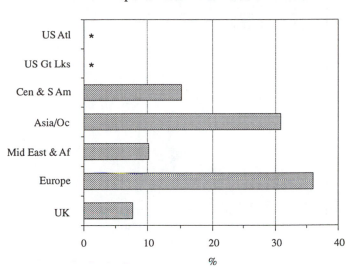

Foreign Destinations of Wheat Exports, 1990
Total exported: 18.44 million tonnes

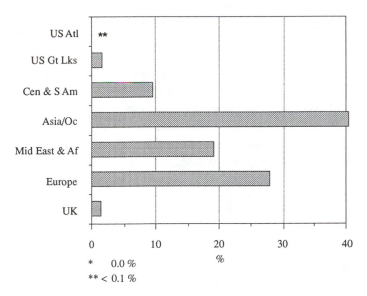

*   0.0 %
** < 0.1 %

Source: Statistics Canada (54–202, 54–205 and 54–209)

Figure 2.5
International Coal Loadings, 1960–1990

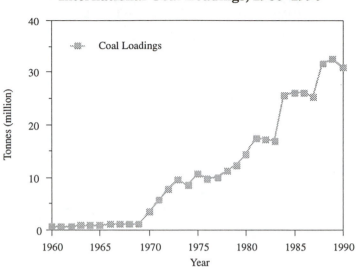

Source: See Figure 2.1

ning in the late 1960s. Up until 1960, very little Canadian coal entered foreign trade. On the East coast, there was a small export trade from Nova Scotia to St. Pierre and Miquelon. Almost all of the coal mined in British Columbia was exported to Japan, but the amounts were small (less than 500,000 tonnes). Between 1967 and 1972, major mines were opened in southeast British Columbia (in the Kootenay area) and in the foothills area of Alberta for the sole purpose of supplying the Japanese steel industry with metallurgical coal. The first large contract was granted by Japanese steel producers to Coleman Collieries (Coleman, Alta): 13.3 million tons over 15 years, beginning in 1967.[3] This was soon followed by long-term contracts with Kaiser Resources (Natal, B. C.) for 75 million tons, Cardinal River Coals (Luscar, Alta.) for 15 million tons, Canmore Mines (Canmore, Alta.) for 3.8 million tons, McIntyre Coal Mines (Grand Cache, Alta.) for 30 million tons, and Fording Coal (Elk River, B.C.) for 45 million tons (*Canadian Minerals Yearbook,* 1969, 171). To handle these increased exports, new port facilities were built at Roberts Bank, Vancouver.

The market for Canadian coal is largely dependent upon Asia and especially Japan, which receives about two-thirds of Canadian coal exports (see Figure 2.6). Australia continues to be the chief supplier of coal to Japan, but in 1984 Canada replaced the United States as the second largest supplier of metallurgical coal to the Japanese steel

---

[3] Tons, and not tonnes, are used here to correspond with the original contract units.

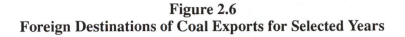

Figure 2.6
Foreign Destinations of Coal Exports for Selected Years

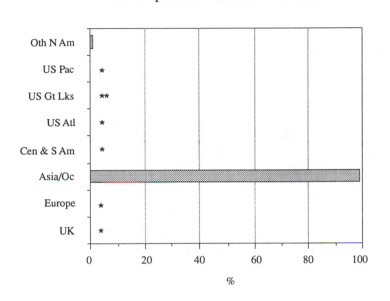

Foreign Destinations of Coal Exports, 1960
Total Exported 0.45 million tonnes

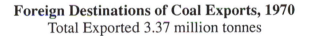

Foreign Destinations of Coal Exports, 1970
Total Exported 3.37 million tonnes

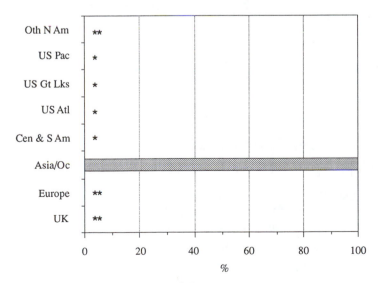

.../ cont'd

Figure 2.6 (cont'd)
Foreign Destinations of Coal Exports, 1980

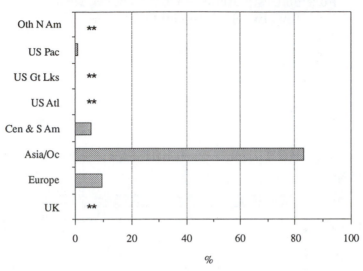

Total Exported 14.34 million tonnes
Source: See Figure 2.1

Foreign Destinations of Coal Exports, 1990
Total Exported 30.91 million tonnes

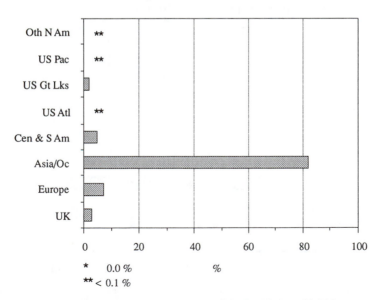

*   0.0 %
** < 0.1 %

Source: Statistics Canada (54–202, 54–205 and 54–209)

Table 2.3:
Regional Loadings of Coal for Export for Selected Years

1960

	A&SLR[1]	GtLks[2]	Pac[3]	Total
mt[4]	<0.1	0.0	0.5	0.5
%	1.3	0.0	98.7	100.0

1970

	A&SLR	GtLks	Pac	Total
mt[4]	<0.1	0.0	3.7	3.7
%	<0.1	0.0	99.9	100.0

1980

	A&SLR	GtLks	Pac	Total
mt	0.6	0.0	13.8	14.4
%	4.1	0.0	95.9	100.0

1990

	A&SLR	GtLks	Pac	Total
mt	1.1	0.5	29.3	30.9
%	3.7	1.6	94.7	100.0

[1] Atlantic and St. Lawrence River ports.
[2] Great Lakes ports
[3] Pacific Ocean ports
[4] million tonnes

Source: See Table 2.1

industry (*Canadian Minerals Yearbook,* 1985). This remains the situation today (*Japan Statistical Yearbook,* 1990). However, new markets also have been developed in an attempt to diversify the destinations of Canadian coal. Coal is now exported from the West coast to Europe (the Netherlands, West Germany, Denmark), South America (Brazil, Mexico) and the United States (both the East coast and the West coast). Canadian coal even passes through Thunder Bay (Table 2.3) destined for USA Great Lakes markets—markets traditionally served by American coal alone. Again, markets for Canadian raw materials are becoming more diversified, or internationalized.

d) Other Exports

While iron ore, wheat and coal make up about one-half of the foreign loadings at Canadian ports, there are hundreds, if not thousands, of

Table 2.4:
The Top Five Export Commodities after
Iron Ore, Wheat and Coal

1960 Commodity	million tonnes	1970 Commodity	million tonnes
Gypsum	3.8	Gypsum	4.4
Lumber and Sawn Timber	2.6	Barley	4.1
Newsprint	2.6	Lumber and Sawn Timber	4.0
Pulpwood	1.3	Newsprint	3.4
Barley	1.0	Rapeseed, flaxseed, soyabeans	2.4
SubTotal	11.3	SubTotal	18.3
Grand Total of Loadings	45.9	Grand Total of Loadings	95.8
% SubTotal	24.6	% SubTotal	19.2

1980 Commodity	million tonnes	1990 Commodity	million tonnes
Lumber and Sawn Timber	6.3	Lumber and Sawn Timber	7.0
Sulphur	5.3	Potash	6.4
Gypsum	4.9	Fuel Oil	5.8
Corn	4.9	Gypsum	5.3
Woodpulp	4.4	Sulphur	4.9
SubTotal	25.8	SubTotal	29.4
Grand Total of Loadings	143.5	Grand Total of Loadings	159.0
% Subtotal	18.0	% SubTotal	18.5

Source: See Table 2.1

commodities which make up the remainder. Water transportation is best at handling the important bulk, high-weight, low-value commodities in this "other" category. An analysis of these remainder commodities indicates that gypsum and lumber and sawn timber always appear in the top five (see Table 2.4). Barley, newsprint and sulphur appear twice in the analysis; potash, corn, woodpulp and pulpwood, rapeseed/flaxseed/soyabeans each appear once. All of these commodities are ideal for the water mode, because most are primary materials and can be handled by bulk-handling devices: conveyor belts, suction, or gravity feed. Newsprint and lumber and sawn timber are neo-bulks; they are processed goods, but they are handled as if they are bulk commodities, placed either in large packages or on pallets and moved by cranes and fork lift trucks.

Table 2.4 also shows that the top five remaining exports consistently comprise one-fifth or so of the total tonnages loaded in

Canadian international waterborne trade. Thus the top eight export commodities constitute approximately 70 per cent of Canadian foreign loadings. With the exception of fuel oil, which is a wet bulk, these commodities are either dry or neo-bulks. It is little wonder that Canada is recognized as one of the leading dry bulk exporting nations of the world—an accomplishment that owes much to the efficiency of the country's water transportation system.

The commodities listed in Table 2.4 originate from across Canada and their destinations are worldwide. However, specific exports are often in demand by a few specific consumers. Gypsum is almost entirely exported from the Atlantic coast—notably Nova Scotia—and its principal destination is the USA Atlantic coast. Sulphur, a by-product of the gas industry of Western Canada, is exported only from the Pacific coast to destinations in Asia, Africa and Europe. Although newsprint does not appear in the two most recent lists of the top five "other" commodities, it has been an important Canadian export since 1960. In recent years, major newsprint exports have been shipped from both the Atlantic and St. Lawrence River area, and from the Pacific coast; Great Lakes loadings have declined in importance. The principal destinations of newsprint include the United States, Europe, Central and South America and Asia. Barley is a product of the Prairies and enters world trade in much the same way as does wheat: it is shipped through Vancouver, Thunder Bay, Churchill, and St. Lawrence ports to destinations scattered throughout the world. Potash is exported from Vancouver primarily to Asian markets, but also to Central and South America; from Thunder Bay to American ports on the Great Lakes; and from Saint John, primarily to Central and South America and the USA Atlantic coast. Lumber and sawn timber, although exported from ports on all coasts, is principally an export of the West coast and is sent to markets throughout the world (especially in Asia, the United States and Europe).

e) Containers

In contrast to single commodity exports such as iron ore or coal or newsprint, containers may hold many different types of goods. But containers are considered to be both carriers of cargo, and cargo itself. Although the tonnages of containers pale beside those of iron ore or wheat, containers are extremely vital to Canadian water trade and to the transportation infrastructure established to service them.

Containerization, the intermodal and standardized cargo handling system that is used today, was established in Canada in 1968 at the port of Montreal. The system's use soon spread to Quebec, Vancouver,

Table 2.5:
Containerized Cargoes Loaded for Export[1] Compared to
Total Exports, 1975–1990

Year	Container Exports (million tonnes)	Total Exports (million tonnes)	Container Exports as % of Total Exports
1975	2.1	102.4	2.1
1976	2.8	114.8	2.4
1977	3.4	119.8	2.8
1978	3.6	116.5	3.1
1979	4.0	146.1	2.7
1980	4.2	143.5	2.9
1981	4.0	145.4	2.8
1982	3.6	125.3	2.9
1983	3.7	129.5	2.9
1984	4.0	145.3	2.8
1985	4.0	143.4	2.9
1986	4.8	144.6	3.3
1987	5.4	159.0	3.4
1988	6.2	131.1	3.6
1989	6.2	159.1	3.9
1990	6.7	159.0	4.2

[1] Container tonnage handled at Halifax, Saint John, Quebec (1975–1978 inclusive), Montreal and Vancouver only.

Source: Container tonnage from Canada Ports Corporation (unpublished data)
Total exports from Statistics Canada (54–202, 54–205 and 54–209)

Halifax and Saint John (Wallace, 1975). These five ports were the first and foremost container-handling facilities in the country, and remain so today (with the exception of Quebec, which ceased container handling in 1978 when CP Ships moved to Montreal). Since 1980, the four ports of Halifax, Saint John, Montreal and Vancouver have handled over 95 per cent of all container tonnage and close to 99 per cent of exported containers in Canadian international trade.

Table 2.5 shows the tonnage of container cargoes loaded for export compared with total exports. Container tonnage has more than doubled in the period 1975 to 1990 and, correspondingly, containers have increased their share of the total exports. However, it should be noted that containerized cargoes represent less than 5 per cent of all Canadian exports by weight.

The proportion of containers handled in each of the five ports is shown in Figure 2.7. Montreal has become the most important con-

Figure 2.7
Proportion of Export Containers Handled at Major Ports

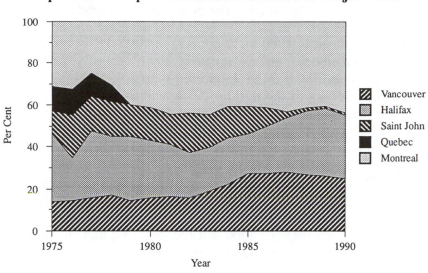

Source: Canada Ports Corporation (unpublished data)

tainer port in Canada handling close to 45 per cent of the container tonnage leaving Canada by water. In earlier years Halifax and Montreal vied for this top spot, but Montreal won the battle when the Quebec traffic transferred upriver to Montreal (and when Montreal developed its mid-West American hinterland). Vancouver's share of total exported containers has been rising slowly as the port improves its facilities and becomes more aggressive in its marketing, especially in South East Asia. Container handling at Saint John has virtually come to a standstill with the decision by Japanese and other Asian carriers to stop calling at the port, because they can better service the Canadian market either through New York or Halifax (see Chapter 4).

The principal destinations of exported containers in 1990 were Europe, including the United Kingdom (which received 52.4 per cent of the Canadian total) and Asia and Oceania (which received 33.4 per cent) (Statistics Canada, 54–205). In 1981 Europe (including the United Kingdom) and Asia and Oceania received 62.0 per cent and 25.1 per cent, respectively, of exported containers. There has been a shift in the destinations of Canadian trade handled in containers, but Europe and the United Kingdom remain the most important destinations. The United States received only 6.8 per cent of all exported container tonnage in 1981, and 8.1 per cent in 1990.

IMPORTS

Canadian waterborne imports have always amounted to less than waterborne exports, by weight. The proportion of imported Canadian international waterborne trade by weight has decreased from approximately 44 per cent in 1960 to 32 per cent in 1990. However the total amount of waterborne imports has risen, albeit unevenly, from about 35 million tonnes in 1960 to 73 million tonnes in 1990 (see Figure 2.8). The setbacks in the middle 1970s and the early 1980s were caused by recessionary trends in the Canadian and world economies.

Canada's principal imports, like its exports, are bulk commodities, the two most important of which are crude oil and coal. Other important imports are bauxite, iron ore and fuel oil. Since their introduction into the Canadian trade in the late 1960s and early 1970s, containers and their cargoes also have become increasingly important, though the tonnages transported are significantly less than those of crude oil and coal. In the period between 1960 to 1990, crude oil and coal together comprised between 41 and 55 per cent of the imports, whereas containerized cargoes have, at most, made up less than 8 per cent of waterborne imports (see Figure 2.9).

a) Crude Oil

Figure 2.8 shows the crude oil imports by water since 1960. The graph is marked by a period of rapid increase in imports in the early 1970s followed by a steady decline, reaching a low in 1983. After 1983, steady increases produced record levels of crude oil imports by the late 1980s.

Although Canada has the capability of producing more crude oil than it consumes and, on many occasions, has done so, for the majority of years since (and including) 1972 Canada was a net importer of crude oil. The reasons for this trade status are geographical: Canada's oil is found in the West, but is needed in greater quantities by the Eastern provinces. But any explanation of the changes in crude oil imports must take into account the complexity of oil production, trade and policy— not only in Canada, but around the world. The management of Canada's oil (until the 1973 OPEC "crisis") exemplifies the way in which supply and demand works in the country. Some of the Canadian demand for oil was met by domestic production; large amounts of crude oil were exported to the United States, and the remaining domestic demand was met with "cheap" imports. The critical dividing line between those areas served by Canadian crude and those areas served by imported crude was the Ottawa River Valley: areas west of the valley were served by Western crude, and areas east of it were served by imported crude.

Figure 2.8
Crude Oil, Coal and Total Canadian Waterborne
Imports, 1960–1990

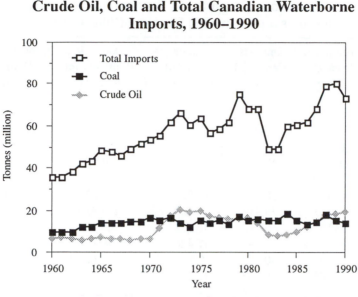

Source: Statistics Canada (54–202, 54–205 and 54–209)

Figure 2.9
Crude Oil, Coal and Container Imports as a
Per Cent of Total Imports

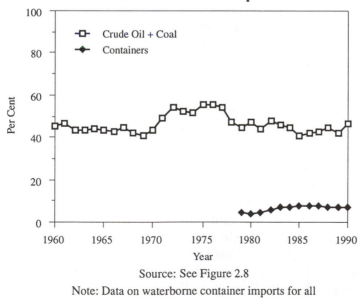

Source: See Figure 2.8
Note: Data on waterborne container imports for all
Canadian ports not published before 1979

Table 2.6:
Canadian Annual Crude Oil Production, Imports,
Exports and Domestic Demand ('000cu m)

Year	Production Crude Oil & Equiv.	Imports Crude Oil & Equiv.	Exports Crude Oil & Equiv.	Domestic Demand (not including exports)	Imports as % of Domestic Demand
1972	106 254	22 683	55 186	93 719	47.6
1973	122 803	52 076	66 073	99 354	52.4
1974	115 778	46 282	52 633	100 886	45.8
1975	100 630	47 413	41 063	99 827	47.4
1976	92 710	41 756	27 265	103 259	40.4
1977	93 148	38 763	18 834	104 536	37.1
1978	91 323	35 916	15 439	107 930	33.3
1979	93 591	35 313	16 728	100 491	35.1
1980	89 522	32 694	12 426	98 714	33.1
1981	80 342	30 738	9 501	92 143	33.3
1982	79 245	19 662	12 158	82 309	23.8
1983	84 047	14 353	16 568	82 331	17.4
1984	89 174	14 850	20 601	82 378	18.0
1985	91 359	16 163	28 309	81 882	19.7
1986	91 413	20 167	33 943	81 218	24.8
1987	95 451	21 767	36 024	83 094	26.2

Source: Canada Year Book (1990 and previous years)

Table 2.6 gives a breakdown of Canadian crude oil production, imports, exports and domestic demand. In 1973, Canada produced more crude oil than its domestic demand could absorb; yet Canada still imported large quantities of crude. In fact, over 50 per cent of the domestic demand for oil in Canada was met by imports, even though the country produced about 22 million cubic metres (cu m) more than it needed. Due to rising world oil prices and apparent instability in world oil supply, steps were taken by Canada to decrease its dependence on oil imports and to increase its self-reliance. One of the first changes made was a decrease in American exports in order to make that oil available to Canadian markets. In order to accomplish this, the crude oil pipeline that had linked fields in the west to Sarnia, Ontario was extended to Montreal in 1976; 13.5 million cu m of crude oil were shipped to Montreal in 1977, and oil imports coming to Montreal through the Portland, Maine - Montreal pipeline were decreased to 13. 6 million cu m (8.7 million cu m less than was imported in the year previous).

A host of policy initiatives was also undertaken in Canada's effort to become less import-dependent: accelerated resource exploration and development of new energy sources; more effective conservation measures; substitution of oil-based energy with energy derived from other sources, notably natural gas; and the adjustment of oil and other energy prices such that the new energy initiatives would be supported. As a result, oil imports fell, oil exports fell, and even oil production and demand fell from 1973 levels—so much so that in 1983, imports fulfilled only 17.4 per cent of Canadian domestic demand for crude oil. However, since 1983 world crude oil prices have fallen, and it is again less expensive for the country to meet an increasing portion of domestic demand with imported crude. A corresponding increase in Canadian exports of crude oil has taken place in amounts approaching those of the post-1973 crisis year.

If 1960, 1970, 1980 and 1990 are considered to be representative years in Canadian oil trade, then there have been only minor changes in the distribution of imports, but major changes in the choice of foreign suppliers. Table 2.7 shows regional breakdowns for imports; Figure 2.10 shows the sources of the imports.

In the four years documented here, virtually all oil imports have been shipped to the Atlantic and St. Lawrence River region, the only area not served by pipeline from Alberta. Of the two regions receiving imported oil, the Atlantic area has received the greatest proportion of the total (see Table 2.8). The 1990 breakdown of quantities sent to the two areas is comparable to that of 1960 in terms of percentage, although the amount imported has more than tripled. The major refineries processing the crude in 1990 are located in Montreal and Quebec/Levis in the St. Lawrence, and in Saint John and Halifax in the Atlantic area.[4]

What is perhaps even more interesting than the change in import reception is the change of crude oil sources, as shown in Figure 2.10. Up until the mid 1980s, the Middle East and Central and South America had been the main sources of imported crude oil. The trade between Venezuela and Eastern Canada, in particular, has been long established; oil has been imported from that country since before 1920. In 1970, Central and South America supplied almost 75 per cent

---

[4] In 1960 and 1970 the crude oil in the St. Lawrence all went to Montreal, but this changed with the opening of the western pipeline, and the building of the Quebec/Levis refinery in 1971. In the period 1970–1980 major refineries were opened, but subsequently closed or cut back in production, at Point Tupper (Port Hawkesbury), N.S. and Come-by-Chance, Nfld.

Table 2.7:
Regional Imports of Crude Oil for Selected Years

1960

	A&SLR[1]	GtLks[2]	Pac[3]	Total
mt[4]	6.0	0.3	0.0	6.3
%	95.2	4.8	0.0	100.0

1970

	A&SLR	GtLks	Pac	Total
mt	6.6	0.1	0.0	6.7
%	98.5	0.5	0.0	100.0

1980

	A&SLR	GtLks	Pac	Total
mt	16.6	0.0	0.0	16.6
%	100.0	0.0	0.0	100.0

1990

	A&SLR	GtLks	Pac	Total
mt	19.4	<0.1	<0.1	19.4
%	99.9	0.1	<0.1	100.0

[1] Atlantic and St. Lawrence River ports.
[2] Great Lakes ports
[3] Pacific Ocean ports
[4] million tonnes

Source: Statistics Canada (54–202, 54–205 and 54–209)

of Canadian oil imports; Venezuela alone supplied about 5 million tonnes. Yet in 1980, oil from the Middle East outweighed the Central and South American totals. Saudi Arabia alone supplied 7.6 million tonnes that year. Two of the most surprising changes in supply have been the rise of the United Kingdom's role (it was Canada's main oil source by 1990), and the increasing dependency on European North Sea oil exports (primarily from Norway). It is not surprising that both the UK and Norway are non-OPEC nations and have priced their oil competitively to capture traditional OPEC markets.

b) Coal

The other major imported commodity handled by Canadian water transport is coal. In the period from 1960 to 1990, between 9.6 and 18.6 million tonnes of coal were imported annually by water (Figure

Table 2.8:
Crude Oil Imports in Atlantic Canada and
in the St. Lawrence River

1960

	Atl	St. Law R	Total
mt[1]	3.7	2.3	6.0
%	62.2	37.8	100.0

1970

	Atl	St. Law R.	Total
mt	6.5	0.1	6.6
%	98.5	1.5	100.0

1980

	Atl	St. Law R	Total
mt	14.1	2.5	16.6
%	85.3	14.7	100.0

1990

	Atl	St. Law R	Total
mt	13.9	5.5	19.4
%	71.7	28.3	100.0

[1] million tonnes

Source: See Table 2.7

2.8). Throughout the 1960s, a slight rise in coal imports was experienced, particularly towards the latter part of the decade and into the early 1970s. However, in 1974 a coal miners' strike in the United States (Canada's chief source of imports) as well as shortages of rail hopper cars and a Great Lakes shippers' strike contributed to a reduction of coal imports in Canada (Canadian Minerals Yearbook, 1974). Coal imports peaked in 1984 because of Ontario Hydro's unexpected shutdown of two units at the Pickering nuclear generating station; coal-fired electricity was necessarily substituted for nuclear-powered. Since 1984 there has been a marked decline in coal imports, such that they are nearly level with the amounts imported in the late 1960s.

The changes in the quantity of coal imported are directly related to the usefulness of the resource. Thermal coal raises steam in the thermal generation of electricity, and coking or metallurgical coal makes coke for the steel industry. Over the past 25 years, thermal coal has become an increasingly important commodity in the import trade.

Figure 2.10
Foreign Origins of Crude Oil Imports for Selected Years

Foreign Origins of Crude Oil Imports, 1960
Total Imported: 6.91 million tonnes

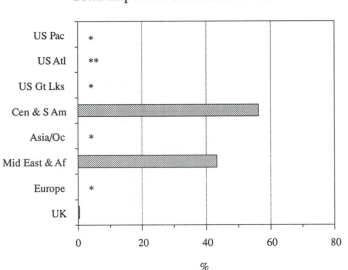

Foreign Origins of Crude Oil Imports, 1970
Total Imported: 6.63 million tonnes

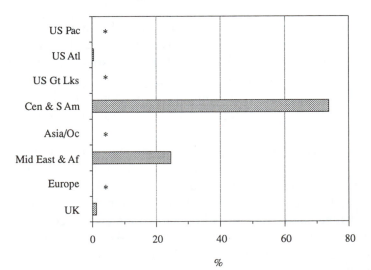

.../ cont'd

Figure 2.10 (cont'd)
Foreign Origins of Crude Oil Imports, 1980
Total Imported: 16.59 million tonnes

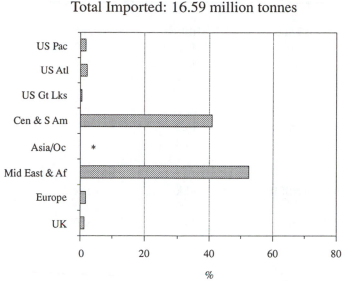

Foreign Origins of Crude Oil Imports, 1990
Total Imported: 19.39 million tonnes

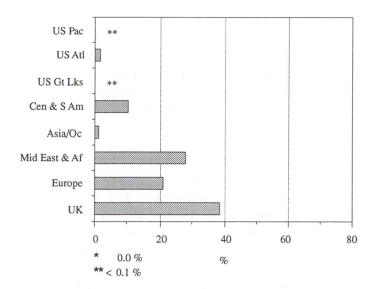

*   0.0 %
** < 0.1 %

Source: Statistics Canada (54–202, 54–205 and 54–209)

Table 2.9:
Regional Imports of Coal for Selected Years

1960

	A&SLR[1]	GtLks[2]	Pac[3]	Total
mt[4]	0.6	9.2	0.0	9.8
%	6.1	93.9	0.0	100.0

1970

	A&SLR	GtLks	Pac	Total
mt	0.3	16.2	0.0	16.5
%	1.8	98.2	0.0	100.0

1980

	A&SLR	GtLks	Pac	Total
mt	0.5	15.0	0.0	15.5
%	3.2	96.8	0.0	100.0

1990

	A&SLR	GtLks	Pac	Total
mt	0.9	13.1	<0.1	14.0
%	6.2	93.8	<0.1	100.0

[1] Atlantic and St. Lawrence River ports
[2] Great Lakes ports
[3] Pacific Ocean ports
[4] million tonnes

Source: See Table 2.7

Virtually all thermal coal imported by water is shipped to Ontario Hydro from the United States. Most of the imported coking coal is also from the United States and is destined for three major steel producers: Stelco, Dofasco and Algoma Steel, all of which are in Ontario. Since the demand for coal imports is primarily in Ontario, well over 90 per cent all of the imported coal comes via the Great Lakes from the Appalachian coalfields in the United States (see Table 2.9).

In the 1960s virtually all coal was imported for the manufacture of steel; but in 1968, the need for thermal coal imports rose considerably. In that year, transportation subsidies were removed from the Nova Scotian thermal coal that was used to produce electricity in Ontario. On the basis of these subsidies, a contract had been signed in 1963 between Ontario Hydro and Nova Scotia coal producers for a five-year supply of thermal coal but, with the subsidy no longer in effect,

Ontario was forced to look elsewhere for cheaper coal. Since most of the accessible hydroelectricity sites had been developed in Ontario, it was necessary that new thermal generating units be established and, initially, Ontario opted for coal-fired plants. In 1968 four coal-fired thermal stations were under construction: Lakeview (near Toronto), Lambton (near Sarnia), Nanticoke (on the north shore of Lake Erie) and Bath (near Kingston). The Bath plant was later changed to an oil-fired station, but in subsequent years new coal-fired plants were built at Thunder Bay (1981) and Atikokan (1985). These, however, were based on West Canadian coal and not on United States imports.

Meanwhile, imports of coking coal continued. In order to secure the supply of this coal, the major steel producers not only entered into long-term contracts with United States suppliers, but they also invested in their own coal mines, taking on American partners. Stelco, for example, has a wholly owned coal mine (the Chisholm mine) at Phelps, Kentucky. It also has partial interests in coal mines in Pennsylvania (Mathies Coal Co.) and West Virginia (LAS Resources Inc.). Up until 1991, Algoma Steel had invested in Appalachian coal also, through its Cannelton Holding Co. headquartered at Charleston, West Virginia.

By 1975 the amounts of coal imported for thermal generation of electricity and for coke production were approximately equal at about 7.4 million tonnes each. In 1990, over 60 per cent of coal was imported for thermal generation (*Canadian Minerals Yearbook,* 1990, 21.8). Imports of thermal coal likely will not grow significantly in the future, however. Increasingly, Ontario Hydro is turning to West Canadian coal for its coal-fired generators. This coal is lower in sulphur content and therefore will better meet the needs of the industry as it becomes increasingly concerned with the effects of sulphur emissions on the environment. In 1990, one-third of the coal used by Ontario Hydro came from the Canadian West, whereas in the mid-1970s Hydro imported all of its coal needs.

c) Other Imports

Crude oil and coal amount to somewhat less than half of Canadian waterborne imports by weight. The remainder are composed of thousands of other products, most of which are bulk goods ideally suited for water transportation.

As Table 2.10 shows, two commodities—iron ore and bauxite (aluminium ores)—have appeared consistently in the "top three imports" list (excluding crude oil and coal) for selected years. Fuel oil is listed in three of the years; corn is cited in the year for which

Table 2.10:
The Top Three Imports after Crude Oil and
Coal For Selected Years

1960 Commodity	million tonnes	1970 Commodity	million tonnes
Iron Ore, Conc. and Scrap	5.1	Fuel Oil	7.9
Fuel Oil	3.5	Bauxite, Alumina and Scrap	3.4
Bauxite, Alumina and Scrap	2.5	Iron Ore, Conc. and Scrap	2.5
SubTotal	11.1	SubTotal	13.8
Grand Total of All Imports	35.5	Grand Total of All Imports	53.3
% SubTotal	31.3	% SubTotal	25.8
1980 Commodity	million tonnes	**1990** Commodity	million tonnes
Iron Ore, Conc. and Scrap	6.1	Fuel Oil	5.7
Corn	4.8	Iron Ore, Conc. and Scrap	4.6
Bauxite, Alumina and Scrap	4.1	Aluminium Ores	3.9
SubTotal	15.0	SubTotal	14.2
Grand Total of All Imports	68.3	Grand Total of All Imports	73.3
% Subtotal	22.0	% SubTotal	19.4

Source: See Table 2.7

fuel oil is not among the top three other imported commodities. Regardless of the lists' components, the total weights indicate that the top three commodities other than oil and coal represent an ever-decreasing proportion of total imports.[5]

It might seem improbable that iron ore, the major **export** of Canadian waterborne trade, is also among the top three Canadian **imports** after crude oil and coal. As has been explained, the iron ore which is exported moves primarily from Lower St. Lawrence River ports to USA Great Lakes ports or to European destinations. The imported iron ore, however, is almost exclusively involved in the trade between American Great Lakes ports in Minnesota and Michigan and the Ontario ports of Sault Ste. Marie, Nanticoke (since 1980) and Hamilton—all of which are major steel producing centres. The remainder of the imported iron ore comes from deep-sea trade

[5] Commodities such as iron and steel products, miscellaneous food products, miscellaneous chemicals, and automobiles have grown at faster rates and have taken on greater significance in the import waterborne trade, but they do not appear in Table 2.10 because they are not yet traded at the bulk level of iron ore, bauxite and fuel oil.

and is destined mainly for Contrecoeur, Quebec. The Great Lakes' trade is one of long standing between Canadian steel interests and American iron ore mining in Minnesota and Michigan. In fact, two of the companies which produce Canadian steel currently have proprietary interests in American iron ore mines. Stelco, with steel plants at Hamilton and Nanticoke, maintains partial ownership of the Tilden mine in northern Michigan, and three other mines in Minnesota; Algoma also has an interest in the Tilden mine.

Bauxite and alumina, the primary resources from which aluminium is produced, are Canadian imports of long standing. Aluminium was first produced in commercial quantities in Canada at Shawinigan, Quebec in 1901 using inexpensive local hydroelectricity and alumina initially imported from England and Germany, though subsequently from the United States. Sources of bauxite have changed somewhat over the years, but the Caribbean and northern South America, including Brazil, continue to be the main suppliers. Today Canada's aluminium-producing smelters are in the Shawinigan area, the Saguenay River - Lac St-Jean region, Baie Comeau, Beauharnois and Bécancour (all in Quebec), and at Kitimat in British Columbia. The alumina smelter at Arvida, Quebec, owned by Alcan (the largest aluminium company in Canada and one of the world's largest producers), was opened in 1926 and for some time processed bauxite from British Guiana (later Guyana) into alumina.

Arvida remains the only Canadian alumina smelter. It sends some of its output to those Alcan plants in Quebec that produce primary aluminium, and it exports the rest. Alumina is also imported from Jamaica, Australia and the United States. The primary aluminium metal smelter in Kitimat, which opened in the early 1950s, was originally supplied with alumina from Jamaica, but more recently its alumina has been imported from Australia and Japan. The Bécancour smelter, opened in 1986 on the south bank of the St. Lawrence River near Trois Rivières, is supplied with alumina from Australia and Texas, while the smelter at Baie Comeau is supplied from Texas alone. Water transportation plays a key role in supplying all of these aluminium-producing plants with raw bauxite or alumina, and in distributing the finished products in Canada and abroad.

The amount of fuel oil imported today is considerably less than that imported in the peak years of the late 1960s. The large amounts imported in the late 1960s—close to 9 million tonnes per year—reflect the lack of Canadian refineries, especially in the Atlantic and St. Lawrence River area, at that time. This problem was alleviated in the 1970s with the construction of new (and major expansions of existing) refineries. Those built include the facilities at: Quebec/Levis (100,000 barrel/day capacity) in 1971; Point Tupper, Nova Scotia (80,000 b/d facility) in 1971, but closed in 1980; Come-by-Chance, Newfoundland (100,000 b/d facility) in 1973, but closed between 1976 and 1987. The Saint John, New Brunswick facility was expanded to 120,000 b/d in 1971 and to 250,000 b/d in 1976, and it became the largest refinery in Canada at the time. With these refineries in place, imports of fuel oil fell, while imports of crude rose—only to fall again with rising oil prices and changes in Canadian government policy. In 1975 and 1976, fuel oil imports fell to less than 1 million tonnes, but in the past few years they have risen again because of low prices on the international market.

The fact that corn appears in the list of "other" top three imports indicates that there has been considerable grain trade passing through Canada. The trade originates in the United States, is off-loaded as imports into Canada, and then is exported from Canada to world destinations. Corn originates in the American mid-West, and is shipped through American Great Lakes ports (particularly Toledo, Chicago and Milwaukee) to St. Lawrence River ports (such as Baie Comeau and Quebec). The amount of corn trans-shipped in this manner depends on the yearly yield, overseas demand, and the ability of the Mississippi River and river ports—especially New Orleans—to handle the American corn. In the late 1970s and early 1980s the corn trade was quite substantial; 3 and 4 million tonnes were trans-shipped annually then, though these figures have since fallen to below 0.5 million tonnes.

d) Containers

In 1990 approximately 5.2 million tonnes of goods transported on water entered Canada in containers, the standardized intermodal form for handling goods. The containers may have held processed foods, manufactured electronics, shoes, books, meat carcasses, or a host of other commodities. Table 2.11 shows that the amount of containerized imports steadily increased until 1989, after which a slight decline was experienced. Though Canada imports less than it exports in waterborne trade, the import and export container tonnage is approximately equal; therefore the proportion of Canadian imports that are containerized has been consistently higher than that of exports. For example in 1990, 7.1 per cent of all imports and 4.4 per cent of exports were containerized; in 1980, the corresponding figures were 3.8 per cent and 2.9 per cent, respectively.

As mentioned previously, the five ports of Halifax, Saint John,

Table 2.11:
Containerized Cargoes Unloaded for Import[1]
Compared to Total Imports, 1975–1990

Year	Container Imports (million tonnes)	Total Imports (million tonnes)	Container Imports as % of Total Imports
1975	1.9	63.8	3.0
1976	2.2	56.5	3.9
1977	2.7	58.9	4.6
1978	2.8	61.8	4.5
1979	2.8	75.4	3.7
1980	2.6	68.3	3.8
1981	3.0	68.2	4.4
1982	2.6	48.7	5.3
1983	3.3	48.9	6.8
1984	4.2	60.1	7.0
1985	4.4	60.7	7.3
1986	4.6	62.0	7.4
1987	5.1	68.0	7.5
1988	5.4	78.9	6.8
1989	5.3	80.3	6.6
1990	5.2	73.3	7.1

[1] Container tonnage handled at Halifax, Saint John, Quebec (1975–1978 inclusive), Montreal and Vancouver only which together handle about 99 per cent of Canadian containerized imports.

Source: Container tonnage from Canada Ports Corporation (unpublished data).
Total imports from Statistics Canada (54–202 and 54–205).

Quebec (until 1978), Montreal and Vancouver have been the dominant container-handling ports in Canada. Figure 2.11 shows the proportion of containerized import cargoes handled in each of these ports since 1975. Clearly Montreal has established itself as the premier container port in Canada handling over half of the imported container cargo in recent years. Halifax rivals Montreal on the East coast, since Saint John plays only a minor and declining role (see Chapter 4).

Vancouver handles between 15 and 20 per cent of Canadian import container tonnage. More containerized tonnage is exported from Vancouver than is imported; for example in 1990, approximately 1.6 million tonnes of containerized cargo was exported, whereas only 1.0 million tonnes was imported. This imbalance of export and import container tonnage at Vancouver is due to the differing types of cargoes handled, and the markets served by each. Vancouver's con-

Figure 2.11
Proportion of Import Containers Handled
at Major Ports

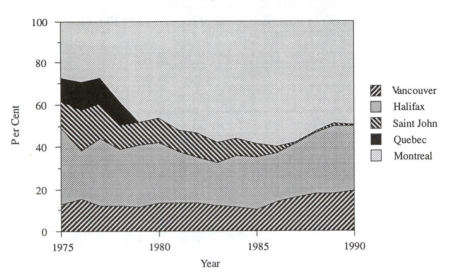

Source: Canada Ports Corporation (unpublished data)

tainerized export cargoes are predominantly wood products and specialty grains which originate locally in the Vancouver region or in
western Canada, and are best handled through the Vancouver port. Its
imports are primarily manufactured goods from South East Asia,
including Japan, which are destined for local markets. Though these
goods also find their way to markets in Western and Eastern Canada
and the United States, American ports on the West coast (such as
Seattle) rival Vancouver for such trade. Vancouver has an advantage
in exporting wood products and specialty grains in containers, but not
in handling import containers, since the market for imported goods is
not primarily local; consequently, Vancouver's container export tonnage is higher than its import tonnage.

Most of the containers imported into Canada originate in Europe
(including the United Kingdom). In 1990, 69 percent of containers
arrived from Europe, slightly less than the 72 percent figure for 1981.
Asia and Oceania contributed over 21 per cent of the tonnage in 1990, a
slight increase from the figure of 19 per cent for 1981. Only about 4 per
cent of containerized imports in 1990 originated in the United States.

Table 2.12:
Principal Commodities Loaded in Canadian
Coastwise Shipping for Selected Years

1960 Commodity	million tonnes	1970 Commodity	million tonnes
Pulpwood	6.0	Fuel Oil	9.1
Wheat	5.7	Wheat	8.0
Fuel Oil	5.1	Iron Ore	6.5
Logs, posts	2.5	Logs	6.3
Gasoline	2.3	Pulpwood	5.4
SubTotal	21.6	SubTotal	35.3
Grand Total of Loadings	37.1	Grand Total of Loadings	57.3
% SubTotal	58.2	% SubTotal	61.6

1980 Commodity	million tonnes	1990 Commodity	million tonnes
Logs	17.0	Wheat	7.8
Wheat	11.3	Logs and Bolts	7.0
Fuel Oil	10.7	Fuel Oil	6.7
Iron Ore	7.3	Iron Ore	6.3
Pulpwood	6.1	Pulpwood	5.9
SubTotal	52.4	SubTotal	33.7
Grand Total of Loadings	82.8	Grand Total of Loadings	60.4
% Subtotal	63.3	% SubTotal	55.7

Source: Statistics Canada (54–204, 54–205 and 54–210)

COASTWISE SHIPPING

The principal commodities transported in Canadian coastwise shipping once again are bulk cargoes, both dry and wet (see Table 2.12). Five commodities have dominated the national principal commodity list for coastwise shipping: wheat, fuel oil, logs, iron ore and pulpwood. The rankings of these commodities differ from year to year, though wheat invariably appears in either first or second position. The top five commodities have consistently comprised substantially more than 50 per cent of all loadings in coastwise shipping, and figures of 60 per cent are not unusual. Although these five goods are dominant at the national level, there are regional differences in their importance.

a)   The Atlantic and Lower St. Lawrence Region

The principal commodities loaded in this area have been fuel oil and, in more recent years, iron ore (Figure 2.12). Since 1960, roughly two-thirds of all fuel oil transported in the Canadian coastal trade moves

Figure 2.12
Principal Commodities Loaded in Atlantic and Lower St. Lawrence River in Coastwise Shipping for Selected Years

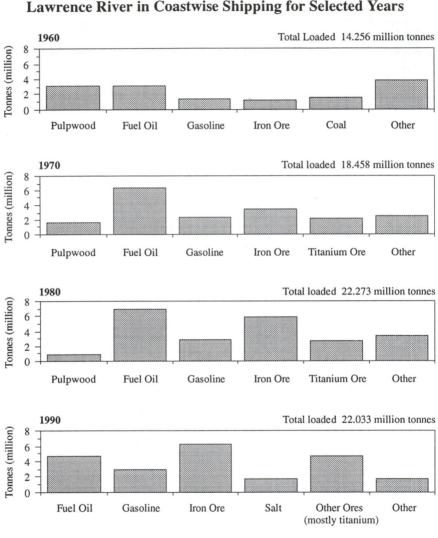

Source: See Table 2.12

through this area. The fuel oil originates from the major refineries in the region (Montreal, Quebec, Saint John and Halifax) and is distributed throughout the lower St. Lawrence River, the Gulf of St. Lawrence, and along the coasts of Nova Scotia, Newfoundland and Labrador. Lesser tonnages of gasoline are also shipped in this pattern. Iron ore, which has become increasingly important in the region's coastal trade, is loaded at Sept Iles and Port Cartier and shipped principally to Contrecoeur and the Great Lakes ports of Hamilton and Nanticoke—both of which are major steel-making centres.

Today, relatively little pulpwood or coal is shipped by water in this region. Coal mined in Cape Breton Island is principally used at the site to produce electricity, or is transported a short distance by rail to be used in steel making. At present very little Cape Breton coal is destined for St. Lawrence River or Great Lakes destinations, since the coal needs of that region are served by imports from the United States or Western Canada. The substantial coal trade between Cape Breton Island and steel makers in Ontario in the early and mid-1960s was curtailed because American coal became less costly to obtain. Pulpwood still moves by water in the area, but not to the same extent as in the past; land transportation—particularly trucking—has taken over as the principal mode of transport since the 1970s, when roads were improved and trucking technology advanced.

Commodities that appear on the principal lists for later years include titanium ore, which is shipped from Havre St. Pierre (on the north shore of the St. Lawrence River) to Contrecoeur for use in the manufacture of steel, and salt, which is principally loaded at Grindstone on the Magdellan Islands and Pugwash, Nova Scotia for distribution in Quebec and Ontario.

Although fuel oil and iron ore are the principal commodities loaded in the region, only fuel oil is one of the two principal commodities **un**loaded there—and it places second in the list to wheat. Loaded at Thunder Bay, the wheat is shipped to various ports on the St. Lawrence River or to Saint John and Halifax, in the Maritimes, for trans-shipment to foreign destinations.

b) The Great Lakes and St. Lawrence River (Above Montreal) Region

The total amount of goods loaded in coastwise shipping on the Great Lakes has increased from 13.2 million tonnes in 1960 to 20.1 million tonnes in 1990 (Figure 2.13), although the peak in tonnage loaded was 28.2 million tonnes in 1983. The principal commodity loaded is wheat, which represents about 40 per cent of the regional total. This wheat is loaded at Thunder Bay and is destined for ports on the Great Lakes—Goderich, Port Colborne, Port McNicholl, Midland, Toronto—or ports further downstream on the St. Lawrence River. The opening of the Seaway in 1959 changed the pattern of the wheat trade (see Chapter 6); the export of wheat through United States Atlantic coast ports was eliminated, as was the transfer of wheat from lake boats to small canal boats at

Figure 2.13
Principal Commodities Loaded in the Great Lakes in
Coastwise Shipping for Selected Years

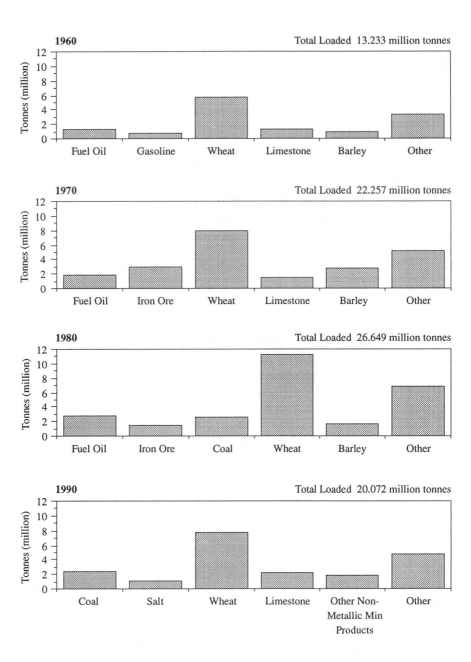

Source: See Table 2.12

Prescott, Ontario for its ultimate passage to Montreal and below. Barley, another of the principal commodities loaded for coastwise transport, follows the same trade pattern as wheat.

Three of the region's principal commodities over the years—limestone, iron ore and coal—are associated with the steel industry; coal is also used for the thermal generation of electricity. Limestone is loaded mostly at Colborne and shipped to Clarkson, where it is used in the cement industry. In the past, iron ore was loaded at Thunder Bay and shipped to the steel-making centres, but this trade declined and then ceased altogether when the Steep Rock mine closed in 1979. The iron ore moving on the Great Lakes today is primarily American in origin, or from the Labrador - Northern Quebec mines. Coal became a major commodity in the coastwise trade in the late 1970s and early 1980s; a coal-handling terminal was opened at Thunder Bay and contracts were signed between coal users in Ontario and coal producers in Saskatchewan and Alberta. Salt, mainly loaded at Windsor and Goderich, is destined for points all around the Great Lakes, including Thunder Bay, Toronto, Sault Ste. Marie, Hamilton and Montreal. Fuel oil is not shipped to the same extent now as in the past because much of its transportation is accomplished by trucking. In 1990 only 1.0 million tonnes of fuel oil were loaded, a reduction that disqualified it from the area's top five list of commodities.

Since the end of the 1960s iron ore has been the dominant commodity unloaded on the Great Lakes in the coasting trade. In 1960, only 5 per cent of unloaded commodities was iron ore, but by 1970 its share had reached 33 per cent (and has stayed at approximately that proportion ever since). Ore is loaded at Sept Iles and Port Cartier and provides a "back haul" to the wheat trade passing downstream through the Lakes and the St. Lawrence River.[6] Coal, fuel oil, limestone, salt, gasoline and wheat traditionally have been the other major commodities unloaded, although the majority of wheat has been unloaded in lower St. Lawrence River ports since the Seaway was opened. For example, in 1960 5.6 million tonnes of wheat were loaded in the coasting trade at Thunder Bay, and 3.1 million tonnes (55 per cent) were unloaded in the Great Lakes while 43 per cent proceeded downstream to Montreal or below. In 1990, however, of the 7.6 million tonnes of wheat loaded at Great Lakes ports in coastwise shipping only 1.0 million tonnes (13 per cent) were unloaded in the the Great Lakes.

---

[6] A "back haul" is the return journey of a ship transporting goods or freight. Often, back haul freight rates are cheaper than normal rates since it costs relatively little more to operate a loaded carrier than an empty one.

c) Pacific Coast

Products for and of the forest industry dominate the coasting trade of the Pacific coast (Figure 2.14). The single most important commodity is logs, although the amount transported in any one year varies according to the demand of the industry. Pulpwood, lumber and timber also enter into coastal water trade. Fuel oil, too, is regularly transported along the West coast, as it is on the East.

The transport of logs along the British Columbia coast has been practiced for over 100 years (Fraser River Estuary Management Program, 1991, 5). The production and consumption of logs in the forest industry of British Columbia are geographically separated. Generally, log consumption is highest on the south coast, in the Lower Fraser River area (around Vancouver and New Westminster) or on Vancouver Island (at places such as Nanaimo, Crofton or Port Alberni). The production of logs for the southern sawmills and pulp mills occurs along the entire coastal area of British Columbia, but forest cutting has moved further and further north, away from the places of consumption, over the years. As a result, coastal water transportation has played an increasingly important role in linking production and consumption sites.

The transportation of logs from the site where they are cut to the place of processing is extremely complicated, and each forest products company has its own intricate coastal delivery system. Almost all of the major forest companies bring logs down the coast to the south; MacMillan Bloedel and Fletcher Challenge get them from as far away as the Queen Charlotte Islands. Fletcher Challenge and International Forest Products (IFP) also bring logs from the West coast of Vancouver Island to fill their needs in the Lower Fraser River (maps of these transport patterns may be found in Fraser River Estuary Management Program, 1991, 6).

Mill location is not the only determining factor in log transport decision; waterways themselves dictate that different types of log transportation must be practiced. In the sheltered waters between Vancouver Island and the mainland, and within sheltered inlets along the coast, logs are mainly towed by tugs in log booms. However, in the exposed waters north of Vancouver Island and on the West coast of Vancouver Island, barges are employed for the purpose. Logs coming from the north by boom or barge usually do not enter into the Fraser River directly; rather, there is usually some intermediate point where booms are broken or barges are dumped, and the logs are stored there until they are required at the mills. Thus areas like Howe Sound, about 40 kilometers north of the Fraser River, have become pivotal points in the coastal transportation of logs. Statistics show

Figure 2.14
Principal Commodities Loaded on the Pacific Coast in Coastwise Shipping for Selected Years

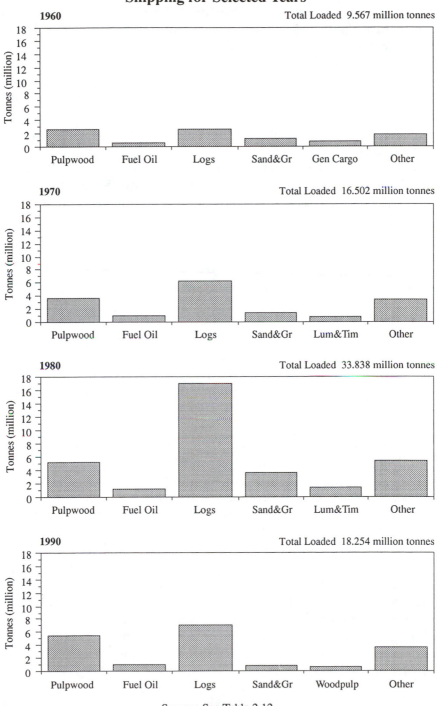

Source: See Table 2.12

that each year Howe Sound is amongst the top five areas on the West coast for both log loading and unloading. Other large log loading areas are the Queen Charlotte Islands, the west coast of Vancouver Island, Jervis Inlet and Johnstone Strait. Large unloading areas are North Arm Fraser River, the east coast of Vancouver Island, Jervis Inlet, Vancouver and Port Alberni.

Another major forest product moving along the coast is pulpwood chips, most of which originates in the Lower Fraser River area (New Westminster and Vancouver). The chips are by-products of the sawmilling operations, and at one time were considered as waste. But with increasingly efficient sawmills and the ability of pulp mills to use the chips as raw material for pulp, the chipping of waste wood has become a major operation. The major destinations for the chips are the pulp mills of Nanaimo, Crofton and Howe Sound. The chips are carried in large barges especially built for their transport, and are towed by tugs.

SUMMARY

Canadian waterborne exports are dominated by dry bulk cargoes, principally iron ore, coal and wheat. Since 1960, there have been shifts in the relative importance of these cargoes as measured by the tonnages handled, and in terms of destination. These goods are sent to all parts of the globe, and to more ports today than ever before. This last point deserves emphasis. The markets for Canadian waterborne exports have become diversified beyond the traditional American, European or Asian destinations. All of the principal trades—iron ore, wheat and coal—have "internationalized" their markets. Canada is one of the premier dry bulk exporting nations of the world and is dependent on the water mode; but Canada's water transportation system is essential for the country's entire economy, an economy that has at its base a major import trade, as well.

Bulk commodities are ideal for water transport. In Canadian trade, imported dry bulk commodities (coal, bauxite and alumina) and wet bulk commodities (crude oil and fuel oil) are significant. Crude oil, fuel oil, bauxite and alumina are primarily received on the Atlantic coast and in the St. Lawrence River; coal and iron ore are principally handled on the Great Lakes. Canada's principal container ports are Montreal and Halifax in the East, and Vancouver on the Pacific coast. During the period from 1960 to the present, the transport of imported and exported commodities has changed with the introduction and growth of containerization.

Coastwise shipping well exemplifies the low-cost efficiency of water transport. Though it may not be very glamorous, the industry is essential to the operation of the Canadian economy in general, and to the well-being of coastal communities in particular. Over the years, the commodities moved by ship have remained much the same: iron ore, coal and limestone are associated with the steel industry, logs and pulpwood with the forest industry. Supplies of commodities such as fuel oil and gasoline depend on the demand of industry as well as that of the final consumer. But whether or not the goods move coastwise by water depends, of course, on the competition for their transportation. For example in the Great Lakes area, fuel oil and gasoline are transported now largely by truck. In the coastal areas of British Columbia and Atlantic Canada, however, water transportation is still the dominant means by which bulk commodities reach the consumer.

CHAPTER 3

THE INFRASTRUCTURE OF THE INDUSTRY

WATERWAYS

The waterways were the early highways of exploration, discovery and commerce in the country that came to be called Canada. The early European explorers arrived by way of the sea and penetrated the continent through two passages into the interior: the St. Lawrence River and its tributaries including the Great Lakes; and Hudson Strait and Hudson Bay, and the waters that drain into it. The fur trade, the first commercial exploitation of the continent's resources, depended on these waterways and, eventually, on the waterways draining into the Pacific and the Arctic Oceans. Waterways have been at the very core of Canada's economic existence since times before the European's arrival. Today, though, waterways as a means of commercial transportation are less prominent in the Canadian imagination. Their place of importance was usurped in the public mind first by the railroad, then the highway, and finally the airplane. However, in some areas—on the coasts, the Great Lakes and the Mackenzie River, for example—the waterways are just as important to our economy today as they were three centuries ago. Certainly, the navigation infrastructure that supports commercial shipping on these waterways is far more sophisticated today than ever before.

The *Canada Shipping Act*, the dominant legislation affecting the operation of ships in Canada, defines Canadian waters as "the territorial sea of Canada and all internal waters of Canada" (Canadian Coast Guard, 1990, 1). The territorial sea extends 12 nautical miles offshore; the inland waters include all navigable fresh waters (including the St. Lawrence River as far seaward as Anticosti Island).[1] The 12-mile limit was unilaterally declared in 1970; prior to that time a 3-mile limit was claimed. Canadian territorial waters are also claimed for the Bay of Fundy, the Gulf of St. Lawrence, Hudson Bay, the Northwest Passage and waters of the Arctic archipelago (see Chapter 8), and the waters comprising the inside passage along the British Columbia coast.[2] Canada's seacoast is the longest in the world; measured on the mainland and offshore islands, it totals nearly 244,000 km (*Canada Year Book*, 1990, 1.7).

Virtually all of Canada's territorial sea is used for commercial shipping, some areas more intensely than others. For example, shipping along the Labrador coast is limited to coastal resupply in the summer, as is Arctic shipping and shipping in Hudson Bay (see Chapter 8). But the Gulf of St. Lawrence, the Bay of Fundy, the Nova Scotian coast, the south coast of Newfoundland and the British Columbia coast undergo year-round commercial use, both from international shipping and coastwise shipping. The St. Lawrence River and the Great Lakes are the main inland waters that serve commercial shipping, but the Mackenzie River and Great Slave Lake are used intensely for the short shipping season of summer. Some inland waterways, such as Lake Winnipeg and Okanagan Lake, experience cruise shipping; but this is limited to the summer season only. There is also intense use of the Rideau Canal and the Trent Canal for recreational boating, but that is not of concern here.

Along the seacoast and within the territorial sea, throughout the Great Lakes and along the commercial inland waterways, a vast network of channel buoys and land-based navigation aids (such as lighthouses, radio stations and vessel traffic centres) operate in order to facilitate the use of waterways for commercial shipping. The government of Canada publishes hydrographic charts and sailing directions to assist with navigation. Assistance is also provided beyond the territorial sea by way of radio navigation aids, ice monitoring and notice to mariners. Shoals, ice, currents and weather pose as great a hazard today as when the waterways were first explored and discovered. The

---

[1] The boundary is determined by a straight line drawn from Cap des Rosiers on the south shore of the St. Lawrence River to West Point Anticosti Island and from Anticosti Island to the north shore of the St. Lawrence along the 63° W meridian of longitude.

[2] This is an area enclosed by a straight baseline drawn across Dixon Entrance, the Queen Charlotte Islands and Vancouver Island and a straight baseline across Queen Charlotte Sound joining the two island groups.

physical characteristics of Canada's commercial waterways have undergone relatively little change since the time of Cartier or Hudson, but our knowledge of physical hazards and our ability to monitor and assist shipping improves each year. Canada has a long history of assisting commercial shipping, but some of the most important navigational infrastructure is relatively new, and has been developed to reduce the negative effects of pollution from ships on marine and coastal environments. These recent innovations have far reaching implications for the operation of ships in Canada's waters.

a) The Traditional Navigational Infrastructure

Traditionally, aids to navigation have included both physical equipment such as channel buoys, radio stations and lighthouses, and published information in the form of hydrographic charts, sailing directions and notices to mariners. In addition, pilotage has been a feature of selected Canadian waters since early colonial times. The traditional navigation infrastructure is in place to assist ship captains in making decisions about where to proceed in their approach to the coast. The hydrographic charts inform them of the depth of water, the presence of shoals or reefs, the markings for channels, and the placement of navigation aids. The navigation aids in the form of lights and radio stations assist in fixing accurate positions. Pilotage is the means by which a captain with limited or no knowledge of the local conditions is assisted in bringing the vessel safely to shore.

The Canadian Coast Guard (CCG), officially named as such only in 1962, was made part of the federal Department of Transport (as Marine Services) in 1936. But the CCG dates back to 1867 when it was called the Marine Branch of the Department of Marine and Fisheries. One of the CCG's major responsibilities is the provision of aids to navigation, which include the approximately 13,000 channel buoys and 10,000 land-based aids in place either permanently or temporarily (*Canadian Encyclopedia*, 1988, 336). A recent public review of tanker safety assessed the system of fixed navigation aids as "one of the most extensive in the world" (Public Review Panel on Tanker Safety and Marine Spills Response Capability, 1990, 29), but it found fault with some of the short range aids in areas prone to freeze-up (such as the St. Lawrence River in winter), where buoys have disappeared under the ice. These aids can be found on all the navigable waters of Canada; they are marked on hydrographic charts and referred to in the published sailing directions. Also included in the land-based aid category are lighthouses, some of which date back to the mid-eighteenth century. The first documented lighthouse was built at Louisbourg in 1734; the oldest existing lighthouse, dating from 1758, stands at the entrance to Halifax Harbour on Sambro Island. A recent undertaking has involved the automation of major lighthouses; the resident lighthouse-keepers are being replaced by itinerant technicians. Well over half of the 266 major lighthouses in the country have now been automated, and the program continues. Canada's greatest lighthouse—the Cape Race, Newfoundland light, which throws a light 48 km into the Atlantic—is yet manned by a resident keeper.

Hydrographic charts have been a feature of Canadian waters for over 200 years; both the French and the British collected hydrographic information. The Canadian Hydrographic Service, founded in 1904, is the federal agency responsible for conducting surveys of all navigable waters, salt and fresh water, and it maintains over 1,000 navigation charts (*Canadian Encyclopedia*, 1988, 1034). As impressive as that number may be, the hydrographic mapping of Canadian waters is not entirely up to modern standards. Some charts still report soundings according to British Admiralty surveys of the last century. Only about 20 per cent of the Arctic waters charts, for example, meet modern hydrographic standards, and the charts are inadequate for the St. Lawrence estuary and the Labrador coast, as well (Public Review Panel on Tanker Safety and Marine Spills Response Capability, 1990, 28).

Four pilotage regions exist in Canada: the Atlantic, the Laurentian (St. Lawrence), the Great Lakes and the Pacific, each of which has a pilotage authority. Pilotage is regulated under the *Pilotage Act* of 1971, but the practice of navigating vessels to and from ports dates back to the early days of the French colony on the St. Lawrence River (*Report of the Royal Commission on Pilotage*, 1968–1970a, 23) and was established immediately upon the founding of Halifax in 1749 (*Report of the Royal Commission on Pilotage*, 1968–1970b, 168). Each of today's Pilotage Authorities has identified compulsory and non-compulsory (recommended) pilotage areas. In the former, it is mandatory that a ship be under the control of a licensed pilot or holder of a pilotage certificate that has been granted by the authority; in the latter, pilot presence is recommended but not compulsory. Table 3.1 lists the compulsory pilotage areas of Canada. One concern to the Public Review Panel on Tanker Safety was the fact that compulsory pilotage is not required for all foreign oil and chemical tankers below Les Escoumins in the St. Lawrence River or in the Gulf of St. Lawrence during the ice season (Public Review Panel on Tanker Safety and Marine Spills Response Capability, 1990, 143). The Panel recommended such pilotage on the grounds that navigating in ice requires special skill and should not be entrusted to those with minimal experience.

Table 3.1:
Compulsory Pilotage Areas of Canada

Pilotage Region	Compulsory Area	Special Restrictions, if any
Atlantic	**New Brunswick**	
	1. Miramichi	
	2. Restigouche	
	a. Dalhousie	
	b. Campbellton	
	3. Saint John	
	Newfoundland	
	1. Bay of Exploits	
	a. Botwood	May 15 – Jan 1. Depending on ice conditions
	b. Lewisporte	May 15 – Jan 1. Depending on ice conditions
	c. Botwood/Lewisporte	Jan 2 – May 14. Depending on ice conditions. Board off St. John's
	2. Clarenville	
	3. Holyrood	
	4. Humber Arm	
	5. Placentia Bay	
	a. Zone A (inner bay)	Compulsory for all vessels
	b. Zone B (outer bay)	Compulsory for vessels over 223 m in length.
	6. St. John's	
	7. Stephenville	
	Nova Scotia	
	1. Cape Breton	
	a. Sydney Harbour	
	b. Bras d' Or Lakes	
	c. Strait of Canso	
	d. St. Peters	
	2. Halifax	
	3. Pugwash	
	Prince Edward Island	
	1. Charlottetown	
Laurentian	**Quebec**	
	1. Les Escoumins to Montreal	Vessels upbound take on pilots at Anse aux Basques near Les Escoumins, then pilots are exchanged at Quebec and Trois Rivières for the trip to Montreal

.../cont'd

Table 3.1 (cont'd)

Pilotage Region	Compulsory area	Special restrictions, if any
Great Lakes	Entire Great Lakes System including the St. Lawrence Seaway, the Welland Canal, the Detroit and St. Clair Rivers and the St. Mary's River.	Pilotage is compulsory for all vessels of foreign registry and other vessels which do not qualify for exemptions. Vessels registered in the United States or Canada whose operations are upon the Great Lakes and ports on the St. Lawrence are exempted from compulsory pilotage.
Pacific	All coastal waters	

Source: Canadian Coast Guard (1989, Notice 23)
Canadian Hydrographic Service (1985, 362)
Canadian Hydrographic Service (1986, 21)

b) Rules and Regulations

Over the past twenty to thirty years, the restrictiveness of the regulations on ship navigation have increased, sometimes to the point where the captain's decision about how to proceed has already been made or is given as an order from shore-based personnel.

Vessel Traffic Services, traffic separation schemes and the regulations pertaining to the *Arctic Waters Pollution Prevention Act*, all have been created or enacted since the late 1960s and early 1970s in order to minimize the risk of marine accidents, and therefore to reduce the negative effects of pollution to the marine and coastal environment.

i)   Vessel Traffic Services

Vessel Traffic Services (VTS) are operated by the Canadian Coast Guard and have the overall responsibility to protect the marine environment and to improve the safety and efficiency of marine traffic movement. The services provided include: distribution of information on traffic movements and waterway conditions; organization of ship movements to facilitate efficient traffic flow; provision of assistance to navigation upon request, and participation in accident response activity (Canadian Coast Guard, 1989, 105). Certain VTS zones have been defined for Canadian waters, each of which has a shore-based station that is responsible for the implementation of the VTS regulations (see Table 3.2).

Table 3.2:
Canadian Vessel Traffic Services Zones

Zone Name	Centre(s)	Number of Sectors	Geographical Extent of Zone
St. John's	St. John's	1	all waters shoreward of a line drawn on a radius of 10 nautical miles from Fort Amherst lighthouse, including the port of St. John's
Placentia Bay	Argentia	2	Placentia Bay and approaches
Port aux Basques	Port aux Basques	1	all Canadian waters adjacent to the west and southwest coasts of Newfoundland between Cape Ray and Rose Blanche Point
Halifax	Halifax	2	Halifax harbour and approaches
Bay of Fundy	Saint John	3	Bay of Fundy and approaches inclu-ing Saint John harbour
St. Lawrence	Les Escoumins	7	all waters of the St. Lawrence exten-ing upstream from 66°W meridian to the upper limits of Montreal harbour including the Saguenay River and other tributary rivers of the St. Lawrence
Sarnia	Sarnia	2	all Canadian waters from Long Point Light on Lake Erie to Detroit Reef light on Lake Huron including the waters of the Detroit River, Lake St. Clair and the St. Clair River
Vancouver	Vancouver	4	all Canadian waters east and south of Vancouver Island in Queen Charlotte Strait, Johnstone Strait, Discovery Passage, Strait of Georgia and Juan de Fuca Strait, including Howe Sound, Vancouver harbour and the Fraser River
Tofino Island	Tofino	1	all Canadian waters west of Vancouver including Alberni Inlet

…/cont'd

Table 3.2 (cont'd)

Zone Name	Centre(s)	Number of Sectors	Geographical Extent of Zone
Prince Rupert	Prince Rupert	1	all Canadian waters north of Vancouver Island to the Alaska/British Columbia border

Source: Canadian Coast Guard (1989, Notice 25)

The first limited VTS operated from under the Lions Gate Bridge at the First Narrows in Vancouver's Burrard Inlet in the early 1960s. Radar surveillance of approaching traffic was undertaken, and limited information on traffic movements was provided to shipping traffic. Also during the 1960s, a VTS system was established on the St. Lawrence River below Montreal, but it, too, had a limited role to play in ship navigation and functioned as a source of information on waterway conditions and other traffic movement for ships. In 1969 a navigation and information service was established in Halifax Harbour and its approaches, and a similar service was established at about the same time for Saint John Harbour and its approaches. None of these initiatives were coordinated; they were developed to serve the needs of the local area, and the development of national guidelines for their operation was not considered at the time.

By the early 1970s a number of factors combined to create the need for a national system of VTS. The greatest impetus was the sinking of the tanker ARROW in Chedabucto Bay, Nova Scotia in February 1970. The ARROW's 16,000 tonnes of oil cargo were released to the sea in what remains as Canada's largest marine oil accident. This accident, which followed the TORREY CANYON disaster of 1967 off the coast of southwest England, served to heighten public opinion about the safety of approaching tanker operations and the need to protect the marine and coastal environments from such accidents. This new public awareness and concern—combined with the general increase in marine transportation, including the introduction of larger and faster vessels to carry not only oil but also containers and all types of bulk cargo—prompted the Canadian government to reassess its VTS program and to develop new policies and programs to monitor and control shipping in its waters.

As a result, national guidelines of VTS operations were developed. In practice today all ships of 20 metres or more in length must seek a clearance to proceed into, through, within or from a VTS zone. To acquire traffic clearance, a ship must inform the VTS centre of its name, master, course and speed; of its intended course, and its destination within the zone; of its cargo and if any dangerous goods or pollutants are carried on board; and of any defects in its hull or with its machinery or navigation equipment. If the centre is not satisfied with the information contained in the report, especially regarding defects, it may refuse the ship entry into, operation within or exit from the zone until defects have been repaired. Moreover, the ship's master must supply all information that is requested and must comply with every marine traffic direction that is issued by the VTS centre. It is not the intention of the VTS regulations, however, to direct ships in their movements to or from a dock within the zone, as is the case for airplane traffic control around airports. For the most part the master or pilot makes decisions about a ship's routing within a zone, but when accidents or equipment failures occur, the shore-based VTS officer does have the emergency authority to order a ship's direction, and the ship must comply. Because of these regulations, the operation of commercial vessels within Canadian waters is very different today than before the advent of the VTS system.

In addition to the individual VTS zones in areas of particularly high risk and high traffic density, there are now three broad geographically based Vessel Traffic Reporting Systems in place. Eastern Canada VTS Zone regulations (ECAREG) apply to Canadian waters on the East coast of Canada south of 60°N and within the Gulf of St. Lawrence, excluding the existing VTS areas of St. John's, Placentia Bay, Port aux Basques, Halifax and the Bay of Fundy. Arctic Canada Traffic Zone (NORDREG) regulations operate in the waters to which the *Arctic Waters Pollution Prevention Act* (see below) apply and in the waters of Ungava Bay, Hudson Bay and James Bay south of 60°N. Western Canada Traffic Zone regulations (WESTREG) apply to the Tofino VTS zone, the Prince Rupert zone and the Vancouver zone. Participation is mandatory in ECAREG alone.

ii) Traffic Separation Schemes

Ships have voluntarily followed predetermined routes on the North Atlantic Ocean for safety reasons throughout this century (International Maritime Organization, 1984, "Forward"). However, the practice of separating opposing traffic in restrictive areas has been operative only since the 1960s. The International Maritime Organization (IMO; formerly the Inter-governmental Maritime Consultative Organization) was instrumental in devising the now internationally accepted regulations. The conduct of vessels within or near traffic separation schemes is now embodied under Rule 10 of the International Regulation for Preventing Collisions at Sea, published in 1972 and subsequently amended.

Canada has adopted these rules with modifications under its own Collision Regulations (Canadian Coast Guard, 1991). The IMO regularly publishes the separation schemes that it has adopted; they are also listed in the annual Notices to Mariners published by the Coast Guard.

The first traffic separation scheme was officially operational on January 1, 1967 in the Dover Strait between France and Britain (Anon, 1969). The wreck of the TORREY CANYON in 1967 prompted the proposal and adoption of traffic separation schemes around the world, not only in waters converging on narrow channels and seacoasts but also in deep water (Oudet, 1979). In the Canadian context, the ARROW incident prompted the first separation scheme to be implemented in the approaches to Chedabucto Bay. Currently, there are three IMO-recognized traffic separation schemes operating in Canada: in Chedabucto Bay, in the Bay of Fundy and approaches, and in the Strait of Juan de Fuca and its approaches. According to the Notices, "ships which depart from these routes and meet with collisions involve themselves in legal liability" (Canadian Coast Guard, 1989, Notice 10). As well, the Canadian Coast Guard recommends routing measures in the Johnstone and Broughton Straits (between Vancouver Island and the mainland), in the St. Lawrence River at Les Escoumins, in the Gulf and River St. Lawrence, in Halifax Harbour and its approaches, and throughout the Great Lakes.

iii) Regulations of the *Arctic Waters Pollution Prevention Act*

Another recent development in the control of commercial shipping operations in Canadian waters has been the creation of Shipping Safety Control Zones in the Canadian Arctic. These regulations are included in the *Arctic Waters Pollution Prevention Act*, which was passed in 1970 and proclaimed in 1972. This Act came about as a direct result of the MANHATTEN voyage (see Chapter 8) and was designed to provide Canada with unilateral control over the type of ship allowed to operate in the Arctic, and aims to guard against pollution in coastal and maritime waters of the Canadian Arctic archipelago. In addition to establishing dimensional criteria for vessels that operate in the Canadian Arctic, the Act established sixteen Shipping Safety Control Zones through an Order in Council. These zones extend from 60°N in Hudson Bay towards the North Pole; from east to west they extend from the Greenland - Canadian border in Davis Strait, Baffin Bay and Kane Basin to the 141°W meridian in the Beaufort Sea, and thence north to follow a line measured seaward from the nearest Canadian land a distance of 100 nautical miles. A shipping season for each zone was designated according to the icebreaking capabilities of vessels. In total, ten classes and four types of vessels are identified in the control zone regulations. For example in Zone 13, which covers Lancaster Sound and adjacent waters, a vessel of Arctic Class 10 can operate year round, but a vessel of Arctic Class 1 is restricted to an operating season of 15 July to 15 October. Work is currently underway to revise these regulations towards "a new ship-categorization system, a more realistic and flexible ice zone system, more stringent structural design requirements and a requirement to separate pollutants from the outer shell" (Public Review Panel on Tanker Safety and Marine Spills Response Capability, 1990, 143). It is expected that shipping regulations will become more restrictive than ever as a result of these revisions.

SHIPS

The past thirty years of world shipping have witnessed a revolution in ship technology and size. Ships have become highly specialized, and very large. The world fleet has grown from about 130 million gross registered tonnes (grt) in 1960 to 436 million grt in 1991 (OECD, 1993). Container ships, which were almost unknown in 1960, have become an integral link in the international intermodal transportation system. In 1960 the largest ship afloat was approximately 100,000 deadweight tonnes (dwt); since then, ships five times that size have been built. In Canada, though, the development of the merchant fleet has not been as spectacular. Certainly specialization has occurred, but the size of the fleet has not changed as dramatically as has the world fleet.

a) The Canadian Registered Merchant Fleet

With less than 1 per cent of the registered world fleet in tow, Canada is now a relatively unimportant registrant of merchant ships. But this was not always the case. At the end of World War 2, Canada possessed the ninth largest tonnage of merchant vessels in the world. Changes since that time, however, have put Canada's fleet in a second- or even third-class position: the rise of the "Flag of Convenience"[3] nations has attracted ship registrations; Canadian government policy has been to treat international shipping services as something to be purchased on the open market, instead of protecting national shipbuilding and shipowning interests; developing nations

---

[3] Those nations that allow the registration of ships owned by non-nationals in order that shipowners may save on lower crew costs, avoid corporate taxes and take advantage of less stringent ship-manning and operating regulations are called "Flag of Convenience" nations. The two most important are Liberia and Panama.

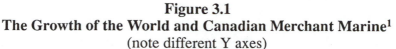

Figure 3.1
The Growth of the World and Canadian Merchant Marine[1]
(note different Y axes)

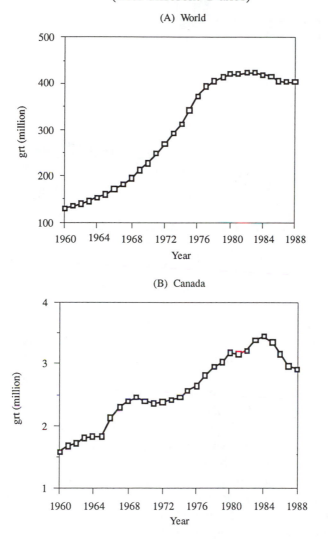

[1] Ships of 100+ grt

Source: OECD (1989)

have established their own merchant fleets; and the Japanese, Soviets, and Chinese have strengthened their fleets.

Figure 3.1a shows the growth of the world fleet since 1960; Figure 3.1b shows what has happened in Canada. Figure 3.2 plots

Figure 3.2
Canadian Merchant Fleet as a Per Cent
of the World Fleet

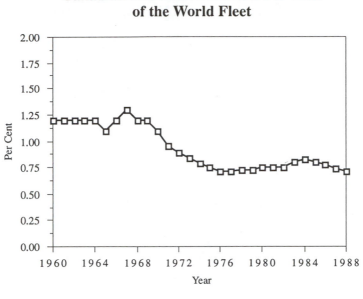

Source: OECD (1989)

that share of the world fleet which is Canadian.

Clearly the Canadian fleet, while expanding its tonnage at substantially the same rate as the world fleet, did so on a very small scale compared to the world fleet. The 1960s and 1970s were periods of fleet growth, while tonnages have slipped in the 1980s as the demand for shipping services declined (this is especially true on the world scene for oil and on the Canadian scene for Great Lakes shipping of iron ore and grain). Some of the overbuilding in the the 1960s and 1970s resulted in laid-up shipping and even scrapping of ships. The recession of the early 1980s was not kind to the shipping industry, either, on the world scale or in Canada; many companies experienced bankruptcy, takeovers, and consolidation.

The Canadian proportion of the world fleet is small and slowly declining. Canada's share had ranked ninth at the close of World War 2, just behind the then USSR and ahead of Sweden, but had slipped to sixteenth in 1960, and thirty-second by 1988, placing between Gibralter and Malta.

The years of World War 2 were important for the Canadian shipbuilding industry. Because of European hostilities and an obvious lack of resources, Britain looked to Canada as a source of ships. The first order for Canadian-built merchant ships to serve in the war was placed by Britain in 1940. By the end of the war, Canada had built 398 merchant vessels (Transport Canada, 1985, 4) and the Canadian government had become a major shipowner—not because of commercial opportunity but because of strategic war-time necessity. Immediately after the war these vessels did serve with commercial success, but by 1948 it was clear that the vessels would have difficulty maintaining profitable positions unless Canada was prepared to subsidize their operation. The Canadian Maritime Commission recommended in 1949 that such subsidization was not feasible, and in the same year Prime Minister Louis St. Laurent announced that the Canadian government would not maintain a shipping industry at the taxpayers' expense (Transport Canada, 1985, 14). Thus the Canadian government's financial policy of non-support for the merchant marine was established—a policy which has remained substantially unchanged ever since. As a result, the Canadian merchant marine has not been a force in international shipping; its function is mainly to supply shipping services to coastal and Great Lakes waterways.

In recent years the government has twice reviewed the feasibility of supporting a Canadian registered deep-sea merchant marine. Both *A Shipping Policy for Canada* (Transport Canada, 1979) and the *Task Force on Deep-Sea Shipping* (Transport Canada, 1985) recommended against the federal government taking steps to establish such a fleet. It was argued that shippers receive adequate service under current government policy, and that there were inadequate qualitative and quantitative reasons to justify the use of scarce national resources for the deep-sea shipping industry. In the 1985 report it was argued that the various benefits that might arise from the creation of a national fleet—an improved balance of payments position, creation of employment for sailors and officers, expansion of employment in auxiliary industries (such as shipbuilding), and the strengthening of national security—would not necessarily materialize. Not all members of the Task Force agreed with these statements. A minority report filed by two of the members representing Canadian labour stated that there were a number of compelling arguments to support a "gradual development of a Canadian-flag deep-sea fleet" (Transport Canada, 1985, 63). Suggestions included the introduction of Canadian registered ships on selected trade routes where a market niche could be established. However, the recommendations of the main report held sway, and few changes in federal government policy have been made.

In the late 1980s there was a discussion of a "second" registry for Canada. This proposal was put forward by Canadian shipowners/operators and labour, and argued that ships be owned, managed and crewed by Canadians. The vessels would not be allowed to operate in Canadian protected trades under the *Canada Shipping Act* but they would be subject to Canadian navigation and safety regulations. The main advantage for the second registry of ships would be that seafarers would be exempt from income tax and companies would not pay corporate tax on the foreign profits from their vessels. According to the Canadian Shipowners' Association, "Transport Canada officials were supportive but the Department of Finance was concerned about tax exemptions associated with exemption from corporate and personal income tax while a ship is engaged in international trade within the second registry" (Canadian Shipowners' Association, 1988, 5–6). It is unlikely that a second registry will be developed in the current Canadian fiscal environment.

In early 1991 the Canadian government took steps to attract foreign shipowners to Canada (especially to Vancouver), but not the ships themselves. The government agreed to "allow foreign shipowners to establish their headquarters in Canada without being taxed on their worldwide business holdings" because their ships would "still sail under foreign registry" (*Globe and Mail*, 22 Feb. 1991: B6). The rationale for the initiative was that foreign shipping companies, especially those from Hong Kong, can create new employment in ship management, banking, law and marine administration. The initiative will do nothing to expand the actual size of the Canadian-registered merchant fleet.

Canada does have a responsibility to develop an ocean-going fleet with expertise in operations in the Canadian Arctic. The *Task Force on Deep-Sea Shipping* recognized this responsibility: "The future exploitation of the Arctic will depend on the availability of reliable and economic shipping services. . . . While Canada already has considerable expertise in Arctic navigation and transportation, it is essential that Canada make a strong and concerted effort to remain at the leading edge of Arctic maritime technology" (Transport Canada, 1985, 58). Chapter 8 reviews Canadian shipping in the Arctic, but here it is worthwhile to discuss the construction of the M.V. ARCTIC, a unique icebreaking, cargo-carrying vessel built to serve two purposes: to undertake commercial bulk shipping from the Canadian Arctic to southern markets in Europe and North America, and to fulfill a research role in the testing and development of technology for Arctic operations and navigation.

The M.V. ARCTIC was commissioned in 1978 and built at Port Weller Drydocks in St. Catharines. She is owned and operated by the

Canarctic Shipping Company, a joint venture between the Government of Canada (51 per cent participation) and the Northwater Navigation Company (made up of Federal Commerce and Navigation, Canada Steamship Lines and Upper Lakes Shipping). The ARCTIC was the first vessel built that complied with the Canadian Arctic Shipping Pollution Prevention Regulations of 1974 (see Chapter 8). She was built as a Arctic Class 2 vessel, able to cut through 60 cm (2 ft) of level first-year ice at a speed of 4 or 5 knots (Webb, 1978, 22). This ability allowed the extension of her normal navigation season in the Eastern Arctic. At 210 m long and 28,000 dwt, the ARCTIC is about the size of a Great Lakes bulk carrier, which is small by ocean-going standards. Nonetheless, she is 100 m longer than the largest Canadian Coast Guard icebreaker, the LOUIS S. ST-LAURENT.

In 1986 the ARCTIC underwent extensive conversion and upgrading. The conversion changed her status to that of an OBO, capable of carrying either wet bulk or dry bulk cargoes. Three of the original five holds were converted to new bulk oil cargo tanks, providing an oil capacity of slightly over 20,000 tonnes (Luce, 1985, 25) The upgrading improved her icebreaking capabilities to that of an Arctic Class 4 vessel, able to continuously move forward through ice 1.2 m (4 ft) thick. A new bow was added to the vessel and the parallel mid-body of the vessel was strengthened. Both improvements came about directly because of the information and experience gained in ice operations during the first seven years of the ARCTIC's work in the north.

In recent years the ARCTIC has been employed principally in the transport of lead and zinc concentrates from Nanisivik and Polaris mines, and light crude oil from Bent Horn. She carries about 25,000 tonnes of concentrates per trip and makes one or two trips per year from Nanisivik and three to five from Polaris, depending on scheduling and demand for her services. The concentrates are shipped to Antwerp, Nordenham (Germany) or Darrow (Louisiana) (Canarctic Shipping Co., 1990). The ARCTIC's movement of crude oil is currently the only sea transport of the product from the Canadian Arctic. About 150,000 barrels or 20,000 tonnes are moved each trip; two trips were made in 1990. The oil has been destined for Montreal and Kalumborg (Denmark) for refining (Canarctic Shipping Co., 1990). Grain, the other bulk commodity carried by the ARCTIC, has not been shipped since 1982 due to a decline in the grain trade and the changed distribution of markets (see Chapter 2).

Technologically, the ARCTIC has been redesigned based on the

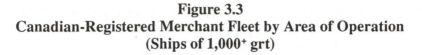

Figure 3.3
Canadian-Registered Merchant Fleet by Area of Operation
(Ships of 1,000⁺ grt)

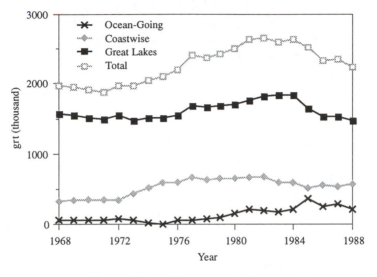

Source: National Transportation Agency and
Canadian Transport Commission (1968–1988)

information collected over its period of operation. A prototype system for ice navigation also has been developed and is especially useful during the long Arctic night. The Shipboard Ice Navigation Support System (SINSS) uses satellite and airborne radar imagery to provide information on ice conditions. This information, when combined with traditional ice navigation aids, ensures that a safe route is planned and followed through extensive and heavy ice cover. The SINSS exemplifies the kind of expertise necessary to Canada's development as a potential leader in Arctic commercial shipping operations. Although the size of Canada's Arctic fleet is never likely to be large, and therefore Canada's success in the area will not affect its rank in fleet registration statistics, it is important that Canada control the development in one of the last shipping frontiers in the world.

b) Components of the Canadian Fleet

The breakdown of the Canadian fleet into its geographical components of operation (Figure 3.3) shows the dominance of Great Lakes shipping. Technically, this category should be called "Inland Waters"; it is reported as such by the National Transportation Agency. However, here it will be referred to as the Great Lakes fleet, because no Inland Waters ship of 1,000⁺ grt operates outside of the Great Lakes and St. Lawrence River. Today about two-thirds of the entire Canadian fleet, including ocean-going and coastwise ships, operates on the Great Lakes. This figure marks a decrease of activity since 1968, when 80 percent of the fleet operated there. The coastwise component remains relatively stable at 25 per cent of the total functioning fleet, and there has been some growth in the ocean-going fleet, which stands at about 10 per cent of the total. The growth in the world fleet has come about not because of policy initiatives on the part of the Canadian government, but because of efficient technology developed for self-loading and self-unloading of bulk commodities on the Great Lakes, technology that has been put to use in international deep-sea trading, as well (see below).

i) The Great Lakes Fleet

Great Lakes shipping is dominated by bulk commodities such as grain, iron ore and coal, and lesser bulks such as limestone, cement and salt. Very little general cargo and a decreasing amount of petroleum products are carried. These cargo types determine the types of vessels that operate on the Lakes. As Figure 3.4 shows, dry bulk carriers dominate. In fact, over 95 per cent of the Great Lakes tonnage consists of dry bulk carriers. In the 1960s and early 1970s, a number of small tankers (twenty to thirty, with 75,000 to 100,000 grt total) operated on the Lakes and in the St. Lawrence River; but by the middle of the 1980s, that number had decreased to two (with less than 10,000 grt total) because trucking has taken over the distribution responsibility. The general cargo fleet has never been large; only eight vessels were designated as such in 1972 (48,000 grt total) and only three were operating in 1988 (14,000 grt total). The passenger vessels are ferries, most of which operate on the St. Lawrence River.

The dry bulk fleet is the mainstay of Canadian registered ships, not only on the Great Lakes, but in general. Table 3.3 shows the importance of dry bulk carriers in terms of number of ships and carrying capacity (dwt). Both number and capacity of the dry bulk carriers have declined, but close to 40 per cent of all Canadian ships are still dry bulk carriers, and about 70 per cent of the fleet's carrying capacity is in these ships.

Though the decline in the number of operating bulkers is quite sharp, there has not been a corresponding decline in the tonnage of bulkers (see Table 3.3 and Figure 3.4). The relative stability in tonnage suggests that bulk carriers have increased in size—which indeed they have. The St. Lawrence Seaway, opened in 1959, enabled larger lake vessels to proceed directly from the Lakes to the St. Lawrence River.

Table 3.3:
Relative Importance of the Great Lakes
Dry Bulk Fleet for Selected Years

Year	Total Canadian Registered Fleet[1]		Great Lakes Dry Bulk Carriers			
	No.	dwt (millions)	No.	% of Total	dwt (millions)	% of Total
1968	287	2.626	152	53.0	2.186	83.2
1974	262	2.613	110	42.0	2.025	77.4
1981	271	3.599	111	40.5	2.476	68.8
1988	209	3.001	81	38.8	2.112	70.3

[1] Ships of 1000+ grt

Source: Derived from National Transportation Agency and
Canadian Transport Commission (1968–1988)

Figure 3.4
Great Lakes Fleet of Ships of 1,000+ grt
(note log axis)

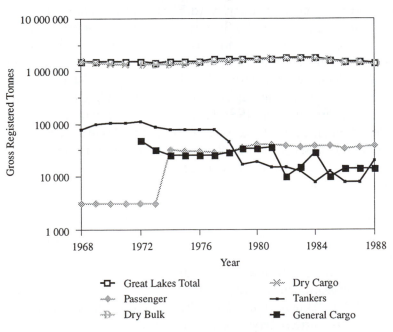

Source: National Transportation Agency and
Canadian Transport Commission (1968–1988)

These larger vessels (Seaway maximum size is 730 feet) "permitted the early retirement of a considerable number of 250-foot "canallers" (Shaw, 1978, 587). Figures from the annual report of the Dominion Marine Association, the organization that represents Great Lakes shipowners, show that for 1968 alone, six new ships of 160,000 dwt total were commissioned, five were on order and eighteen of 115,000 dwt total were scrapped (Dominion Marine Association, 1968). This trend in building new Seaway-size vessels to replace aging and less efficient bulkers continued throughout the 1970s and into the 1980s. Between 1961 and 1986, federal government policy encouraged the construction of new ships with shipbuilding subsidies, though towards the end of this period the subsidies had been reduced to token amounts. The first subsidy program, called the Ship Construction Assistance Regulations (SCAR), began in 1961 and provided 40 per cent of approved costs for non-fishing vessels built in Canadian shipyards. This was later reduced to 35 per cent of costs. More than one-third of the $137 million paid out in this program between 1961 and 1966 went to the construction of bulk carriers (de Silva, 1988, Table 3.2).

Beginning in January 1966, SCAR was replaced by Ship Construction Subsidy Regulations (SCSR), which first allowed a 25 per cent subsidy of approved costs for non-fishing vessels; the amount declined to 17 per cent for vessels constructed after 28 February 1973. The Shipbuilding Temporary Assistance Program (STAP) was introduced in 1970, but it only allowed shipbuilding subsidies for ships constructed for export, and these subsidies ranged from 17 to 12.5 per cent of approved costs depending on the size of the vessel and the date of construction. Between 1975 and 1986 the federal government operated the Shipbuilding Industry Assistance Program (SIAP), which brought together the existing export subsidy program and domestic subsidy programs. Subsidies were originally set at 14 per cent of approved costs, in 1976, and declined by 1 per cent per annum, staying at 8 per cent for vessels built after 31 December 1980.[4] In the period of its operation SIAP paid out $480.3 million. The largest single vessel type receiving shipbuilding assistance was the bulk carrier, which was granted $98.5 million. Shipbuilding subsidies were abolished in 1986, but other forms of support for the shipbuilding industry still exist: tariff protection, procurement policies and subsidies for modernization provide some financial assistance (de Silva, 1988, 81).

A significant change in shipping on the Lakes has been the rise in the number of self-unloaders in operation. These ships carry their

[4] An exception to this pattern occurred between 1977 and 1979, when subsidies were raised to 20 per cent.

own unloading mechanism, allowing the ships to serve ports that lack such equipment and improving ship turnaround in ports with such equipment. Self-unloaders had been part of shipping in the Lakes for many years prior to the opening of the Seaway, but the Seaway gave impetus to their development because of the maximum sized vessel the Seaway allowed. As Figure 3.5 shows, 31 of the 81 dry bulk carriers operating in the Great Lakes were self-unloaders in 1988. This is a great increase from the 16 self-unloaders of the 186 dry bulk carriers in 1960, and 24 of 122 in 1970 (Shaw, 1978, 588). The self-unloaders tend to be maximum sized vessels, as Figure 3.6 shows.

Self-unloaders are particularly efficient at handling coal, and as the demand for coal increased at steel mills (in Hamilton, Sault Ste. Marie and Nanticoke) and at power stations (at Nanticoke and Lakeview), the maximum-sized self-unloader was adopted. The self-unloaders were not especially advantageous in handling grain since it is destined for elevators complete with sophisticated handling equipment. However limestone, salt, cement and iron ore, along with coal and grain, are all handled by self-unloaders.

The self-unloading ship technology, along with certain modifications in ship construction, has enabled some Canadian Great Lakes shipowners to operate part of the year on the Great Lakes and part on deep-sea trades. Ships that participate in fresh water/salt water trades have been termed "salty-lakers". The two companies which pioneered this activity in the late 1970s and early 1980s were Canada Steamship Lines (CSL) and Upper Lakes Shipping. Their original plan was to operate the ships within the Great Lakes during the Seaway season, carrying Canadian cargoes (coal, iron ore, grain) between Canadian points or across the Lakes to the USA; then, during the winter months, they planned to operate on deep-sea trades. At first the ships were Canadian-registered in order to take part in Canadian cabotage trade.

The drawback to the operation of salty-lakers in the ocean trades is their relatively small size. They must be built to Seaway dimensions which means that their ocean-carrying capacity is restricted to about 35,000 tonnes. Also, because the ships are Canadian-registered, they are subject to Canadian shipping and taxation laws, and must be Canadian crewed. This adds about $1.0 to $1.25 million (at 1990 cost levels) to the ship's operation (Misener Shipping Co., 1990). But the advantage of the self-unloader is the quick turnaround time of the ship while in port. Unloading rates of 4,400 to 6,000 tonnes per hour (depending on the commodity) allow a ship to be fully unloaded in hours instead of days.

With a softened Canadian economy and the subsequent decline in the Great Lakes shipping (see Chapter 6), many of the salty-lakers

Figure 3.5
Great Lakes Dry Bulk Fleet of 1988 by Year of
Build or Latest Upgrade

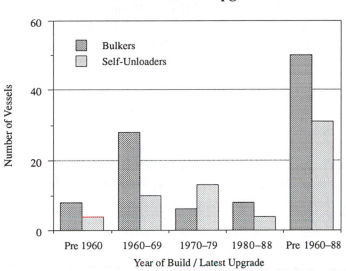

Source: National Transportation Agency and
Canadian Transport Commission (1968–1988)

Figure 3.6
Great Lakes Dry Bulk Fleet of 1988 by Size

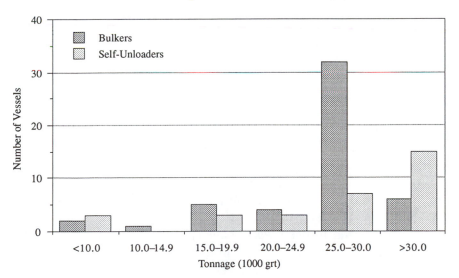

Source: National Transportation Agency and
Canadian Transport Commission (1968–1988)

have transferred to foreign registry and now concentrate entirely on foreign trades. For example, Upper Lakes Shipping does not operate any Canadian-registered vessels in deep-sea trades. Both the M.V. PIONEER and the M.V. AMBASSADOR, built for Great Lakes and ocean trading in 1981 and 1983, respectively, now operate only on the deep sea, concentrating on bulk trades in Eastern North America, Caribbean, USA Gulf and South American north coast markets (ULS Marbulk Inc., 1990). Originally, these ships were Canadian-registered, but they were "flagged out" to foreign registry in 1987 (M.V. PIONEER) and 1988 (M.V. AMBASSADOR). Another Great Lakes operator, Misener Shipping, had three salty-lakers operating from 1983–1987. All three ships, SELKIRK SETTLER, CANADA MARQUIS and SASKATCHEWAN PIONEER, were foreign-built but were placed on Canadian registry. With the increased costs of operating under Canadian registry and the decline of Great Lakes cargoes, the vessels were flagged out over the three year period from 1988-1990. Typical cargoes carried and trading routes served included grain, transported from the Lakes to western and eastern Europe and the Mediterranean; steel products from north and south Europe, brought into the Lakes; potash, moved from the Lakes to Europe; iron ore and coal from Canada, taken to the USA east coast and Gulf; and salt and fertilizers transported from north Africa to Europe and the Baltic Sea. Despite the change in ship registry, trading on the Great Lakes is still part of the operation of these ships.

Canadian Steamship Lines (CSL), the largest Canadian dry bulk carrier, has taken its Canadian-developed self-unloading technology to the deep-sea trades. In fact, in 1988 international operations comprised 25 per cent of CSL's marine revenues (Ryan, 1989, 11). Self-unloaders such as the ATLANTIC SUPERIOR and ATLANTIC ERIE (launched in 1984 as HON. PAUL MARTIN, but renamed) were built and originally registered in Canada, and were intended to operate both on the Great Lakes and in deep-sea trades; but they have been taken off Canadian registry, re-registered in the Bahamas, and now operate only on foreign trades. One of the operations which CSL pioneered in the early 1980s was the use of the self-unloaders to "topoff" large ocean-going bulkers that were too large to enter American ports. The self-unloaders load coal at Norfolk, Virginia and then proceed to deep water havens at the Strait of Canso or in the Gulf of St. Lawrence where mid-stream transfer of the coal to the partially-loaded, large ocean-going bulkers takes place (Ryan, 1989, 11 and *Seaports and the Shipping World*, 1984, 34). CSL self-unloaders are also active in the trans-shipment trade of bulk commodities, especially coal and ores, in Western Europe. Commodities that land in Rotterdam and other European ports on the largest ocean-going ships are taken aboard the self-unloaders and trans-shipped, for example, to Portugal or Bremen, Germany (Ryan, 1989, 11). CSL has built new self-unloaders in Brazil that are too large to enter the Great Lakes; these are dedicated to deep-sea trades. Thus, a technology that was developed for Great Lakes shipping has been taken outside of its original realm of operation and has had a significant impact on the conduct of shipping business worldwide.

iii) The Coasting Fleet

This fleet consists of two geographical sub-fleets: one on each of the Atlantic and the Pacific Coasts. There are more ships of 1,000[+] grt (and hence more ship tonnage) operating on the Atlantic Coast than on the Pacific, a reflection of the much greater diversity of goods handled there. Figures 3.7 and 3.8 show the tonnage of the fleet operating on respective coasts.

No one type of ship dominates the Atlantic coast fleet. Dry cargo ships, tankers and ferries are all well represented. Generally, shipping on the Atlantic coast has experienced tonnage increases since 1972, though the figures for the late 1980s are somewhat lower than those of the middle 1970s. The decrease reflects a weakened Atlantic economy in the 1980s and an increase in competition from other means of transport (principally trucks). In the early to middle 1970s there was an increase in the dry cargo ship tonnage, but tonnage again declined in later years. Tanker tonnage has always been important in the Atlantic Coast, since it is the principal means of distributing fuel oil and gasoline between the refineries (Holyrood, Halifax, Saint John, Quebec, and Montreal) and coastal communities.

Since the ferry system between the eastern provinces and along the coasts has been well established for many years,[5] it is not surprising to see that annual ferry tonnage has remained relatively stable. The principal ferry operator is Marine Atlantic, Inc. a federal Crown Corporation created in 1986. Before that year, Marine Atlantic operated as CN Marine, also a Crown Corporation, created in 1985 and operated by a subsidiary of Canadian National. The subsidiary, in turn, was created in 1979 from a CN department known as East Coast

---

[5] The Prince Edward Island ferry was established in 1873 under the terms of union between Prince Edward Island and Canada and remains a federal government obligation; similarly, the provision of freight and passenger service between Newfoundland and Canada was established as a federal government responsibility upon the entry of Newfoundland into Confederation in 1949.

Figure 3.7
Atlantic Coast Fleet (Ships of 1,000⁺ grt)

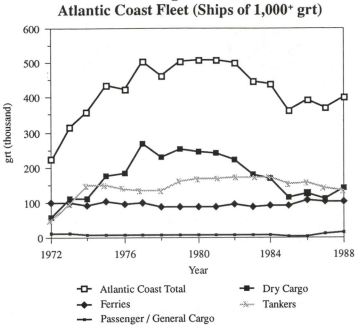

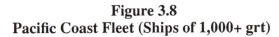

Source: National Transportation Agency and
Canadian Transport Commission (1968–1988)

Figure 3.8
Pacific Coast Fleet (Ships of 1,000+ grt)

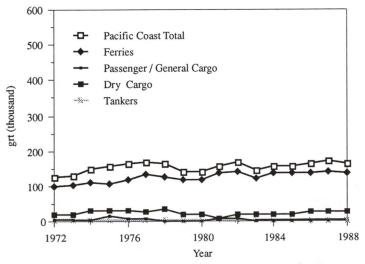

Source: National Transportation Agency and
Canadian Transport Commission (1968–1988)

Marine and Ferry Services (established in 1973). Before that, Canadian National Railway operated all services using vessels and facilities provided by the Ministry of Transport (Abbott and Mockus, 1986, 121). Even though the corporation names have changed, the federal government has remained responsible for much of the ferry and coastal services operated in the Atlantic provinces.

The auto ferry services operated by Marine Atlantic are:

- Cape Tormentine, N.B. - Borden, P.E.I. — year round

- North Sydney, N.S. - Port aux Basques, Nfld. — year round

- North Sydney, N.S. - Argentia, Nfld. — June to late October

- Lewisporte, Nfld. - Goose Bay, Labrador — June to mid-September

- Digby, N.S. - Saint John, N.B. — year round

- Yarmouth, N.S. - Bar Harbour, Maine — year round

In addition Marine Atlantic operates coastal services for passengers and goods on the south coast of Newfoundland, running ferries from Port aux Basques to Terrenceville year-round; and in the summer season, an operation is run on the north coast of the province serving Lewisport, St. Anthony and the Labrador coast north to Indian Harbour. In 1987, Marine Atlantic acquired a subsidiary company—Coastal Transport Limited—which operates an auto ferry service to Grand Mannan Island from the New Brunswick mainland. In total, Marine Atlantic operated 16 vessels in 1990, including vehicle ferries, passenger and cargo ships and freighters.

The other major ferry routes in the Atlantic provinces are privately operated, although two are subsidized by the Canadian government and one is partly owned by the province of Nova Scotia. The Canadian government subsidizes ferry operations from Souris, P.E.I. to Magdalen Islands, Que. (Co-opérative de Transport Maritime et Aérien), and Caribou, N.S. to Wood Islands, P.E.I. (Northumberland Ferries). The Nova Scotia government has an interest in the seasonal (May to October) ferry from Yarmouth, N.S. to Portland, Maine.

Although the tonnage of ferries operating on the Atlantic coast has been stable over time, the number of actual ships operating has been

Table 3.4:
Changes to Ships Added since 1960 in the Marine Atlantic Ferry Fleet

Year	Ship	Deployment	Capacity	Status Today
1965	PATRICK MORRIS	North Sydney to Port aux Basques	38 rail cars	lost at sea, April 1970
1966	LEIF ERIKSON	North Sydney to Port aux Basques	124 autos or 22 tractor trailers	sold, 1976
1967	FREDERICK CARTER	North Sydney to Port aux Basques	39 rail cars	retired and sold, 1986
	AMBROSE SHEA	North Sydney to Argentia and to Port aux Basques	525 passengers; 175 autos, or 14 tractor trailers	retired and sold, 1990
1968	JOHN HAMILTON GRAY	Cape Tormentine to Borden	516 passengers; 165 autos, or 18 tractor trailers, or 18 rail cars	operating on Cape Tormentine to Borden winter service
1971	PRINCESS OF ACADIA	Digby to Saint John	650 passengers; 155 autos, or 33 tractor trailers	operating on Digby to Saint John year round service
	HOLIDAY ISLAND and VACATIONLAND (sister ships)	Cape Tormentine to Borden	485 passengers; 155 autos, or 16 tractor trailers	operating on Cape Tormentine to Borden summer service
1974	MARINE CRUISER	North Sydney to Port aux Basques and to Argentia	76 autos or 10 tractor trailers	discontinued service, 1982
	MARINE NAUTICA	North Sydney to Port aux Basques	180 autos or 42 tractor trailers	charter discontinued, 1986
1975	MARINE ATLANTICA	North Sydney to Port aux Basques	180 autos or 42 tractor trailers	charter discontinued, 1986

.../cont'd

Table 3.4 (cont'd)

Year	Ship	Deployment	Capacity	Status Today
	SIR ROBERT BOND	North Sydney to Port aux Basques, but switched to Lewisporte to Goose Bay in 1978	200 passengers; 124 autos, or 26 tractor trailers, or 34 rail cars	operating on Lewisporte to Goose Bay summer service
1976	STENA NORDICA	North Sydney to Port aux Basques	180 autos or 42 tractor trailers	charter discontinued, 1982
1982	STENA JUTLANTICA (renamed BLUENOSE in 1983)	North Sydney to Port aux Basques, but switched to Yarmouth to Bar Harbor in 1983	1,000 passengers; 255 autos, or 28 tractor trailers	operating on Yarmouth to Bar Harbor year round service
	ABEGWEIT	Cape Tormentine to Borden 40 tractor trailers, or 20 rail cars	974 passengers; 250 autos, or to Borden year round service	operating on Cape Tormentine
1986	CARIBOU	North Sydney to Port aux Basques	1,200 passengers; 350 autos, or 91 tractor trailers	operating on North Sydney to Port aux Basques year round service
	ATLANTIC FREIGHTER	North Sydney to Port aux Basques	12 passengers; 110 tractor trailers	operating on the North Sydney to Port aux Basques year round service as a freight vessel only
1990	JOSEPH and CLARA SMALLWOOD	North Sydney to Argentia and to Port aux Basques	1,200 passengers; 350 autos, or 91 tractor trailers	operating on North Sydney to Argentia summer service and North Sydney to Port aux Basques year round service

Source: Marine Atlantic (1991)

far from static. As Table 3.4 shows, the Marine Atlantic vehicle ferry fleet has added eighteen ferries since 1960, of which nine are still operating. The tendency over time is to replace smaller less efficient ferries with larger ones (the replacement of the AMBROSE SHEA by the JOSEPH and CLARA SMALLWOOD is one example; the replacement of the original ABEGWEIT, built in 1947, with the modern ABEGWEIT in 1982 is another). Chartered vessels such as the MARINE ATLANTICA, MARINE NAUTICA and the STENA NORDICA have been replaced with Canadian-built and -registered vessels. Also, the newer ferries are built to handle road vehicles, both auto and tractor trailer, in an efficient drive-through manner; the older ferries, built to handle rail cars as well as road vehicles, required side-loading or one-way loading and off-loading. With the abandonment of rail service in Newfoundland (in 1988) and in Prince Edward Island (in 1989), the ferries no longer need to accommodate rail car transport.

The Pacific coast fleet of 1,000⁺ grt is dominated by ferries (Figure 3.8). There is very little transport of dry bulk or wet bulk commodities on the West coast in vessels of 1,000⁺ grt. Even the transport of logs and pulpwood, the principal commodities moved in coastwise transport, is handled by tugs and barges much smaller than 1,000 grt. The predominant ferry operator is the British Columbia Ferry Corporation, created as a Crown Corporation of the British Columbia government in 1977. Its predecessor, the British Columbia Ferry Authority, was created in 1960 with the introduction of the Tsawwassen (mainland) to Swartz Bay (Vancouver Island) service. In 1961, BC Ferries purchased the Gulf Island service, the Horseshoe Bay to Nanaimo service, and the Horseshoe Bay to the Sunshine Coast service—all of which had been privately owned. In 1966, a service from northern Vancouver Island to Prince Rupert (via the Inside Passage) was begun. Finally, fourteen saltwater ferries that had been operated by the provincial Ministry of Transportation and Highways were transferred to BC Ferries in 1985. The continual growth of the existing fleet has made BC Ferries one of the largest ferry operators in the world, with thirty-eight ships (not all of which are over 1,000 grt) and twenty-four routes (British Columbia Ferry Corporation, undated, 5–7). In 1990 another route was added: it links Tsawwassen to Nanaimo, thereby enabling users to by-pass Vancouver itself when travelling from or to areas south of Vancouver.

Currently, the largest car-carrying ferry is the recently commissioned SPIRIT OF BRITISH COLUMBIA, the first of the new S (super) class ferries, with a capacity for 470 cars and 2,100 passengers and crew. At the other end of the scale, the smallest ferry, DOG-WOOD PRINCESS II, cannot carry any vehicles and has a passenger capacity of 38.

PORTS

Situated at the interface of land and water, ports enable the transfer of goods from ship to shore and vice versa. Their importance is felt both in the immediate area and far beyond—at regional, national and even international levels. Locally, ports act as a generator of direct and induced employment; beyond the local level, port activity influences hinterland activity such as wheat growing, forestry, manufacturing and final consumption. The port is but one link in the chain of international transportation that joins one continental interior to another. As such, how well the port functions is not only of immediate concern to those who live in the city or town where it is found, but also to the many inland industries and individuals who depend upon the port to facilitate trade. Over time, the breadth of a port's impact has been extended as inland transportation has improved. Ports no longer only serve the needs of the immediate port area and surrounding region; the port's influence now can spread from one seacoast to another. Today, ports often compete not only against other ports on the same seacoast, but also against ports on different seacoasts. Over the past thirty years the influence of ports has become far reaching, but the relationship between ports and the urban areas they occupy, too, has changed. Before a discussion of the changing relationship of the city and port is undertaken, a brief description of the Canadian port system will be of use.

a)   The Canadian Port System

The administration, management and development of ports in Canada is a federal government responsibility carried out primarily through the Ministry of Transport. Commercial ports are administered by the Canadian Marine Transportation Administration division (McCalla, 1982). In addition, the Department of the Environment administers about 1,700 non-commercial public harbours and wharves used for fishing and recreational purposes under the terms of the *Fishing and Recreational Harbours Act*.

The commercial ports administered by the Marine Transportation Administration fall under the control of either the *Canada Ports Corporation Act*, the *Harbour Commission Act of 1964*, or the *Public Harbours and Port Facilities Act*. There are three Harbour Commissions (in Toronto, Hamilton and Belleville), which operate under their own separate federal legislations. In terms of sheer numbers, most commercial ports—approximately 720 in total—are classed as public harbours and facilities. In terms of tonnages of goods handled, Canada Ports Corporation (Ports Canada) ports and Harbour Commission ports are the most important. Included under the former are ports which are either local port corporations (LPC), which have a high degree of local autonomy under a local board of directors, a chairman and a port manager; or non-corporate (NC) ports, which are administered directly by Ottawa. The ports under the umbrella of Ports Canada include St. John's (LPC), Halifax (LPC), Saint John (LPC), Belledune (NC), Sept Iles (NC), Chicoutimi/Baie des Ha!Ha! (NC), Quebec (LPC), Trois Rivières (NC), Montreal (LPC), Prescott (NC), Port Colborne (NC), Churchill (NC), Vancouver (LPC) and Prince Rupert (LPC). The Harbour Commission ports include Belleville, Oshawa, Toronto, Hamilton, Windsor, Lakehead (Thunder Bay), Fraser River (New Westminster), North Fraser, Nanaimo and Port Alberni. In 1989, the twenty-four Ports Canada and Harbour Commission ports handled 60 per cent of all cargo at Canadian ports.

The fact that so few ports handled the majority of cargo indicates that the vast majority of ports are small and limited in what they do. But the size and scope of these ports are appropriate for their function. Only a small number of ports like Vancouver, Montreal and Halifax serve the international, national and regional interests of the country; the majority are small because they need to serve local markets. Ports such as Corner Book, Nfld., Newcastle, N.B., Yarmouth, N.S., Summerside, P.E.I., Chandler, Que., Port Stanley, Ont., Port Alice, B.C., or Nanisivik, N.W.T. are representative of the norm in Canadian ports; they permit the bulk transportation of local and regional produce by shipping. The few major ports are vitally important to the Canadian economy, but the many minor ones are also essential.

b)   The Influence of the Port

Ports employ people, generate expenditures, and facilitate trade both locally and beyond. From the economic point of view, the study of port influence involves "economic impact analysis," with its own specific methodology and terminology. Unfortunately, it is extremely difficult to make temporal comparisons of the economic impact of ports because of the differing methodologies and terminologies used in different studies. These are expensive studies to conduct, as well; consequently, relatively few studies of Canadian ports exist. The most

Table 3.5:
Job Creation by Canada Ports Corporation Ports, 1990

	Atlantic[1]	St. Lawrence[2]	Central[3]	West Coast[4]	Total System
Direct Jobs (D)	6 873	13 168	229	16 526	36 796
Induced Jobs (I)	4 850	11 521	214	12 172	28 757
Subtotal (D + I)	11 723	24 689	443	28 698	65 553
Related Jobs	n/d	n/d	n/d	n/d	367 000

[1] Ports of St. John's, Halifax, Saint John and Belledune
[2] Ports of Sept Iles, Chicoutimi, Baie des Ha! Ha!, Quebec, Montreal and Trois Rivières
[3] Ports of Prescott, Port Colborne and Churchill
4 Ports of Vancouver and Prince Rupert

Source: Canada Ports Corporation (1991a)

recent was conducted by the Canada Ports Corporation (1991a), which updates an earlier 1988 report. Individual economic impact studies were completed for the ports of Montreal (1973), Vancouver (1974), Quebec (1974) and Halifax (1977). The most thorough and rigorous is the CPC study; the individual port studies were more exercises in public relations than sound economic impact analyses.

The CPC's study showed that the impact of the ports operated by the Canada Ports Corporation reaches far into the Canadian economy. "Direct jobs" are those which exist solely because of the port activity, and include, for example, jobs in maritime services (longshoremen, tug boat operators, pilots, chandlers, forwarders), in surface transportation (trucking and railroad), in labour (shippers/consignees working directly at the port,) and in the banking and insurance sector. "Induced jobs" are created locally, regionally and nationally as a result of purchases made by those individuals directly employed in port activity. Finally, there are the "related" (sometimes referred to as "indirect") jobs that are held by the users of the port. They include the grain farmers, the coal miners, the potash workers, and people employed in manufacturing that depends for sales on export markets, or on imports for materials used in the manufacturing process. Table 3.5 shows the type and regional distribution of the jobs estimated to be have been created by the Canada Ports Corporation ports in 1990.

In practical terms, a regional breakdown of the location of the related jobs would be difficult since the entire Canadian economy would have to be accounted for by such statistics. People dependent on the activity of ports are found where grain is grown, where miner-

Table 3.6:
Tonnage of Canadian Container Cargo Diverted through
USA Ports (million tonnes)

	1984[1]	1989
Canadian Exports via USA Ports	0.6	1.2
Canadian Imports via USA Ports	0.7	1.1

[1] Estimated from data appearing in Archambault (1986).

Source: Archambault (1986) and Canada Ports Corporation (1991b).

als are mined, where timber is cut or where export-related manufacturing occurs. However, such dependence is not necessarily tied to one port, and one port alone; nor is it consistent in its port associations year after year. Competition between ports can be intense, and Prairie grain, for example, can be exported through Vancouver or Prince Rupert; Eastern Townships forest products can go by way of Quebec or Saint John; Central Canadian containers can pass through Montreal or Halifax. Fluctuations in the container trade prove how vulnerable ports are to competition and to decisions over which the port has very little influence.

The Central Canadian market receives and sends containers that might pass through any of a dozen ports, including Halifax, Montreal or Saint John on Canada's East coast; New York, Philadelphia or Baltimore on the USA Eastern seaboard; Vancouver or New Westminster on Canada's West coast; and Seattle, Tacoma or Los Angeles/Long Beach on the American West coast. The shipper, the freight forwarder, and the shipping company itself decide which port to use depending on the actual origin or destination of the goods. All the port can do is provide as reliable a service as possible at a competitive rate.

Containers which originate in or are destined for Canada are regularly handled at United States ports, to the detriment of Canadian ports. However, containers originating in or destined for the United States pass regularly through Canadian ports. This practice of diverting traffic is one of long standing, and it seems to be increasing in frequency. Table 3.6 shows the amount of Canadian diverted container cargo handled in USA ports for 1984 and 1989. In 1989 the diverted cargo amounted to an estimated 270,000 twenty-foot equivalent units, or teu (Canada Ports Corporation, 1991b, 56). The estimated annual volume of USA container traffic handled at Canadian ports was approximately the same, estimated at between 250,000 and 300,000 teu (Canada Ports Corporation, 1991b, 56). The ports of Tacoma, New York and Seattle handled over 80 per cent of Canadian import trade and over 70 per cent of Canadian export trade trans-shipped through the United States in 1989 and 1990 (National Transportation Agency of Canada, 1992, 210). The diversion of containers between USA and Canadian ports benefits Canadian ports in the East—principally at Montreal, which handles those USA mid-West based containers to/from Europe that could pass through New York, or Baltimore or Hampton Roads. Conversely, Vancouver on the West coast loses imported containers that originate in Asia and are handled at USA West coast ports such as Seattle, Tacoma and increasingly Los Angeles and Long Beach. What is even more interesting is that the Canadian East coast ports of Saint John and Halifax are also experiencing the negative impact of diversion through West coast USA ports (see Chapter 4). Containers from East Asia and destined for Central Canada, for example—which at one time passed through Saint John or Halifax—often arrive in Los Angeles, Long Beach, Oakland, Tacoma or Seattle and then continue to Central Canada by rail.

Thus the influence of a single port is not confined to the coastal region, or even to the country in which it is found.

c) The Relationship between Ports and Urban Areas

In the last thirty years, a major change has taken place in the waterfront land use of both major and minor Canadian ports. Gone from central waterfronts are the rotting wooden piers, the obsolete warehouses, and the derelict buildings associated with port activity between the last century and the beginning of the 1960s. In their place, office buildings, hotels, shopping arcades, public open space, marinas and condominiums have been built. Many cities have rediscovered their central waterfronts, once port operations moved to open spaces with better land and sea access. Chapter 5 presents a case study of this phenomenon as it took place in Montreal; here it is worthwhile to refer to a few of the developments in several Canadian port cities, so that the generalized nature of the change might be appreciated.

In Vancouver, the False Creek redevelopment (including Granville Island) and the continuing development of the site of EXPO 86 have made new use of the waterfront, as have Canada Place and Gastown on Burrard Inlet. Toronto's Harbourfront, Montreal's Le Vieux Port, Saint John's Market Square, and Halifax's Historic Properties have accomplished similar goals. Smaller ports such as Kingston and Collingwood, both in Ontario, have also experienced the same phenomena (Tunbridge, 1988).

Why have waterfronts changed so drastically in recent years? There are many forces at work, but all explanations must take two major factors into account: economics and the environment. On the economics side, new shipping technology has changed how cargo is handled on the waterfront, so that economies of scale prevail; as ships became larger, cargo handling was necessarily mechanized. Consequently, small piers with gangs of labour and storage sheds gave way to new cargo terminals that use large cranes or conveyor belts and open storage areas. The size of these new facilities dictated that they be constructed at sites removed from the central waterfront. Consequently, the old facilities were abandoned by the industry, and their use for more people-oriented activities became possible. On the environment side, people rediscovered that the waterfront, once cleaned up, is a desirable area in which to work and relax, even to live. The central port waterfront was transformed from a dirty, industrial cargo-handling, closed area to a clean extension of the central city, newly available for business, residential and recreational use. As a result, the relationship between ports and the cities they occupy changed. The waterfront is not solely the domain of the port and its related cargo activities and, increasingly, it has taken on a greater human orientation.

d) The Development of the Canadian Port Infrastructure, 1960–1989

Not all Canadian ports have grown at the same rate. Some have expanded; some have declined; some have ceased operations altogether; others have been created. The change in their geographical distribution has been caused by several factors: a tendency to concentrate cargo at fewer and fewer ports, and changes in port performance are two of the most important. The statistics published each year by Statistics Canada list tonnage of cargoes and types of commodities handled, whether loaded or unloaded, as well as the designation of the cargoes as international or coastwise. From this listing it is possible to estimate the number of ports operating in any one year.

In 1960, there were 249 ports handling some type of cargo in waterborne commerce. In 1989 there were 238. Table 3.7 shows the total number of operational ports for several selected years.

The total number of ports operating in Canada has decreased somewhat since 1960, particularly the number of ports engaged in both coastwise and international cargo handling. Interestingly, ports

Table 3.7:
Number of Canadian Ports Handling Coastwise Cargo Only,
International Cargo Only or Both Types of Cargo, 1960–1989

Year	Coastwise Only	International Only	Coastwise and International	Total
1960	63	17	169	249
1965	53	12	146	211
1970	78	19	143	240
1975	83	11	133	227
1980	95	39	122	256
1985	69	44	122	235
1989	68	50	120	238

Source: Derived from Statistics Canada (54–203, 54–204, 54–209, 54–210 and 1989)

which handle only international cargo have increased in number. This may be because more ports are increasingly involved in direct shipments overseas; or it may be that ports which at one time were involved in coastwise and international shipping have lost their coastwise business to land transportation competition. The number of ports handling only coastwise cargo has fluctuated over time.

It is probable that the decline in the total number of ports is even greater than is represented in Table 3.7. Up until 1980 Statistics Canada maintained a port category called "All Other Ports Not Elsewhere Stated" (NES) for international shipping in the provinces of Newfoundland, Nova Scotia, Prince Edward Island, New Brunswick, Quebec, Ontario, British Columbia and the Northwest Territories. This NES category collectively reported on the activities of very small ports and on non-ports such as bays or sheltered areas where cargo transfers occurred. But in 1980 Statistics Canada eliminated its NES category for international shipping ports. Thus for 1980, 1985 and 1989 the number of ports listed in Table 3.7 engaged in international shipping either exclusively or in combination with coastwise shipping is more accurate than the number listed for previous years, when the NES ports distort the figures. The NES category still exists for coastwise shipping ports, but over the years the number of ports in that category has become smaller.

A regional breakdown of the data shows that three of the five regions in the country have suffered port declines, whereas the other two have seen increases (see Table 3.8). Although there has been an overall decline in the number of ports in Eastern Canada, the number of International Only ports in the Atlantic region has increased. The

Table 3.8:
Regional Breakdown of Ports Handling Coastwise Cargo Only (C), International Cargo Only (I), or Both Types of Cargo (B), 1960–1989

	Atlantic[1]				St Lawrence[2]				Great Lakes[3]				Pacific[4]				Other[5]			
	C	I	B	Total	C	I	B	Total	C	I	B	Total	C	I	B	Total	C	I	B	Total
1960	17	7	72	96	20	3	21	44	11	6	47	64	15	1	27	43	1	0	1	2
1965	4	7	47	58	11	0	20	31	7	4	42	53	30	1	36	67	1	0	1	2
1970	10	9	50	69	13	3	23	39	10	6	33	49	45	1	35	81	0	0	2	2
1975	13	9	46	68	15	0	21	36	12	2	32	46	42	0	33	75	1	0	1	2
1980	12	25	47	84	13	3	21	37	15	5	27	47	54	6	26	86	1	0	1	2
1985	9	21	40	70	11	3	20	34	10	9	30	49	38	7	31	76	1	4	1	6
1989	8	20	45	73	11	6	18	35	6	10	30	46	42	8	27	77	1	6	0	7

[1] Atlantic region includes the ports of Newfoundland, Nova Scotia, New Brunswick and Prince Edward Island.

[2] St. Lawrence region includes the ports along the St. Lawrence River and north shore of the Gulf of St. Lawrence in Quebec and ports in the Gaspé region of Quebec.

[3] Great Lakes includes ports on the Great Lakes and along the St. Lawrence River in Ontario.

[4] Pacific region includes the ports of British Columbia.

[5] Other is the ports of Manitoba (Churchill) and the Northwest Territories.

Source: See Table 3.7

increase in ports in the Pacific region is even more dramatic: in 1960, the area boasted only 17 per cent of Canadian ports, but in 1989 one-third of all Canadian ports were found in British Columbia. Increased coastwise shipping of forest materials and other raw materials as well as increases in direct shipping to international markets of British Columbia products necessitated the construction of new ports. The overall decline in the East reflects the decline in Great Lakes shipping activity and increased transport competition with road transport, especially in the Atlantic provinces.

Ports including Carbonear, Curling and Hare Bay in Newfoundland, Georgetown and Victoria in Prince Edward Island, Arichat, Chester and Louisbourg in Nova Scotia, Moncton, Fredericton and Campbellton in New Brunswick, Cap Chat, Oka and Donnacona in Quebec, and Brockville, Killarney and Port Hope in Ontario all handled coastwise cargoes in 1960 but not in 1989. In other cases, new ports have been built since 1960, especially in British Columbia, but also in other regions. For example in British Columbia in 1989, port activity was reported at Jervis Inlet, Tasu, Port Alice and Butterfly Bay, none of which appear in the 1960 statistics. In the East, Nanticoke in Ontario, Becancour in Quebec, Come-by-Chance in Newfoundland and Belledune in New Brunswick are examples of new ports active in 1989.

Although the total number of operative Canadian ports has declined since 1960, the amount of cargo handled in the existing ports has grown significantly. A total of 151.153 million tonnes of international and coastwise cargo were handled in the 249 Canadian ports of 1960; in 1989, 362.263 million tonnes were handled in the 238 existing ports (ports in the category "All Other Ports Not Elsewhere Stated" [NES] were not included in this calculation). Obviously Canadian ports are, on average, handling more cargo now than ever before. It is to be expected, of course, that some ports have grown at faster rates than others, but are there any regional patterns to port growth and decline? Which ports are the big winners in cargo handling? Which are the losers?

Answers to these questions might be derived from Table 3.9, which shows the changes in ranking of Canadian ports between 1960 and 1989 based on their share of all cargo handled. Not every port's position is shown on the scale; only the "major ports"—defined quite arbitrarily as ports handling 1 per cent or more of the total cargo tonnage—are cited. The major ports are then divided into two groups: Tier I handles 5 per cent or more of the total cargo and Tier II handles between 1 and 5 per cent of the total. There were 22 major ports in both 1960 and 1989 but their total share of cargo tonnes handled

Table 3.9:
Ranking of Canadian Ports1 According to Share of Cargo Tonnes Handled, 1960 vs 1989

1960	1960 Rank with % of cargo tonnes	1989	1989 Rank with % of cargo tonnes
249 ports 151.153 million tonnes		238 ports 362.263 million tonnes	
Major-Tier I Ports Each port handles at least 5.00% of all cargo tonnes	4 Major-Tier I ports handling 33.51% of all cargo	4 Major-Tier I ports handling 35.54% of all cargo	
	1 Montreal 11.49		1 Vancouver 17.61
	2 Vancouver 7.84		2 Sept Iles 6.44
	3 Thunder Bay 7.27		3 Port Cartier 5.88
	4 Sept Iles 6.91		4 Montreal 5.61
Major-Tier II Ports Each port handles between 1.00 and 4.99% of all cargo tonnes	18 Major-Tier II ports handling 41.55% of all cargo	18 Major-Tier II ports handling 42.52% of all cargo	
	5 Hamilton 4.89		5 Halifax 4.51
	6 Halifax 4.56		6 Quebec 4.24
	7 S.S. Marie 2.82		7 Saint John 4.03
	8 Toronto 2.74		8 Thunder Bay 3.70
	9 Saint John 2.67		9 Hamilton 3.45
	10 Quebec 2.54		10 Prince Rupert 3.20
	11 New West'r 2.24		11 Nanticoke 2.63
	12 Port Alfred 2.18		12 Howe Sound 2.06
	13 Sydney 1.99		13 Come-by-Chance 1.75
	14 Sarnia 1.98		14 Baie Comeau 1.72
	15 Bell Is. 1.92		15 S.S. Marie 1.72
	16 Trois Rivières 1.65		16 Sarnia 1.57
	17 Sorel 1.63		17 New Westm'r 1.53
	18 Port Colborne 1.56		18 Sorel 1.48

.../cont'd

Table 3.9 (cont'd)

	19 Hantsport	1.31	19 E. Cst. Van. Is.	1.41
	20 Victoria	1.10	20 N Arm Fraser R.	1.34
	21 Windsor	1.09	21 Windsor	1.17
	22 Baie Comeau	1.00	22 Port Alfred	1.01

Minor-Tier III Ports

Each port handles between 0.10 and 0.99 % of all cargo tonnes

70 Minor-Tier III ports handling 23.30% of all cargo	52 Minor-Tier III ports handling 18.05% of all cargo
	24 Toronto 0.90
44 Prince Rupert 0.39	34 Sydney 0.53
45 Howe Sound 0.39	35 Trois Rivières 0.47
	36 Hantsport 0.47
	42 Victoria 0.35
	43 Port Colborne 0.35

Minor-Tier IV Ports

Each port handles less than 0.10% of all cargo

1960 Rank with % of cargo tonnes

157 Minor-Tier IV ports handling 1.64% of all cargo	164 Minor-Tier IV ports handling 3.89% of all cargo
97 Port Cartier 0.09	229 Bell Is. <0.01

1 Excludes ports in the category entitled All Other Ports Not Elsewhere Stated (NES).
Note: Montreal includes Contrecoeur, Quebec includes Levis, Toronto includes Lakeview, Sept Iles includes Pointe Noire.
Source: Statistics Canada (54–203, 54–204 and 1989)

Table 3.10:
Relative vs Absolute Decline in Canadian Major
Ports Engaged in Cargo Handling, 1960 vs. 1989

Ports Experiencing Relative Decline but Absolute Tonnage Increase	Ports Experiencing both Relative Decline and Absolute Tonnage Decrease
Montreal	Toronto
Thunder Bay	Sydney
Sept Iles	Bell Island
Hamilton	Trois Rivières
Halifax	Hantsport
Sault Ste Marie	Victoria
New Westminster	
Port Alfred	
Sarnia	
Sorel	
Port Colborne	

Source: derived from Statistics Canada (54–203, 54–204 and 1989)

increased from 75 per cent in 1960 to 78 per cent. The other main group of ports is the "minor" tier (ports handling less than 1 per cent of total international cargo), which in turn is divided into Tier III and Tier IV ports. The number of minor ports has declined from 227 (25 per cent of cargo) to 216 (22 per cent of cargo). There is some evidence here that fewer ports are handling more cargo; that the cargo is becoming concentrated in the larger ports; and that the decline in the number of ports and their share of cargo handled is taking place at the bottom end of the scale.

In 1989, as shown in Table 3.9, concentration or gains in cargo share are recorded for the major ports of Vancouver, Port Cartier, Quebec, Saint John, Prince Rupert, Nanticoke, Howe Sound, Come-by-Chance, Baie Comeau, East Coast Vancouver Island, North Arm Fraser River and Windsor. Interestingly, Nanticoke, Come-by-Chance, East Coast Vancouver Island and North Arm Fraser River were not reported as "ports" in 1960 (the latter two are statistical reporting areas and not individual ports). The performances of Vancouver, Port Cartier and, to a lesser extent, Prince Rupert are especially remarkable. The fact that two of these ports (Vancouver and Prince Rupert) are on the Pacific coast is an indication of how much the trading pattern of Canadian waterborne trade has shifted to the West coast, mainly because western Canadian resources (grain, coal, potash, sulphur, and timber) have become increasingly important in world trade—especially to the Pacific Rim area. Port Cartier, too, experienced a large gain in cargo share. Having started in a minor port position in 1960, Port Cartier has grown to become the third-ranked Canadian port in tonnage terms. The principal cargoes are iron ore from northern Quebec, destined for American, European and other international markets, as well as grains trans-shipped from Thunder Bay and destined for international markets. Iron ore loadings began there in 1961; grains were first handled in a significant amount in 1968.

Seventeen major ports have shown a decline in their share of cargo handled since 1960 (see Table 3.10). For the most part, these ports did not experience declines in actual tonnages handled; the declines are indicative of their reduced share of the total Canadian waterborne commerce. The six ports which experienced both relative decline and absolute tonnage decrease are mainly in Eastern Canada; three of them (Sydney, Bell Island and Hantsport) are found on the Atlantic coast. Two of these Atlantic ports, Bell Island and Hantsport, either were or are one-commodity ports. As the fortunes of that one commodity change, so the cargo handling at the port changes. Bell Island was a major iron ore producing centre up until 1966 when the mine closed; by early 1970 no shipments of iron ore were being made. Hantsport is a gypsum exporting port, and over time gypsum handling has decreased. It still approaches 1.5 million tonnes annually, but this is a reduction from the over 2 million tonnes handled in the early 1960s. Sydney has lost much of its coal trade, especially domestically, but it retains domestic gasoline and fuel oil trade as well as international coal and steel shipments. The dependency on limited raw materials (pulpwood, fuel oil, grain and coal) and a decline in their shipments accounts also for the relative and absolute decline at Trois Rivières, Victoria and Toronto.

Most of those ports that have lost relative ground but have experienced an absolute tonnage increase are found either on the Great Lakes or the St. Lawrence River (exceptions include Halifax on the Atlantic coast and New Westminster on the Pacific coast). The shift of the grain trade from the Great Lakes and the East coast to the West coast (see Chapter 2) accounts for the relative decline in tonnage at Montreal, Thunder Bay, Sorel, and Port Colborne. The relative decline in Hamilton, Sault Ste. Marie and Sept Iles tonnage is accounted for by changes in the steel industry and the decreased handling of either iron ore or coal or both. Relative declines in major port activities are not geographically determined, since all regions of the country have ports which have lost ground relative to the overall waterborne commerce increase.

Peter Rimmer (1966) shows a way to measure the geographical pattern of port performance. Following common methods for measuring changes in the concentration of industrial activity, Rimmer ranked ports according to their share of cargo tonnage handled in an initial year and a terminal year, and compared their relative increase or decline. These relative changes in concentration are then translated into absolute terms by calculating the difference between the actual tonnage of a port in the terminal year and the expected tonnage in that year if the port had grown at the national rate between the initial and terminal years. By comparing the actual and expected tonnage, Rimmer identified which ports performed at growth rates greater than the national rate, and which performed at growth rates of less than the national average.

Using this methodology in application to the Canadian port scene, the expected port tonnage for 1989 can be determined by multiplying the actual 1960 port tonnage by the national growth rate of total cargoes handled at all ports (excluding ports in the NES category) for the period between 1960 and 1989. This national growth rate was 2.3966. Table 3.11 shows those ports which outperformed the national rate and thus show a positive tonnage value (actual tonnage is greater than that expected) and those which underperformed the national rate and show a negative value (actual tonnage is less than that expected). Not surprisingly, given the discussion above, Vancouver, Port Cartier and Prince Rupert are three of the biggest "winners". Saint John and Quebec also show major gains due to the growth of crude oil imports and the handling of petroleum products. In addition, Saint John has developed a potash export trade and Quebec continues to be a major player in the grain trade.

Oil imports also explain the inclusion of Come-by-Chance as a major "winner." Come-by-Chance oil terminal did not exist in 1960; it was established in 1971, but closed from 1976 to 1987, at which time it re-opened under new ownership and management. Increases in log transport explain the higher than expected tonnages at Howe Sound, East Coast Vancouver Island and North Arm Fraser River. As was pointed out earlier, the latter two cargo-handling areas were not even listed as such in 1960, but were included in the B.C. NES category then. Nanticoke also was not listed in 1960; it first appeared in Statistics Canada shipping publications in 1975, when a coal-burning electrical generating station had been built at the port, soon to be followed by a steel mill—both of which have allowed Nanticoke's port to prosper.

A regional breakdown of the top ten winners gives an indication

Table 3.11:
Top 10 "Winners" and Top 10 "Losers" Among Canadian Ports Engaged in Cargo Handling, 1960 vs 1989

"Winners"[1]	Actual 1989 Tonnes (million)	Expected 1989 Tonnes(million)	Tonnes Difference (million)
Vancouver	63.752	28.400	35.352
Port Cartier	21.290	0.332	20.958
Prince Rupert	11.601	1.464	10.137
Nanticoke	9.532	0	9.532
Come-by-Chance	6.332	0	6.332
Quebec	15.367	9.217	6.150
Howe Sound	7.461	1.457	6.004
East Coast Van. Is.	5.100	0	5.100
Saint John	14.589	9.685	4.904
North Arm Fraser River	4.866	0	4.866
"Losers"[2]			
Sault Ste. Marie	6.221	10.220	-3.999
Port Alfred	3.677	7.897	-4.220
Trois Rivières	1.709	5.984	-4.275
Port Colborne	1.251	5.661	-4.410
Hamilton	12.507	17.720	-5.213
Sydney	1.922	7.223	-5.301
Toronto	3.266	9.912	-6.646
Bell Island	<0.001	6.962	-6.962
Thunder Bay	13.387	26.340	-12.953
Montreal	20.295	41.600	-21.305

[1] Defined as ports outperforming cargo expectations based on 1960 cargo levels multiplied by national growth rate of 2.3966 in total cargo handled at Canadian ports, 1960 vs. 1989.

[2] Defined as ports underperforming cargo expectations using the same criteria as above.

Note: Quebec includes Levis; Montreal includes Contrecoeur; Toronto includes Lakeview; Sept Iles includes Pointe Noire.

Source: See Table 3.9

of where ports have prospered in Canada in the last twenty-five years. Five of the ports—Vancouver, Prince Rupert, Howe Sound, East Coast Vancouver Island, and North Arm Fraser River—are on the Pacific coast; only one, Nanticoke, is on the Great Lakes. The St. Lawrence River and the Atlantic area each has two winners.

The regional breakdown of the major "loser" ports presents a different geographical pattern for 1989. There were two losers on the

Table 3.12:
Regional Breakdown of All "Winner" and
"Loser" Ports, 1960 vs. 1989

"Winners"[1]	Pacific	Great Lakes	St. Lawrence	Atlantic	Other	Total
Number	58	18	18	34	5	133
%	43.6	13.5	13.5	25.6	3.8	100
"Losers"[1]						
Number	19	28	17	39	2	105
%	18.1	26.7	16.2	37.1	1.9	100
Total Ports						
Number	77	46	35	73	7	238
%	32.4	19.3	14.7	30.7	2.9	100

[1] See Table 3.11 for definition of ports referred to as "winners" and "losers."

Atlantic coast, Bell Island and Sydney, which balanced the number of winners on that coast. The St. Lawrence River had three losers: Port Alfred, Trois Rivières and Montreal. The Great Lakes had five loser ports: Sault Ste. Marie, Port Colborne, Hamilton, Toronto and Thunder Bay. Finally, the Pacific coast was not represented by a loser port. The top loser port was Montreal, but this definition of a "loser" is a relative one, and the entire analysis is based on tonnage of cargo handled. In absolute terms, Montreal handled more cargo in 1989 than it did in 1960; however, its increase fell far short of what was expected, if the port's tonnage had increased at the national rate between 1960 and 1989.

The regional representation of winners and losers gives evidence of increased port performance on the Pacific coast and decreased port performance on the Great Lakes. The Atlantic region and the St. Lawrence River ports have struck a balance in terms of winners and losers. These conclusions are drawn by only looking at the top ten winners and top ten losers, though by expanding the analysis to include all ports in 1989, the conclusions are further verified (see Table 3.12). Clearly the Pacific region had a disproportionate number of winners compared to losers, and the Great Lakes had the opposite imbalance.

SUMMARY

Canada has an enormous water area available for commercial shipping. In order to facilitate shipping, the country has established an elaborate infrastructure, some of which is long-standing and traditional in function, other portions of which are more recent in origin and impose greater restrictions on ship operations.

Great changes in the operation of Canadian commercial waterways have taken place in terms of assistance given to ship navigation, the monitoring of ship traffic performance and the regulations imposed that restrict where shipping is allowed. Consequently, the autonomy enjoyed by ships' masters as they bring their ships through Canadian waters has been diminished. Masters are still responsible for the actions of their ships, but they must proceed cautiously in order to satisfy the regulations which are now in place. This is as it should be. With ever-larger tonnages transported in larger ships, and with increased public sensitivity to the needs of the environment, it is not surprising that the operation of ships in the commercial waterways has come under such scrutiny and control. The ARROW oil spill of about 8,000 tonnes is still Canada's largest marine pollution incident, though it is relatively insignificant on the world scale of such incidents. It could be argued that this record is the result of good luck and not of any safety steps that Canada has taken; but some credit must be given to the system of navigational infrastructure that is in place. The Public Review Panel of Tanker Safety and Marine Response Capability has found much to criticize within the navigational infrastructure, and it has made recommendations for its improvement; but the fact that such an elaborate infrastructure exists attests to Canada's concern for safety within its commercial shipping waterways.

The size of the Canadian-registered fleet is insignificant in world terms. It exists not to serve Canadian deep-sea interests, but rather to serve domestic trades. By far, the most important area of operation, as measured by tonnage of ships devoted to it, is the Great Lakes. Some interesting developments have happened in the Arctic with the M.V. ARCTIC, and there is a substantial passenger and vehicle ferry fleet on the coasts, as well, but Canadian-registered ships have not distinguished themselves on the world scene.

Over time, the fleet has become more modern and individual ships have become larger and more specialized, following world trends. Some worthy technological innovations have been developed and/or adopted in the fleet, including self-unloaders and the M.V. ARCTIC; and even the construction of very large ferries for the

Atlantic and Pacific coasts is indicative of Canada's expertise in the construction and operation of very modern vessels.

On a negative note, it would appear that the Canadian government has resigned Canada to being a second- or third-rate power in terms of international ship registration. Canada will never be a Japan, or a France, or a South Korea in its shipping abilities. Nor will it be allowed to be a haven for shipping in the guise of Liberia or Panama. International shipping is one of the most competitive businesses of the modern world, and the Canadian government has indicated that it will not become involved in a subsidy program in order to allow Canadian shipyards and shipowners to enter into that competition; nor does it wish to compromise its high standards of ship operation by trying to attract foreign vessels for Canadian registration. The government of Canada seems to be satisfied to see Canadian shipping requirements purchased in the international marketplace. But this policy may cause much money to leave the country; the loss was estimated at $5 billion in 1985, but an exact figure is not known (Transport Canada, 1985, 4). The government would rather not create an inefficient and expensive merchant fleet, and has maintained this position for thirty years. And as long as the international shipping scene remains competitive, it is unlikely that the policy will change in the future.

The following changes have also occurred in the Canadian port infrastructure in terms of number of ports and their performance:

- There has been a decrease in the total number of Canadian ports, particularly in those dedicated to the combination of coastwise and international shipping.

- The decrease in ports is most pronounced in the East, whereas the Pacific coast area has run counter to the trend, and has recorded an increase in ports.

- Fewer ports are handling more cargo. The major ports (those handling at least 1 per cent of total cargo) have increased their proportion of cargo handled from 75 per cent to 78 per cent.

- As indicated by "winners" and "losers," there has been increased port performance on the Pacific coast, and decreased performance particularly on the Great Lakes.

- The major port winners are Vancouver, Port Cartier and Prince

Rupert; the major losers are Montreal, Thunder Bay and Bell Island.

Overall, there has been a negative national shift in port numbers and performance in the past thirty years. Ports have had to adapt as new markets have opened, as old raw material sources have closed and new sources have been developed; competition from land transport has evolved to challenge water transportation's traditional activity in coastwise shipping, as well. Waterborne commerce is still concentrated in a limited number of larger ports, and the vast majority of ports handle small amounts of cargo. This was true in 1960 as well as 1989, and it will likely continue to be true in the future. The trend towards larger and larger ports and the concentration of more cargo in fewer ports will continue, based on competition and shifting markets and sources of commodities. There will always be a place for the small port as it serves the limited needs of its immediate area. The small port, however, may be the outlet for a local mine or locally produced forest products, or it may be the point of entry for bulk materials such as fuel oil or gasoline consumed locally. Individual ports, both large and small, will either decline in importance or grow in stature as the national and international needs of producers and consumers change. Ports can themselves affect their performance through the nature of their facilities and their performance, but much of what a port does is controlled by factors outside of its control. The analysis presented here shows that some ports have prospered extremely well in the past thirty years, as the Canadian economy has grown; but other ports have declined as their particular service has not been needed or as competing ports and land transportation have taken customers away from them. The conclusions drawn, however, are all based on cargo tonnage handled. Ports handling exclusively iron ore, coal, grain, crude petroleum and other dry and wet bulk commodities thus gain advantage in the analysis, whereas those ports that are high in break bulk shipping (characterized by low-weight, high-value commodities) have not fared as well. Montreal, for example, is cited as a loser port since it did not live up to expectations of cargo tonnage, but the fact that Montreal has grown to be the most important container port in Canada should offset this negative connotation.

The Canadian port system is vast and subject to change. In the past thirty years, Canada's ports have expanded their sphere of influence and have had to deal with increasing competition. This is particularly the case for the major ports. Within the immediate waterfront area of the port and the urban areas which they occupy, there has been an ongoing change of land use as the port has sought, or been forced to find, new locations for modern cargo-handling needs. The central city waterfront has taken on an urban, as opposed to an industrial, port orientation. Finally, some ports have grown enormously in size as measured by tonnage of cargo handled, while others have languished or closed altogether. The dynamic nature of the port is expected to continue. By the very nature of what ports do and because so much of the Canadian economy depends on waterborne trade, it is a certainty that Canada's port system will continue to evolve.

CHAPTER 4

HALIFAX AND SAINT JOHN CONTAINERIZATION: DOES GEOGRAPHY COUNT?

This Chapter concerns the development of containerization at the two Canadian East coast ports of Halifax and Saint John, and attempts to explain that development in the context of basic geographical principles. Containerization, along with the trend toward economies of scale in bulk shipping, have been the two major "revolutions" in modern shipping since the end of World War 2. The handling of general cargo in a uniform containerized system is now the accepted manner in which processed and semi-processed goods— and even some raw materials, such as stone, asbestos or peat moss— pass from one continent to another. In this way, general cargo is treated as bulk cargo and water transport has become much more efficient as a result. This method of cargo-handling has created inter-modal transportation, such that land transportation is linked to sea transport; each complements the other and "door-to-door" service is thereby practiced. The seaport and its inland "load centre" play key roles in intermodal transportation, efficiently transferring the container from land to water. Halifax and Saint John have developed as container ports, and they therefore compete against each other.

a)   Containerization at Halifax and Saint John

Containerization on the Canadian East Coast began officially in November 1970 in Halifax (Wallace, 1975), although containers had been handled there on a regular scheduled basis since July 1969. At Saint John official containerization began in September 1971. The fact that Halifax pre-dated Saint John in this regard is important in explaining the subsequent development of containerization in the two ports.

It has been said that containerization "saved" the port of Halifax (Lotz, 1974, 26). This is an exaggeration; but it is certainly true that containerization revitalized the general cargo trade in Halifax and is responsible for the port's growth into a legitimate rival to Montreal, and even New York, serving the Canadian market with traditional general cargo goods. Prior to the adoption of containerization at Halifax, it was feared that the port would lose all of its general cargo trade to Montreal. Both Halifax and Saint John acted as "winter" ports for the St. Lawrence ports when the latter were closed to shipping because of ice in the St. Lawrence River and the Gulf of St. Lawrence. Winter navigation with icebreaker support began in the St. Lawrence in the late 1950s. In the first years, ships went only as far as Quebec City and only irregularly; but by 1964 one line was advertising regular sailings to Montreal, and by 1967 at least ten lines were advertising regular Montreal service (*The Mail-Star*, 5 Dec. 1967: 15–16).

In order to devise strategies that might combat the loss of cargo at Halifax, reports were commissioned by the port, the city and the province of Nova Scotia. The Kauffeld Report recommended that Halifax become a "superport" for the North American continent, handling such diverse goods as California oranges and Saskatchewan potash (*Financial Post*, 24 June 1967: M2). Needless to say this plan did not come about, but the idea of consolidating cargo at Halifax and sending/receiving it by unit train and large "supership" is essentially the "containerization concept," but applied to general cargo. A provincial crown corporation was established in Halifax to encourage the development of containerization at the port (*Financial Post*, 23 Nov. 1968: 43). In 1969, Dart Container Service (a consortium of Clark Traffic Services, Bristol City Lines and Compagnie Maritime Belge) began to call at the port of Halifax on its North Atlantic service. In quick order, other lines also served Halifax, and by

November 1972 eight container-shipping services were using the port. Dart, Atlantic Container Lines, and Hapag-Lloyd served the North Atlantic trade route; Columbus Line traded to Australia and New Zealand; Zim served both the Mediterranean area and the Far East; Japan Line, NYK Line and "K" Line (three parts of the Japanese "five" line consortium) also served the Far East; and Trident Steamships was providing a feeder service to St. John's, Newfoundland (Atlantic Provinces Transportation Commission, 1972–1990).

Saint John was slower to adopt containerization and has always played a secondary role to Halifax. This inferior position can be accounted for by a number of factors, including the initial advantage held by Halifax; but the difficulties in constructing a modern container terminal in the early 1970s were great. The first regular container service at Saint John was that of Associated Container Transportation (ACT), serving Australia and New Zealand beginning in September 1971. The first gesture toward using Saint John as a container port was made by ACT in June 1968 (Oland, 1969). After considerable discussions with Halifax and Saint John about the merits of each, the decision to call at Saint John was made in the fall of 1969, but it was not until two years later that ACT fully cellular ships began calling. Originally, the ships called at the one-crane Brunterm terminal which was to be upgraded immediately to a combined forest products, autoport and container-handling facility on the west side of harbour. Because of cost overruns and the withdrawal of federal government support, the new two-berth container facility was not opened until 1975 (Wallace, 1975, 441); in the end, it was built only because the provincial government had committed $30 million to the project. After ACT began to call at Saint John other lines were slow to follow. By the end of 1972 only three container services were calling at Saint John: ACT/PACE, Atlantica Line (serving the Mediterranean) and YS and Mitsui - OSK consortium serving the Far East (Atlantic Provinces Transportation Commission, 1972–1990).

The tonnage of container cargo handled at the two ports since the beginning of containerization at each is shown in Figure 4.1. Figure 4.2 shows the proportion of containerized cargo handled in each port. In both cases, Halifax has outperformed Saint John. Two points about containerization development are not evident in Figures 4.1 and 4.2. First, the Halifax port has always serviced a wider geographical area, with early concentration on the North Atlantic and later emphasis on round-the-world service; and second, Halifax and Saint John have

Figure 4.1
Container Cargo Tonnage at Halifax and Saint John

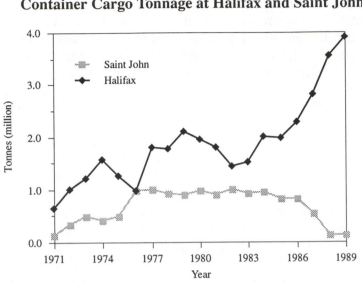

Source: Port of Halifax (unpublished data)

Figure 4.2
Container Cargo Tonnes as a Per Cent of Total Cargo
Tonnes Handled at Halifax and Saint John

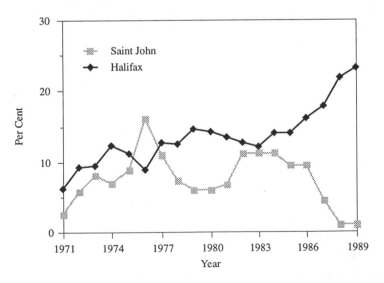

Source: Port of Halifax (unpublished data)

always competed against each other for shipping lines and, at times, each has "stolen" shipping lines from the other, though Halifax has ultimately won most battles.

Table 4.1 shows that Halifax, in its early years, served mainly the North Atlantic trades (principally North Europe), with three competing services. Other areas were serviced by few competing shipping lines; for example in 1978, although six deep-sea foreland areas were served, five of the six were serviced by one line. In 1983 competition became more intense, and in 1990 there were competing shipping lines for all the deep-sea foreland areas served. The expansion of deep-sea services and the competition of services to various foreland areas is indicative of the maturity of Halifax as a container port and of the status that Halifax has gained over Saint John. Other signs of this maturation and status are the round-the-world services that call at Halifax (five in 1990) and the development of feeder services from the "mother" port to short-sea destinations.

Saint John has not developed the maturity and status of Halifax in container handling. This is evident in the tonnage figures; it is also evident in its deep-sea and short-sea connections. In 1972, three services (for Australia/New Zealand, the Mediterranean, and the Far East) called at Saint John. By 1980 these three areas were still the principal forelands served, but competition on the Australia/New Zealand and the Far East routes developed, and Central/South America - Caribbean became an additional foreland. Significantly, it was not until 1985 that Saint John acquired a North European service, and also very telling is the fact that, by 1990, no container services traded to/from the original deep-sea foreland area of Australia/New Zealand. No round-the-world services call at the port. Saint John has been reduced to serving mainly the Central/South American - Caribbean foreland (one not served well by Halifax). In the short-sea trades, Saint John has never developed a feeder system of shipping. Only Greenland is served, and only infrequently. Although there was a feeder service to New York very briefly in 1987 (after the Japanese lines left the port), that service was discontinued less than six months later due to a lack of cargo.

The documented number of services calling and the foreland areas served indicate that Halifax and Saint John have developed in very different ways as container ports. The former has expanded its foreland areas both geographically and in the number of services to each; the latter has seen a contraction of the geographical areas served by containerization through the port.

Through the years there has been a rivalry between the two ports

Table 4.1:
Forelands Served by Halifax and Saint John Container Services (Numbers represent Number of Services to/from that Geographical Area)

HALIFAX	1972	1975	1977	1978	1980	1982	1983	1985	1987	1988	1990
Deep-sea											
Australia/NZ	1	1	1	1	1	1	1	2	4	4	3
Mediterranean	1	1	2	1	1	1	2	3	3	4	3
Far East	2	2	1	1	1	1	1	1	1	3	3
C/S Amer - Carib.			1	1	1	1	2		1	1	
N. Europe	3	3	3	3	4	3	4	4	3	4	5
West Africa			1	1	2	1	1				
Round-the-World									3	4	5
Sub-Total	7	7	9	8	10	8	11	9	15	20	19
Short-sea											
USA East Coast[1]		2	1	1	2	2	1	1	1	2	4
Newfoundland	1	1	1	2	2	2	1	1	1	1	1
St. Pierre					1	1	1	1	1	1	1
Iceland							1	1	1	1	1
Sub-Total	1	3	2	3	5	5	4	4	4	5	7
Total Services	8	10	11	11	15	13	15	13	19	25	26

.../cont'd

Table 4.1 (cont'd)

SAINT JOHN	1972	1975	1977	1978	1980	1982	1983	1985	1987	1988	1990
Deep-sea											
Australia/NZ	1	2	2	2	2	2	2	1			
Mediterranean	1	1	2	1	1	1	1	1			
Far East	1	2	2	2	2	2	2	2	1		1
C/S Amer - Carib.					2	3	3	1	2	5	7
N. Europe									2	2	2
Round-the-World						1	1	1		1	
Sub-Total	3	5	6	5	7	9	9	6	5	8	10
Short-sea											
Greenland										1	1
Total Services	**3**	**5**	**6**	**5**	**7**	**9**	**9**	**6**	**5**	**9**	**11**

Source: Atlantic Provinces Transportation Commission (1972–1990)

[1] Dedicated feeder service as opposed to regular deep-sea services which call at Halifax and then proceed to the USA East Coast

Table 4.2:
Container Lines Switching Between Halifax and
Saint John and Vice Versa[1]

From Halifax to Saint John	From Saint John to Halifax
Japan Line - NYK - "K" Line (1975)	Atlanttrafik (1984)
Saguenay (1985)	ACT/PACE (1985)
	OOCL/NOL (1986/87)

[1] This is only a partial list based on Atlantic Provinces Transportation Commission (1972–1990) which appears intermittently, either every year or every second year. Therefore some lines which began calling at one port and switched to the other between the times of the directory's publication may not be cited as having done so. For example, Galleon Shipping Corp. of the Philippines began a service to Halifax in the fall of 1980 but switched to Saint John in the spring of 1981 and was not shown in either the 1980 directory (published in September 1980, before Galleon began calling at Halifax) or in the next (January 1982) directory, because Galleon had since left the port of Saint John.

in their efforts to attract shipping lines. As an indication of the rivalry that would develop because of containerization, Saint John and Halifax eliminated their common Ports Day event in 1969. Saint John claimed that the conference was loaded in favour of Halifax (*Financial Post*, 15 Feb. 1969: 2). The port promotion conference was an annual event that had alternated between the two cities since 1957. This parting of the ways was complete before any container line called at either of the two ports. The rivalry has meant that container lines have been able to use the two ports to get the best possible "deal" for the handling of containers. Table 4.2 shows those container lines that switched from one port to the other.

As a result of the switches, Saint John has suffered more so than Halifax. The loss of ACT/PACE, the original container service in the port of Saint John, was both a psychological as well as a commercial blow. At the time of the switch, ACT/PACE accounted for about 10 per cent of Saint John's container business (*The Mail-Star*, 25 Jan. 1986). Of even more significance, from the commercial point of view, was the switch of OOCL/NOL which had acted in a cargo-sharing agreement. The OOCL (Orient Overseas Container Line) first began serving Saint John in 1975 and, with NOL (Neptune Orient Lines), it operated a round-the-world service that focused on the Far East. At the time of the change to Halifax, the lines accounted for nearly 50 per cent of container volume in the port of Saint John (*The Mail-Star*, 5 Sept. 1986). Saint John's big coup in attracting container lines away from Halifax occurred early in the rivalry when the Japan Line - NYK - "K" Line, a cargo-sharing consortium, left Halifax in 1975 to join the other members of the Japanese "five" lines consortium (YS Line and Mitsui - OSK). At the time, the new container terminal at Saint John, Brunterm, had just opened and was aggressively seeking new business, whereas the terminal at Halifax had all the business it could handle. There was speculation that the lines received some type of "sweetheart" deal from Brunterm to come to Saint John (*The Mail-Star*, 13 Sept. 1982: 6-P). The Japanese presence was felt in Saint John until 1987 when they left the port for good; the lines now serve the Eastern Canadian container market with feeder shipments from New York to Halifax.

That New York functions as a alternative to Saint John suggests the wider sphere of competition within which Saint John and Halifax operate. Lines have not only switched back and forth between Halifax and Saint John, but they have also gone from each of these ports to either New York, Philadelphia or Montreal. Consider the following:

- Dart moved from Halifax to Montreal in 1980 to join with CP Ships and Manchester Liners

- Trans Freight Lines dropped Halifax as a port of call in favour of New York in 1981

- Barber Blue Sea dropped Saint John as a port of call in favour of New York in 1984

- Italian Line moved from Saint John to Montreal in a slot charter agreement with Canada Maritime in 1985

- ACL and Hapag-Lloyd moved over half of their business from Halifax to Montreal in a slot charter agreement with Canada Maritime and OOCL in 1991

- Columbus/ACT moved from Halifax to Philadelphia in 1991.

Ironically, while Halifax and Saint John have competed for container lines, and while Halifax has won most of the important battles, both ports compete in a wider market where New York and Montreal are their newest rivals. But what role does geography play in accounting for these containerization developments?

b) The Role of Geography

Before this question can be answered, the term "geography" itself requires some explanation and definition. "Geography," in this context, refers both to the physical attributes of a site (what one might term the inherent or created properties of the place) and, secondly, to the relative properties of location; in other words, no place is isolated, because any location may be defined according to its position relative to some other location. (This second concept of "geography" has been previously termed geographical "situation"). The degree of separation and the quality of connections between two locations can be measured in terms of actual distance, cost of transport, or time needed to move from one to the other. In technological terms, the stage coach has been usurped by the railroad, the railroad by the airplane, and the airplane by electronic communications, so that places seem to be much closer together today than ever before. But not all places have advanced uniformly in their ability to "converge" with other places by increasing their transportation efficiency in terms of cost or time. The more advanced the transportation technology adopted, the more quickly the relative location of a place changes.

In terms of the "site" factor, or the physical attributes of the harbours on which the ports of Halifax and Saint John sit, Halifax has the advantage (see Figure 4.3). The harbour is a natural one without the need for dredging. The harbour at Saint John, although natural, does require periodic dredging because of siltation caused by river and tidal deposits. Halifax's entrance has a constraining depth of 15.24 m at low water (*Lloyd's Ports of the World*, 1989, 77); although depths at the container terminals are less—13.41 m at Ceres, and 12.2 m at Halterm—they are sufficient to berth the largest container ships operating today. At Saint John the dredged constraining depth is 9.14 m at low water (*Lloyd's Ports of the World*, 1989, 95) though Rodney Terminal depth is 12.2 m. The tidal range at Halifax is 1.98 m at spring tide, and 8.53 m at Saint John. The high tidal range at Saint John is one of the limiting features of the harbour, since fully laden container ships must time their arrival at the port according to the state of the tide. Low tides also negatively affect ro-ro (roll on - roll off) operations, which must be suspended when ramps are too steeply pitched for safe cargo transfer. On the positive side, port officials suggest that the tidal range can be beneficial in handling containers since there is less need for an "up and down" movement of the container from the ship's hold to the terminal; instead there is simply an

Figure 4.3
The Ports of Halifax and Saint John: Site

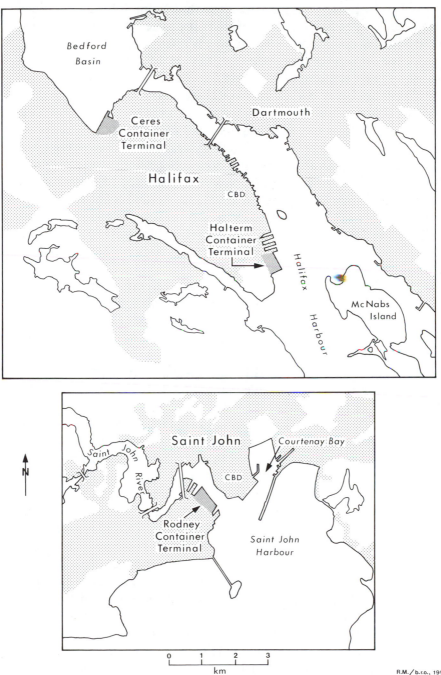

R.M./b.r.o., 1993

"across" movement from the hold to the apron at half tide (when the top of the deck of the ship is close to the apron of the dock), and a limited "up and across" movement at low tide (*Financial Post*, 20 April 1968: J7). Both harbours are ice free, but Saint John experiences strong currents because the river feeds it (especially at spring melt) and the tidal action is continual. Halifax is relatively current free.

As for the actual container facilities, Halifax has two common user terminals: Halterm (24 hectares, or ha) has four gantry cranes; and Ceres or Fairview Cove Container Terminal (21 ha) in the Bedford Basin has three gantries, the most recent of which was added in 1991. Saint John has one common user facility: Rodney Terminal (also known as Brunterm; 20 ha) on the west side of the harbour has three cranes. All terminals have rail connections right at the terminal. There really is very little difference in the efficiency of operations at the terminals, although figures in 1989 showed that Saint John had a slightly higher labour productivity of 2.5 moves per hour (per gang member) versus 2.1 moves at Halifax (Canada Ports Corporation, 1989, 37). Interestingly, these productivity figures are more than twice those of New York and Montreal.

A drawback to both ports is the lack of flat, empty land for terminal construction. All three existing terminals were built on fill. Any new terminal construction will have to be built either on existing port facilities—which will entail the destruction of existing sheds and filling in of piers—or on costly, newly filled land.

Both ports are administered by the Canada Ports Corporation, the federal crown agency that handles all major ports in the country. The CPC took over this responsibility from the National Harbours Board (NHB) in 1983. Halifax was declared a Local Port Corporation (LPC) in 1984, as was Saint John in 1986. With LPC status, both ports enjoy greater autonomy in their operations than was possible under the NHB; for example, both now set their own rates and are free to borrow and spend money without national approval. It is telling that Halifax reached this status before Saint John did. Halifax was then able to make local decisions on issues such as the Fairview Cove Terminal extension, which had an immediate and positive impact on container handling in the port. Moreover, Halifax was judged to be in a better financial position than was Saint John, which still carried a heavy debt to the New Brunswick government for the construction of the expanded Brunterm in the 1970s. It may be coincidental that the decline of Saint John as a container port took place before 1987, when the port was in the process of application for LPC status, but the federal government's resistance to the idea may have been a major factor in Saint John's decline. At the same time, Halifax had already gained its autonomy and container tonnages had increased quite rapidly (see Figure 4.1).

In retrospect it would seem that the self-promotion of the port of Halifax has been more aggressive than that of Saint John; this was certainly the case in the late 1960s, when containerization was being established. But some of the responsibility for marketing ports lies beyond the ports themselves. Promotion is undertaken by municipal agencies that work closely with port officials. In Halifax this agency is termed the Port of Halifax - Dartmouth Port Development Authority, which took over from the previous Halifax - Dartmouth Port Development Commission. In Saint John, port promotion is accomplished by the Saint John Port Development Commission. The fact that, together, the Province of Nova Scotia and the City of Halifax initially held one-third ownership in the first terminal built in Halifax shows the commitment of the local levels of government in the port.[1] Local government has also supported the port of Saint John in terms of marketing and financing, but Halifax's "site" has benefitted from promotional efforts to a greater extent.

Would these site advantages be strong enough on their own to attract shipping lines to Halifax instead of Saint John? Probably not, though they certainly help. Halifax serves well those ships that require deep water and cannot afford delays, requirements that are becoming more the norm in container shipping operations (especially as they turn to round-the-world service of few ports on a very tight schedule). Geography, in the form of site characteristics, **does** count in attracting shipping lines to Halifax to some extent, then, but other factors are involved as well.

The other geographical factor that influences a port's success in attracting and keeping business is its relative location, or geographical "situation." As explained earlier, relative location identifies a site according to other locations nearby, and it notes how well it is connected (by sea or land) to other places. "Sea connections" refer to a port's proximity to shipping lanes; "land connections" include links (by water, rail and road) between ports and the hinterland. The relative nature of location can be measured in terms of actual distance (km), time and cost, but from the commercial point of view, time, and cost are the most meaningful measures.

For each of Halifax and Saint John, there are advantages and disadvantages to the relation between the port and its sea and land connections. Halifax is better located for most sea connections, but Saint

---

[1] This share in ownership was sold in 1986.

John is more efficient for land connections (see Figure 4.4). However, in both cases it is not clear if these so-called advantages and disadvantages ultimately work in favour of or against the port concerned.

Consider the sea connections. Halifax's chief advantage here is the fact that it is very near the great circle route linking New York to northern Europe. In the words of its own advertisement, Halifax is "the most easterly commercial port on the mainland of North America, and the port closest to Europe, the Mediterranean, Africa and much of South America in terms of distance and time" (Halifax - Dartmouth Port Development Commission, 1986, 16). It is a simple matter for ships coming from northern Europe to divert their path to Halifax to service the Central Canadian market and even the mid-West market of the United States, and then to proceed to their ultimate destination of the American Eastern seaboard. It is no accident that every Halifax container line dedicated to the North Atlantic trade route also goes to New York. Often Halifax is both the first port of call **from** Europe and the last port of call **to** Europe. Containers that land in Halifax can be on their way to Montreal by rail, for example, within six hours, and they can arrive there before the carrier ship docks in New York. Two dedicated container trains per day connect the port to Central Canada, and beyond. Saint John, on the other hand, is not as well situated for the North Atlantic trade route (see Table 4.3). It is a further 200–300 nautical miles removed from the North Atlantic great circle route, which adds an extra 12–16 hours' steaming to the trip, one way. Because of these very simple geographic relationships, Halifax has always focused on the North Atlantic trade route; its first container line, Dart, served this route and, as Table 4.1 shows, the North Europe foreland has always been a significant market. Saint John, on the other hand, had to wait until 1985 to acquire a North Atlantic service, and in 1990 only two such services existed. Significantly, neither one of them served New York or other ports on the USA Eastern seaboard.

On the round-the-world services, Halifax has the advantage over Saint John from the perspective of sea connections, as well. All five of the round-the-world services calling at Halifax either come from or go to the Mediterranean, and two call at North European ports on the way. The North European services use the great circle route and find Halifax advantageous, as do other services; for example Alexandria (Egypt) is 250 nautical miles closer to Halifax than Saint John (see Table 4.3). Halifax is the deeper harbour, too, and is able to accommodate the very largest container vessels serving in round-the-world services.

Figure 4.4
The Ports of Halifax and Saint John:
Situation on the Landward Side

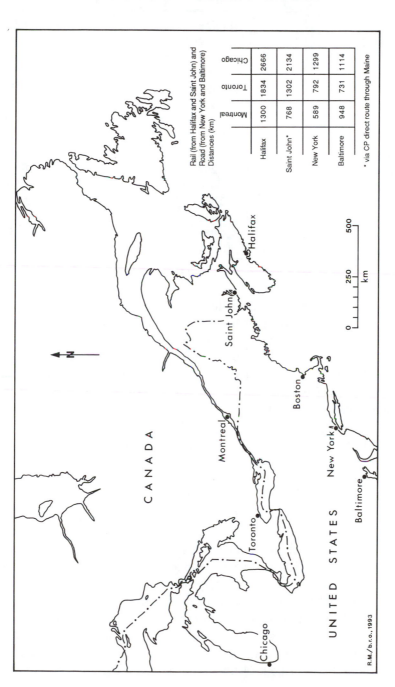

Rail (from Halifax and Saint John) and Road (from New York and Baltimore) Distances (km)	Montreal	Toronto	Chicago
Halifax	1300	1834	2666
Saint John*	768	1302	2134
New York	589	792	1299
Baltimore	948	731	1114

* via CP direct route through Maine

R.M./b.r.o. 1993

Table 4.3:
Sailing Distances from Halifax and Saint John to
Selected World Ports (in nautical miles)

	Halifax	Saint John
Alexandria	4,472	4,722
Auckland	8,849	8,848
Bermuda	753	801
Buenos Aires	5,731	5,853
Hamburg	2,923	3,176
Havana	1, 640	1,621
Hong Kong	11,057	11,296
Marseilles	3,362	3,612
Melbourne	10, 267	10, 66
New York	600	486
Panama	2,339	2,338
Rotterdam	2,758	3,017
Valparaiso	4,955	4,954
Yokohama	10,021	10,020

Source: Canadian Ports and Seaway Directory (1986), 50–51

For other sea connections, Saint John is not as badly placed (see Table 4.3), especially on North - South routes coming up from the Panama Canal (these include Far East and Australia/New Zealand routes, as well as Caribbean connections). The early emphasis on Australia/New Zealand and Far East trade routes, and the later emphasis on the Central/South America - Caribbean routes, can be partly explained by the advantage that Saint John has over Halifax in distance, time and ship operation costs. However, both Saint John and Halifax suffer losses on the North - South trade routes because of their location relative to New York. New York operates as an intervening opportunity for trade coming up from the south, trade such as that of the Japanese "five" lines consortium, which pulled out of Saint John in 1987. New York is closer to Central Canada than is Saint John, so why go to Saint John? Productivity at Saint John was high, land connections were good, and there were local markets and cargo which required containerization service at Saint John; but because the revenue derived from local cargoes (woodpulp, asbestos, peat moss, for example) was low, and because New York could offer the same service to Central Canada with lower ship operating costs, Saint John lost out.

Both ports are a long way from the primary hinterland, Central Canada and the American mid-West. Studies have shown that between 65 and 80 per cent of the containers passing through Halifax and Saint John are destined for Central Canada (Quebec and Ontario); the remainder are either destined for local markets in Atlantic Canada or distant markets in the American mid-West (Brown and Brooks, undated and Canadian Transport Commission, 1984). Regardless of the exact dimension of the hinterland, there is no doubt that the very existence of Halifax and Saint John as container ports is based on efficient rail connections. The distance to Montreal is 1,300 km by rail from Halifax, 768 km from Saint John, and only 600 km from New York. CN serves Halifax; Saint John is served by both CN and CP, but the CN service requires that containers be railed to Moncton in order to connect with the Halifax train. There is also an interlining charge at Saint John since CP rail owns the rail lines that lead onto the terminal. There is no time savings in using CN service from Saint John or from Halifax, but using CP from Saint John is faster, since the CP line connects that city directly to Montreal via its route through Maine.[2] However, Saint John's geographical advantage in its land connections does not lead to financial advantage for anyone since the door-to-door price between Europe and Toronto, for example, is the same whether the shipping line uses Halifax and CN, or Saint John and CP. Since the turn of the century, rail rates for transporting goods between Central Canada and Saint John and Central Canada and Halifax have been equal, regardless of the differing distances involved.

Interestingly, studies show that Saint John may even have been penalized for its favourable geographical position. Table 4.4 shows the published rail line haul rates for containers sent from Halifax and Saint John to Montreal and Toronto. These rates are based on an annual minimum movement of 18,000 containers. The cost per kilometre of moving a 20-foot container from Saint John to Montreal is between 1.66 and 1.75 times more than the cost from Halifax to Montreal. Rates to Toronto do not differ as greatly, though the Saint John - Toronto route costs 1.33 and 1.44 times more than the Halifax route. With the deregulation of rail rates (effective 1 January 1989), it is likely that container line-haul rates from Halifax to Central Canada are even cheaper than before deregulation (Port of Saint John, 1990). The large volumes of containers being shipped from Halifax, along with the introduction of double-stacking on the CN route from Halifax to Montreal, have created an even greater rate differential in favour of Halifax—despite the fact that Halifax is 532 km **further** from Montreal than is Saint John. So, does geography count? Not, it seems, in this case.

[2] With the proposed abandonment of this line by CP Rail, Saint John port will be limited to the use of the CN connection to Central Canada; as a result, much of the port's land advantage over Halifax will be lost.

Table 4.4:
Published Rail Line-Haul Rates on a 20' Loaded Container
From Halifax and Saint John to Montreal and Toronto

| | Halifax | | | | Saint John | | | |
| | to Montreal[1] | | to Toronto[2] | | to Montreal[3] | | to Toronto[4] | |
Year	$	$/km	$	$/km	$	$/km	$	$/km
1969	75	0.06	110	0.06	75	0.10	110	0.08
1975	118	0.09	163	0.09	118	0.15	163	0.13
1980	189	0.15	271	0.15	189	0.24	271	0.21
1985	266	0.20	372	0.20	266	0.35	372	0.28
1989	306	0.24	426	0.23	306	0.40	426	0.33

[1] 1,300 km
[2] 1,834 km
[3]   768 km
[4] 1,302 km

Source: Derived from information supplied by Atlantic
Provinces Transportation Commission

This geographical anomaly suggests that, when it comes to inland container shipping relative location based on distance alone is not always meaningful for costing purposes. Rather, location is deemed favourable according to economic principles, not operating costs based on distance. Back haul economics, economies of scale, base point pricing and area freight rates have always distorted the relationship between distance and freight rates. In the case of container handling from Eastern Canadian ports, the relative locations of Halifax and Saint John on the land side are relatively insignificant as determinants of success.

Although Halifax benefits from rate distortion in this case, and although the impact of its relatively disadvantageous position (1,300 km away from Montreal and over 1,800 km away from Toronto) has not been strongly felt, Halifax is still very aware of its peripheral position vis à vis its market. It may not have to worry about Saint John as a competitor, but it surely is aware that Montreal and New York, and even West coast ports, are competitors for the Central Canadian and mid-American markets.

In the spring of 1991, ACL and Hapag-Lloyd announced plans to re-route over half of their containers that passed through Halifax and to ship them, instead, directly to the port of Montreal (Sadler, 1991, 3). Montreal's advantages and disadvantages in handling containers are discussed in Chapter 5 but, to summarize, its greatest advantage is its position in the heart of the "heartland"; consequently land transportation, with its related high cost, is minimized and water transportation, with its related lower cost, is maximized. The great disadvantage for Montreal is that it stands at the end of the line, as far as water transport is concerned. All container ships operating to and from Montreal have Montreal as their only North American port of call, because there is no opportunity to load/unload cargo at other ports along the way. Halifax, however, is on the way to/from American Eastern seaboard ports. Thus, the container lines view Halifax as a "convenient" port of call where it is possible to serve the Canadian market as well as the lucrative East coast American market. This type of service works well only if the CN rail link to Central Canada operates efficiently and effectively, though, and here is the nub of Halifax's problem. The railroad is the lifeblood of the port; not only does it largely determine whether shipping lines use the port of Halifax to serve the Canadian market, but it also affects Halifax's competitive position in relation to New York.

Just as New York has operated as an intervening opportunity for ships going to Saint John, it could fulfill such a function for ships destined for Halifax. So far, high port charges, the dominance of trucks handling containers to and from the terminals, and poor train service between New York and Montreal/Toronto have been deterrents. Greater efficiency in container handling at New York might justify the high port charges, as might special rates for Canadian cargo and better container train services. However, Halifax has lived with this threat since its inception as a container port, and it will continue to successfully meet New York competition as long as CN continues to offer efficient and effective service at competitive rates.

The importance of the railroad link has been the subject of much discussion in the past five years, as Halifax has agitated for the introduction of double-stack container service and CN has delayed its implementation. Double-stacking—the loading of one container on top of another on the same rail car—began in the early 1980s on the American West coast. Savings have been estimated at 30 to 40 per cent per container unit carried by double-stacked cars (Fleming, 1989). Such reported savings stimulated railroads and ports to adopt double-stacking throughout the United States. Canada was much slower to introduce the new technology, mainly because cargo volumes here are lower; also, increased efficiency in rail container-handling in comparison to that of the States prior to double-stacking reduced the pressure to implement the technology. However, now that the American system is widespread and the cost savings have been demonstrated, it is only a matter of time until the service will be a feature of Canadian container ports and the railways that service them. Double-stacking did begin on the Vancouver - Toronto rail run in the summer of 1990, and it had been promised for the Halifax - Montreal - Toronto service by the end of the 1990 (Mason, 1990, 25), but it was not until August 1991 that double-stacked rail cars made their first appearance in Halifax. The delay for their start-up had been blamed on a variety of financial reasons; the high cost associated with start up, mainly in track improvements and bridge re-construction, was the major problem, and CN was financially strapped and unable to meet the costs of the new equipment. The Province of Nova Scotia was willing to contribute to the cost of the new service, but the amount and terms were not easily arrived at (Temple, Barker & Sloane, 1988; Sadler, 1991; Peters, 1991).

The slow introduction of double-stacking has concerned Halifax port officials, but other rail services are equally worrisome to Halifax. Since the introduction of containerization at Halifax, the port has been able to market its relative location as the first port of call in North America after the Atlantic crossing. Consequently, New York was not seen as a major threat in handling containers crossing the Atlantic and destined for Central Canada. Container delivery to and from New York was truck-based; there were very poor loading and unloading facilities for containers moving by rail. But recently, changes have occurred that threaten Halifax's position vis à vis containers and that enhance New York's position in the container trade.

In 1990, Canadian Pacific Railway (CP) acquired the Delaware and Hudson Railway which served the south Philadelphia, New York and New Jersey port areas. CP also negotiated trackage rights with the Consolidated Rail Corporation (Conrail) to move trains over Conrail track between Buffalo and Niagara Falls, N.Y. in order to connect the CP rail lines in southern Ontario to the newly acquired Delaware and Hudson lines (Atlantic Provinces Transportation Commission, 1991, 2). Thus CP had created its own railway with intermodal services from the Central Canadian markets, which Halifax depends on, to rival American East coast ports—ports which are 800 km closer to this market than is Halifax. The move by Columbus/ACT to Philadelphia in 1991 was made because of this proximity. Therefore the move highlights the practical impact of the geographical concept of "relative location," and demonstrates the changing dimensions of location as transportation services are improved or introduced.

SUMMARY

Halifax and Saint John have been keen port rivals for over a century and the introduction of containerization is the most recent ingredient in this rivalry. There were very good reasons why both ports introduced container facilities, and why shipping lines chose one of the two ports. Based on site factors alone, Halifax has an advantage in the competition; but site alone has not established Halifax's superiority over Saint John. Rather, relative location as determined by connections across the sea and to the inland markets has been the key factor. Because of its location, Halifax has always had the advantage in handling European containers and round-the-world services. Saint John has been cut out of container shipping services coming from the south because of the intervening service offered by New York, and because of the decision of shipping lines to consolidate services at one Eastern Canadian port: Halifax. The major advantage Saint John had in terms of relative location was its closer proximity to inland markets, but this has always been negated, in economic terms, by the equalization of rail rates to the central markets. However, Halifax is not immune to competition. Its tardiness in providing double-stack rail service and the competition for inland markets through American East coast ports has already affected it negatively. It is likely that other shipping lines will move from Halifax in the future as they attempt to "rationalize" their services. But as some lines leave, others are attracted, and this pattern is likely to continue in the future.

Does geography count, then? Yes, and no. The sites of the two ports may have attracted container lines, but site factors alone have not determined whether container services thrive; in this regard, geography does not count. However, Halifax's relative position as the first port of call for European services has been a geographically advantageous factor, since the equalization of rail rates between the central markets from both Saint John and Halifax has kept land transportation costs down; thus Saint John's favourable land geography has not been realized. However, the least expensive way to service the markets may be directly by water through Montreal, or by rail from New York, and Halifax's gain over Saint John would then be threatened. But the geographical proximity of Montreal and New York to the central markets is not the only factor taken into account by the shipping lines, some of which decided to serve Central Canada directly rather than indirectly through an East coast port. Regardless, Halifax's land geography will be a factor in determining its future status as a container port. Geography does, indeed, count.

CHAPTER 5

MONTREAL'S CITY-PORT: PORT EVOLUTION AND WATERFRONT REDEVELOPMENT

It was suggested in Chapter 3 that Montreal serves well as a case study of a changing urban waterfront. In a book about revitalization of port waterfronts, one of the authors speaks of such change in the context of challenge (Hoyle, 1988, 3). On the one hand, he notes, ports must evolve to reflect changes in technology: this is the port evolution challenge. On the other hand, the urban area must seize the opportunity to redesign and revitalize a decaying part of the city: this is the urban waterfront redevelopment challenge. The City and Port of Montreal have faced these challenges for over fifteen years, and continue to do so. Two relevant questions have arisen during this time: Where does the Port of Montreal expand to serve containerization? and, What is to be done with Le Vieux Port (The Old Port)? The former search for new land is part of the port's evolution challenge; the redevelopment of old port land is its redesign challenge. Not surprisingly, the two issues are related.

The search for and development of new port land leaves the old port land available for redevelopment. In the mid-1970s the Port of Montreal drew up plans for the construction of a new container-handling facility on Jacques Cartier Pier in the heart of the old port of Montreal (see Figure 5.1). At least $3.2 million was spent for land fill between Victoria Pier and Jacques Cartier Pier, but work was stopped on this project in 1977 when these piers were given over to Public Works Canada, to be included in the redevelopment of Old Montreal Harbour. Le Vieux Port project is still under construction today. Rather than redevelop a portion of the old port for containerization, it was decided instead to construct a new container facility, the Racine Terminal, in east end Montreal. This was opened in the fall of 1978, but because the port continues to expand, the question of where to build new port facilities remains a crucial one.

It is typical that as a port grows it needs new port facilities which are usually built on new land located downstream or "down harbour" from the original port area. And, typically, this new port development is never smooth, because it creates tension with other users of the waterfront, including recreational and residential interest groups. What is not so typical in the case of Montreal is the length of time it has taken to resolve the redesign challenge. Even after fifteen years have passed and at least $30 million have been spent (Semanak, 1986, A6), Le Vieux Port of Montreal largely consists of empty space. At least a dozen engineering firms and urban design teams have worked on development plans for Le Vieux Port, but little concrete change has been accomplished. Among the causes of delay is the fact that the land is owned by the federal government, but it rests in the heart of Canada's second largest city in the province of Quebec, and therefore three levels of government have been involved in the plans to redevelop the waterfront. Moreover, there have been two extensive public consultation processes to determine the wishes of the people in the redevelopment of this valuable property.

The expansion of the port for container facilities is also atypical in the Canadian context, though not in the world one. The effort to develop new container facilities has followed the typical pattern of moving "down harbour', but the planned jump to a location removed from the Island of Montreal, and downstream a distance of 40 kilometres, is unprecedented in Canadian container port development.[1]

---

[1] Such large scale moves have occurred elsewhere; for example, the port of London, England was moved to Tilbury; the port of New York changed with the development of Port Elizabeth, New Jersey; and in Sydney, Australia, the port of Botany Bay is far away from Sydney Harbour.

Figure 5.1
The Montreal Waterfront

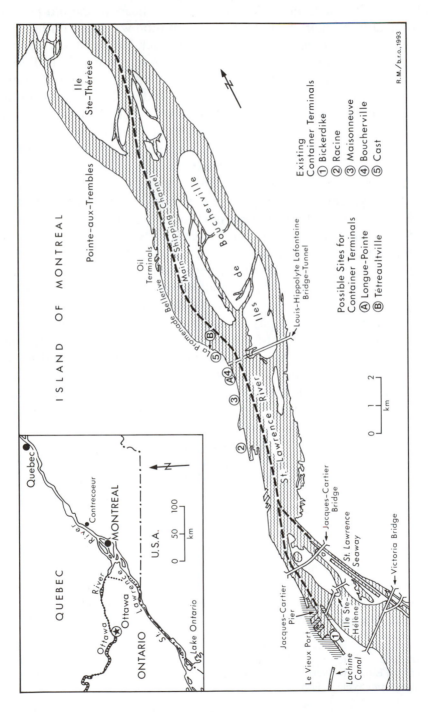

a) Port Expansion

In tonnage terms, the Port of Montreal has not grown greatly over the past twenty-five years. In 1960, 16.0 million tonnes of cargo were handled; in 1989, 20.3 million tonnes passed through the port, representing an average annual growth rate of slightly less than one per cent. However, when compared to 1970, when 22.7 million tonnes of cargo were handled, or to 1980s 24.9 million tonnes, the 1989 figure is, in fact, quite low indeed. What is noteworthy is the change in the type of commodities handled. Figures 5.2 and 5.3 show the changes in the major commodities handled by the port. General containerized cargo has grown greatly over the years, while non-containerized general cargo has declined. There have not been great changes in liquid or dry bulk cargo tonnages, though both were somewhat lower in 1989 than in 1975.

The growth in container cargo at Montreal is one of the great success stories of Canadian ports. In 1989 Montreal handled about 5.5 million tonnes of containerized goods which represents well over one-third of all container cargo handled at Canadian ports and makes Montreal the largest container port in the country. Halifax was its nearest rival, handling slightly less than 4 million container tonnes that year. On the North American East coast, Montreal—like every other North American Atlantic port—trails New York in container tonnage; but it is in the same "league" of ports as Baltimore, Hampton Roads, and Charleston, South Carolina in terms of number of containers handled.

The reasons for Montreal's success with containers are many, and they can be grouped under four categories: geographical, historical, economical and institutional. Montreal is an inland port, situated over 1,600 km from the Atlantic Ocean. The St. Lawrence River (facing, as it does, towards Europe) is ideally suited to handle cargoes originating from or destined for that continent. The inland location puts the Port of Montreal in the midst of the Canadian heartland, the main area it services. It is the nearest container port to much of New England, upstate New York and the American mid-West; almost half of the containers passing through Montreal originate from or to the United States. There are excellent road and rail links to both the markets of Central Canada and the Northeast/mid-West United States

This inland location has its disadvantages, though. While it is a gateway to traffic, the port can also be thought of as a cul-de-sac, the end of the line, off the beaten path of world shipping routes (Slack, 1988). No container ship which serves Montreal makes any other calls to handle containers in North America. If a container line decides to use Montreal, it does so with the full knowledge that the service must be dedicated to that port, while the container lines that serve Halifax also have New York and other American East coast ports of call (see Chapter 4). Consequently, any disruption at the Port of Montreal means that the North American operations for its shipping lines are disrupted. The location on the St. Lawrence, although ideal for European service, is disadvantageous for service to and from other parts of the world, especially Japan and the Far East. No container lines that serve Montreal also serve the Asian market; to do so means extra steaming time and expense. Cargoes moved on the Central Canada - mid-West - Far East route are either dropped off or picked up in East coast Atlantic ports, or they make the long rail journey across the North American continent from West coast Pacific ports. Geographically, the Port of Montreal is ideally located to serve the Europe - Central Canada - mid-West United States trade, but other trade routes are better served from other American or Canadian ports.

Historically, Montreal was the first Canadian port to handle containers in a significant amount using International Standards Organization (ISO) containers. Manchester Liners, a well-established general cargo carrier serving Montreal and the Great Lakes, introduced containers at Montreal in 1968 after a special container-handling facility had been constructed. This early start in containerization gave Montreal an advantage over its rivals, and especially Halifax, which did not officially open a container facility until 1970. Over the years, the transfer of container lines from competing ports also reinforced Montreal's position as the premier Canadian container port. CP Ships moved from Quebec to Montreal in 1978, and Dart moved there from Halifax in 1981; the two companies joined Manchester Liners to form Canada Maritime, one of the two major lines now serving Montreal. The other major Montreal line, Cast, was also a transfer from Halifax where it had originally set up a Europe - Halifax service in 1970. In 1972 the company built its own terminal in Montreal. The decision by Cast to use Montreal as its North American base was an important one for the port. Cast brought an innovative influence to containerization that not only benefitted the line, but also the port. Also, Cast originally operated outside of any shipping conference, which meant it was free to implement its own shipping rates. It since has become a conference operator, but since it serves only one route (Antwerp - Montreal - Antwerp) and charges one rate per box tariff (in contrast to conference lines, which can have as many as 3,000 different rates and routes), Cast's administrative costs were lowered (Marcus, 1987, 120–121).

Figure 5.2
Port of Montreal Cargo Tonnages

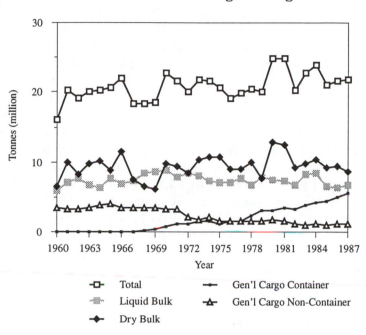

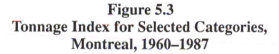

Source: Port of Montreal (unpublished data)

Figure 5.3
Tonnage Index for Selected Categories,
Montreal, 1960–1987

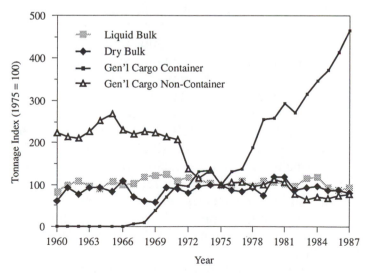

Source: derived from Port of Montreal (unpublished data)

Shipping by water has always been more economical than ship-ping by land. Because of economies of scale, greater efficiency in fuel use and natural routeways, the per unit cost of shipping goods by water is less than that by rail or road. Because of Montreal's inland location, the water portion of the trip from inland Europe to inland North America is maximized. However, trade at the inland location is limited by the size of vessels that can enter the St. Lawrence River. The very large container vessels—third- and fourth-generation types that carry up to 4,000 teu—cannot come to Montreal. The largest container vessels calling at Montreal carry about 2,000 teu. The inland location also ensures that pilotage charges to reach the port are the highest of any major port on the Eastern seaboard. For example in 1988, pilotage charges were almost $8,500 (U.S. dollars) based on a 2,400 teu vessel (in the winter they accumulate to over $17,000 U.S.) (Canada Ports Corporation, 1989, 50). This compares to fees of $1,500 (U.S.) for Halifax and $7,000 (U.S.) for New York. In port labour costs, Montreal does have the advantage over New York, one of its main rivals in the container trade serving the mid-West United States. In 1987, the total cost for one man-hour in Montreal was about $26 (Canadian) whereas the average man-hour cost at the Port of New York/New Jersey was $41 (Carey, 1987, 30). The utilization ratio of the Cast Terminal in Montreal (in terms of the number of teu per hectare) is the highest in Eastern North America at over 12,000; terminals in New York and Baltimore achieve 2,000 (Canada Ports Corporation, 1989, 40).

Even with these economic advantages and disadvantages of ship-ping containers through Montreal, it is unlikely that transport costs (land and marine) are significantly different for Montreal and its rival ports (Dagenais and Martin, 1985, 17). Any single cost advantage is usually offset by a disadvantage in another cost. Other factors that lie beyond economics also help to determine the rate of use for a given port. These factors could be termed "institutional," because they are related to the operational milieu in which ports or companies find themselves. Dagenais and Martin (1985) identify two such institu-tional factors that have had a beneficial impact on the Port of Montreal: the changing modes of behaviour of transport companies, and government regulations. The former refers to the degree of coop-eration between shipping companies and land transport (largely rail) companies in the handling and pricing of container shipping; the lat-ter refers to the different government regulations in effect in Canada and the United States.

Two key phrases are used to describe the degree of cooperation between land and water carriers: "intermodality" and "door-to-door pricing." Intermodality refers to the ability to transfer a container smoothly and quickly from ship to rail, or from ship to truck. In order to facilitate such a practice, it is often the case that transportation companies are vertically integrated and hold partial ownership in a land transportation company (either trucking or railway), in the shipping terminals (both inland and at the ports), and in the shipping line itself. Containers pass quickly from overseas origins or to overseas destinations when fully under the control of a single transportation company. This system allows the company to quote, with confidence, a door-to-door price for the handling of its containers. Intermodality lends itself to door-to-door pricing, and containerization lends itself to intermodality.

Both of Montreal's major lines, Cast and Canada Maritime, negotiated intermodal service and door-to-door pricing for the shipment of containers into and from North America. The two Canadian railways, Canadian National (CN) and Canadian Pacific (CP), had financial or equity participation in either Cast or Canada Maritime. CN had as much as 18 per cent ownership of Cast, and CP ships—part of Canada Maritime consortium—is linked to CP rail through the parent Canadian Pacific Co. Moreover, Cast owned its own trucking fleet and Canada Maritime had access to the trucks owned by CP. This intermodality led to competitive attitude of Canadian railways in setting container rates and "increased considerably their business in the USA mid-West, from 1971 to 1982, to the prejudice of the USA railways linking Chicago to the USA East coast" (Dagenais and Martin, 1985, 18). These agreements not only benefitted the two major shipping lines, but smaller lines also took advantage of favourable rail rates through the Port of Montreal.

Government practices within the two countries were advantageous for the Port of Montreal as well. The USA's *Shipping Act* did not require Canadian based carriers to file rates with the Federal Maritime Commission, whereas it did require American based carriers to do so. Consequently CN and CP, on behalf of Cast and Canada Maritime, knew what American land carriers were charging for the transport of containers, and thus could set their rates accordingly; but the USA carriers did not know what the Canadians were charging. Intermodalism was also less practical and less efficient in the United States where laws forbade the vertical integration of USA carriers. However, much of these initial Canadian advantages have been lost as American railroads have become more competitive and as intermodality has grown in the USA. Under the Staggers amendment to the Act, railways were deregulated in the USA in 1980, and this allowed secret intermodal rates to be negotiated and the vertical integration of transportation companies to become established. Moreover, the introduction of double-stacked containers on American railroad cars has allowed the railroads to become more competitive by lowering their prices. Hence, the mid-West market is much more competitive today than it was in the past, and the Port of Montreal and its carriers do not have all of the advantages it had initially when containerization was growing in the 1970s. Still, the port continues to increase the number of containers it handles, and forecasts show that that growth will continue, albeit at a lower rate (see below).

In order to accommodate the expansion in container trade at the port, several investments were made in container-handling terminals and equipment. Table 5.1 shows the development of container-handling facilities at Montreal necessitated by containerization growth. In 1988 there were five container terminals in the port (Figure 5.1) with thirteen gantry cranes. The five terminals are: Racine (16.8 ha), Cast (10.9 ha), Maisonneuve (17.8 ha), Bickerdike (5.4 ha) and Boucherville (5 ha). Overall, 55.9 hectares (ha) of the port surface area (or almost 40 per cent of the 142 ha of port land on the Island of Montreal) was devoted to container handling. According to port promotional material, "As containerized traffic grew, it occupied an increasing amount of space on land that offered less and less opportunities for expansion. It soon became clear that the Port would be caught in a squeeze between the river and the city" (Port of Montreal, 1988a, 6).

The problem facing the Port of Montreal today is that it appears to have run out of land with which to accommodate growth in containerization. From the eastern entrance to the Lachine Canal in the southwest of the Island of Montreal to its northeast tip—a distance of more than 20 km—the waterfront on the St. Lawrence River is fully occupied by port facilities, industries and residences (see Figure 5.1). There are three areas of exception: Le Vieux Port, near the central area of Montreal; La Promenade Bellerive, between the Cast Terminal and the oil terminals of East Montreal; and Ile Ste-Thérèse, a largely uninhabited island across from Pointe-aux-Trembles. If port expansion does not take place on these sites, then the Port will be forced either to convert industrial and/or existing port land to container operations, or to find land off the Island of Montreal. At one time the port did own what is now Le Vieux Port land, and had even developed plans to construct a container terminal on a portion of this land; but between 1978 and 1983 it transferred these 44 ha to Le

Table 5.1:
The Development of Container Handling Facilities at the Port of Montreal

Year	Facility	Details
1968	Manchester Terminal, Section 70	Canada's first container terminal, 5.8 ha, 2 gantry cranes, initial cost $2.5 million
1970	Manchester Terminal, Section 68	Expansion to 7.8 ha at a cost of $0.7 million
1972	Cast Terminal, Sections 76–77	New terminal construction, 5.0 ha, initial cost $4.2 million, 2 gantry cranes
1972	Boucherville Terminal, Sections 73–74	New terminal construction, 5 ha, 1 gantry crane, ro-ro ramp, $2.0 million
1976	Cast Terminal, Sections 76–77	Expansion to 9.5 ha, at a cost of $3.2 million
1978	Racine Terminal, Sections 59–60	New terminal construction, 2 gantry cranes, 7.3 ha, $4.3 million
1979	Cadillac Terminal, Section 66	New terminal construction, 1 gantry crane, 4.1 ha, $0.9 million
1980	Reliance Marine Terminal, Wharf B-7, Bickerdike Pier	Erection of a 35 ton gantry crane to handle containers, 5.3 ha terminal area
1981	Racine Terminal, Sections 59–60	Expansion to 11.3 ha at a cost of $16 million
1983	Racine Terminal, Section 63	Expansion to 16.8 ha, addition of a gantry crane, total cost of $5.4 million
1984	Cadillac Terminal, Section 66	Expansion to 4.7 ha as a cost of $1 million
1984	Cast Terminal, Sections 76–77	Expansion to 10.9 ha at a cost of $8 million
1986–88	Maisonneuve Terminal	Redeployment to create 17.2 ha of container handling facilities, at a cost of $10 million, 2 gantry cranes
1988	Wharf B-8, Bickerdike Pier	Redeployment and joining with Wharf B-7 to create a 9.6 ha handling area with 2 gantry cranes and a ro-ro ramp, $4 million
1989	Cast Terminal, Sections 76–77	Expansion of terminal area to 15.5 ha at a cost of $5 million

Note: Capital expenditures indicated are for infrastructure only and do not include cranes, which are purchased and owned by terminal operators and not by the port

Source: Port of Montreal (personal communications)

Vieux Port. The port once attempted to purchase Ile Ste-Thérèse, but the Quebec government bought the land instead, for reasons that are not altogether clear. La Promenade Bellerive, a vital piece of land adjacent to the Cast Terminal in the east end of Montreal, has been a topic of conflict between the port and the people of the area, who value the open space along the river for recreation. However, it would appear that the Port has given up hope of acquiring this land for the purpose of container terminal expansion.

The search for new container-handling property has been an ongoing one in the port since the mid-1970s. The Port of Montreal, the Quebec government and the City of Montreal all have been involved, either separately or in conjunction with each other, in studying the issue of port expansion. In 1976 a study undertaken for the Quebec government recommended that the only possible place for new development was Ile Ste-Thérèse (Côté, 1987, 3). A Committee of the Port of Montreal—made up of representatives of the Quebec government, the city of Montreal, La Communauté Urbaine and the Port of Montreal—concluded that, in the short and medium terms, increased containerization could be handled by expanding Racine and Cast terminals, but that the latter would involve some land of La Promenade Bellerive. Two major studies commissioned by the Port of Montreal were undertaken in the early to mid-1980s: the Dessau study of 1981 and the Lavalin study of 1985. Their recommendations were not without controversy.

The Dessau study, the conclusions of which were not made public until 1983, focused on possible port expansion sites downstream of the Island of Montreal. Eleven sites were studied in the search for one with the least resistance to port development, and environmental considerations were weighed equally with technical and operational factors. Three sites on the South Shore of the St. Lawrence River were deemed the most promising. The Ile Ste-Thérèse site was ranked tenth due to the high cost of land acquisition and construction of access, which was estimated at $34 million (Côté, 1987, 11). Of the three South Shore sites, Contrecoeur was judged the best prospect for port development. This site, 40 km downstream of the Island of Montreal, had very good quality road access, a railway was already in place, and there were good marine navigation conditions; it was primarily an industrial zone with virtually no residential or recreational areas nearby and, importantly, land was available a low cost (see Table 5.2). But the reaction of some of the Montreal business community to the potential move away from the city was negative. The community, represented by a committee of the Montreal Chamber of

Table 5.2:
Summary of Estimated Parameters Associated with
Container Terminal Expansion at Four Sites: L'Ile Ste-Thérèse,
Contrecoeur, Longue-Pointe and Tétreaultville ($1985)

	L'Ile Ste-Thérèse	Contrecoeur	Longue-Pointe	Tétreaultville
Surface Area (ha)	42	42	30	20
Additional Capacity (t)	3.3 million	3.3 million	1.3 million	1.5 million
Cost of Land, Clearing and Access	$34 million	$4 million	$37.2 million	$1.4 million
Cost of Terminal (excluding paving and services)	$42 million	$36 million	$19.3 million	$22.8 million
Total Cost	$76 million	$40 million	$56.5 million	$24.2 million
Unit cost per additional Capacity	$23/t	$12.2/t	$43.5/t	$16.1/t
Residences Destroyed	0	0	118	0
Industries Forced to Move	0	0	10	0
Parkland Eliminated	0	0	0.7 ha	13 ha

Source: Côté (1987)

Commerce and the Montreal Board of Trade, feared another "white elephant" for Montreal similar to the Mirabel Airport development if Contrecoeur were to go ahead (Harris, 1983, C3). The City of Montreal, the government of Quebec and La Communauté Urbaine de Montréal moved to support the expansion of the port on the Island of Montreal and not at Contrecoeur (Côté, 1987, 4).

The later Lavalin study was an in-depth look at possible sites on the Island of Montreal. Two were studied: Longue-Pointe and Tétreaultville (La Promenade Bellerive). The development of the Longue-Pointe site would entail the relocation of approximately one dozen industrial plants, at the risk of the loss of jobs, the removal of about a hundred homes, and the loss of a small park. Estimated costs of land acquisition and clearing alone were $37.2 million, compared to $4 million for Contrecoeur. The construction of a new terminal at Longue-Point was not possible, though the land area of existing terminals could have been expanded. Even so, only 30 ha of new port land would be created. The Tétreaultville site, although not disruptive to existing industries or housing, and superior to any other site in the Montreal waterfront from technical and operational viewpoints, was considered too risky in terms of potential negative effects on the environment. Thirteen ha of green space would be lost, including about 800 m of riverfront. This part of the waterfront is the last remaining "window on the river" for public recreation. The area has been the focus of public concern in the past, most notably when the area was suggested as a dump for waste snow removed from Montreal streets. This plan was rejected by Le Bureau des Audiences Publiques de la Commission Environnementale du Governement du Québec in 1982. The threat of container operation expansion into the area prompted Le Comité de la Promenade Bellerive, a local group of concerned citizens opposed to port expansion in the park area, to declare that La Promenade Bellerive would not become a port facility; that the Port of Montreal and its consultants would not be able to change the minds of the people who live there; and that the Committee would not let the matter rest (La Comité de la Promenade Bellerive, 1988).

In August 1988 the Montreal Port Corporation announced its decision that, based on the studies it had commissioned and public reaction to them, future port expansion would take place at Contrecoeur. The development strategy was given the title "Horizon 2010." The decision to develop at Contrecoeur was based on the fact that more land was needed to handle not only containers, but also dry bulk cargoes other than grain. It was estimated that nearly 150 ha of new land were required by the Port to meet projected cargo flows in the year 2010: 120 ha for container handling, and another 32 ha primarily for handling dry bulk. Thus, the amount of container-handling land required was estimated to be more than double the 55.9 ha used in 1988. Correspondingly, the Port forecast that the tonnage of containerized cargo would increase by a factor of 2.4, from 5.5 million tonnes in 1987 to 13 million in 2010. New land was required, and a lot of it, considering that, presently, the entire land area of the Port of Montreal is 142 ha.

In assessing its needs, the Port dismissed the Longue-Pointe site because it was not large enough and because it would be too disruptive of existing economic activity to develop the site. The reasons behind the rejection of the Tétreaultville site were not as simple. The site fulfils all technical, operational and economic criteria of the port;

it is, however small—only 20 ha—and would not meet long-term requirements of the port. The major stumbling block to its development, though, is the fear of the negative impact it would have on the human environment: namely, the removal of parkland and access to the river in one of the few places that such access is available on the Island of Montreal. In rejecting the site, port officials said: "Because of foreseeable negative impact on the environment, the Port of Montreal will not insist on building a terminal on the Tétreaultville site. Nevertheless, the Port of Montreal is prepared to build a container terminal on the Tétreaultville site if the environmental commission so recommends following the environmental impact study" (Port of Montreal, 1988b, 6). Thus the door has been left open for the development of the Tétreaultville site. This impact study was officially announced in June 1989 under the terms of the federal Environmental Assessment and Review Process. The stated objectives of the review are "to examine the environmental and social impact of the Montreal port expansion project" through a consideration of "the site selection process for the long-term expansion of the Port with due regard for technical, economic and environmental criteria" (Federal Environmental Assessment Review Office, 1989). Guidelines for the preparation of an Environmental Impact Statement by the Port of Montreal were released by the review panel in March 1990, but the actual environmental impact statement has not yet been prepared. The assessment continues.

The announcement that the port would not go ahead with the Tétreaultville site was greeted with the following headline in a local East End Montreal paper: "Le Port n' insisterait pas pour s'emparer de la Promenade Bellerive!" ("The port will not insist on seizing the Promenade Bellerive") (Lecours, 1988, 2, 3). The article noted that, although the City of Montreal wished to preserve the access to the river through La Promenade Bellerive site, the port had not entirely rejected the possibility of container terminal development at the site depending on the recommendations of an environmental impact assessment. In an accompanying article, a spokesman for the City of Montreal said that the city is not going to give the port its park for development, and that although the port can legally expropriate the land, it would do so against the wishes of the city and there would be a great fight ("... s'il le fait, ce sera contre la volanté de la Ville. Il ya aurait donc une grande bataille ...", Lecours, 1988, 3). However, one is left wondering about the possibility that the Port of Montreal will expand to Contrecoeur in the manner envisioned. The Port has said that it will do everything it can to expand, redeploy and make more efficient use of its current facilities; this might include the acquisition of land on the Island of Montreal if, and when, it becomes available. Moreover, any expansion at Contrecoeur will only proceed under signed contractual commitments from those port users who will ultimately provide the revenues required for the development of the terminal(s). There are those in the Montreal business community who feel "that building new port facilities at Contrecoeur would adversely affect the economic vitality of Montreal;" that "traffic congestion would be a serious problem if Contrecoeur were chosen" since "the bridges and tunnel linking Montreal and the South Shore already are being used to capacity" (Kucharsky, 1988, 25). However, the real achilles heel of the Contrecoeur expansion is whether or not the Port of Montreal has projected correctly the growth in containerized traffic and its subsequent land requirements.

There is no doubt that containerized cargo has increased rapidly at the Port of Montreal, but what will the rate of expansion be in the future? From 1980 to 1987, the average annual rate of increase in container tonnage at the port was a phenomenal 11 per cent, but from 1987 to 1989 there was no growth at all.[2] For the period from 1987 to 2010, the port forecasts an average annual rate of 5.9 per cent (Port of Montreal, 1988c, 9). While this figure is substantially below those of the halcyon days of the mid-1980s, how realistic is it? No one knows for certain. As outlined above, the port grew because of geographical, economic and institutional factors. The economic and institutional factors are different today than they were ten or even five years ago. There are no guarantees that Canada Maritime and Cast, the two big shipping companies using the Port of Montreal, will continue to expand their trade. About 50 per cent of the Port's container business is with the USA (about one-half of which is in the USA mid-West; but it is impossible to say with certainty that the Port of Montreal will retain its large American market in the face of competition from Halifax, New York, Baltimore and Hampton Roads. Intermodal improvements that will speed the transfer of containers from ship to shore and vice versa are ongoing within the ports of New York and Baltimore (Robertson, 1988, 41), and these changes will perhaps threaten Montreal's intermodal advantage. That double-stack trains now operate from Chicago to/from New York and Baltimore changes the economics of moving containers through the USA, to the disadvantage of Montreal. And the fact that some of the largest container-shipping companies in the world, including Evergreen, Maersk, and SeaLand, call at East coast Atlantic ports and not at Montreal will

---

[2] Between 1989 and 1991 there was an annual growth in container tonnage of about 2.75%.

ensure that economies of scale will result for those East coast ports— scales that cannot be achieved for Montreal.

The only certainty in the shipping world is the uncertainty about what cargo will be shipped where, and by which company. Past trends cannot predict the future of container trade. The validity of Montreal's prediction for a 5.9 per cent annual growth rate figure over 23 years is questionable, especially given the recession experienced in the Canadian and world economies since the announcement of the Horizon 2010 planning document in 1988.

There are also some compelling details about the site of Contrecoeur that may limit its projected use. Over half of the containers leaving and arriving at the Port of Montreal do so by rail; of that total about 90 per cent are handled by CP (Slack, 1989), but CP does not connect to Contrecoeur. This leaves CN with a glorious opportunity to increase its container-handling ability and market share but, in the past, it has demonstrated no particular interest in handling containers to/from the Port of Montreal. Will shipping companies be reluctant to make long-term agreements with CN in order to enhance the intermodality of shipping through Montreal? The answer to this question could pose serious problems for Contrecoeur.

In 1978 Montreal benefitted because CP Ships moved its container operations from Quebec to Montreal, but it is quite possible that the decision may be reversed in the future. In November 1988 it was announced that the Port of Quebec would develop a small container terminal at its Beauport facility designed to handle less than 20,000 teu annually (*Canadian Sailings*, 1988, 28). The project was never completed because of changes in the demand for container services at Quebec. A year later, there were extensive discussions between the Port of Quebec and Cast concerning the feasibility of Cast using Quebec as a container terminal. These discussions did not lead to any concrete decision in terms of new facility construction at the Port of Quebec, but they imply that Quebec could, at some date, attract some of the Montreal container traffic. There is room for expansion at Quebec; the port has excellent road and rail services, including CP, and it could accommodate any of the major users of the Port of Montreal. Even if Cast or any other current user continues to use Montreal, there is always the possibility that Quebec would attract any new container shipping companies which might be reluctant to establish at Contrecoeur, if the terms of its terminal construction and operation, and the service and cost of CN rail, are not to their liking.

Consequently, the projected move to Contrecoeur is not without its drawbacks. It is proper that the Port of Montreal plan for its future needs, but plans thus far are fraught with problems. A development at La Promenade Bellerive would satisfy present and mid-term needs of the Port, and such a breathing space would make the next decision— to move to Contrecoeur—an easier one. It may be that the port will need even more new land in the future, but to think of expanding the port by 150 ha from its present size of 142 ha is to take a big leap of faith in the future prospects of the port. To expand beyond the Island of Montreal may not be necessary in the short to medium term, and it is right that the port and city continue to coexist (after all, they have been doing so since 1642). It would seem that in planning the move to Contrecoeur, the Port of Montreal is wiping the slate clean and starting again in its thinking about its future land requirements, in contrast to previous port expansions that have involved piece by piece additions to satisfy immediate and short to medium term needs. The port has grown progressively downstream with relatively little thought about overall planning and development, but eventually it will run out of land on which to expand.

In terms of port expansion plans, the objectives of the port and the city often may be in conflict. The port needs a waterfront location, but the waterfront must satisfy other demands, as well. From the view-point of the people who live in the city and who have little knowledge about or contact with it, the port is often seen as a usurper of prime waterfront property, property desirable for recreational or residential purposes, for transportation routes, for offices and services, or for manufacturing sites. Which use is the most important? The answer partly depends on the other options that exist for the various purposes mentioned. The port can look for other sites, but so, too, can other needs be accommodated elsewhere. What is unique about the port's need for a waterfront location is that it is a necessary condition of the port's operation; obviously, it cannot operate anywhere else.

On the other hand, all other activities can be accommodated else-where. Certain manufacturing processes need water as a raw material, and it is aesthetically pleasing to have residences or parks which have water frontage, but these needs are not integral to the existence of the respective businesses or lifestyles, as water is to that of a port. Some expanded or new sites may be detrimental to the operation of the port itself, however, and may not be advantageous to the long-term health of either the port or its host city. If a port moves away from the city, for example, causing job losses and leaving current port users dissat-isfied with the new non-city location, then both the city and the port lose. The decision to use land in a particular way is both an economic and political one and, because of the latter, is subject to pressure from interest groups. To opt for a port use of the waterfront is to reinforce the importance of the port in the local economy of the city; to opt for other uses works to the detriment of the port. But such are the ways of the relationships between ports and their cities. At one time, ports and cities were one and the same thing; but now cities have outgrown the ports, so much so that the port must be prepared to give up its favoured status on the waterfront. This may mean it expands beyond the city, and the city must then be prepared to lose its expanded port function, or even the entire cargo operations of the port. This has already happened in London; the City and Port of Montreal are at the crossroads now.

b) Le Vieux Port

The other major issue on the Montreal waterfront is redevelopment of obsolete port space. For over fifteen years the old port waterfront of Montreal has been the subject of study, debate and expense but, until recently, of very little redevelopment. Like most modern-day ports in western economies, the Port of Montreal has had to develop new cargo-handling facilities to accommodate the changes in ships and trade; because of these new port developments, land that is no longer used or required by the port has been abandoned. Unlike most city-ports, Montreal's old port land has not been turned into shops, hotels, residences, recreational space, or museums. It is not for lack of trying that Le Vieux Port, the Old Port of Montreal, has not taken on an urban orientation. Some might say there has been too much trying, too much study, too much delay; but others argue that it is essential for planners and developers to get it right, regardless of delay. Given the potential for redevelopment of Montreal's old waterfront and the impact such redevelopment will have on the city, it is important that the redevelopment reflect the wishes of all parties involved. This goal has demanded time and intense study by many, but in the end, it is hoped that the new waterfront will be unlike any in Canada, with an orientation to people and their activities and not to developers and their profits.

The area involved encompasses 53 ha of land extending from the Bonaventure Autoroute in the west to the cold storage facility at the foot of Amherst Street in the east (Figure 5.4). Its landward extent is marked by Rue de la Commune running parallel to the water. Working from north to south, it includes the de l'Horloge Basin and Pier (formerly the Victoria Pier), Jacques Cartier Basin and Pier, King Edward Pier, Pier No.1, Alexandra Pier (still owned by the Port of Montreal, but included in Le Vieux Port for planning purposes), and

Figure 5.4
Le Vieux Port

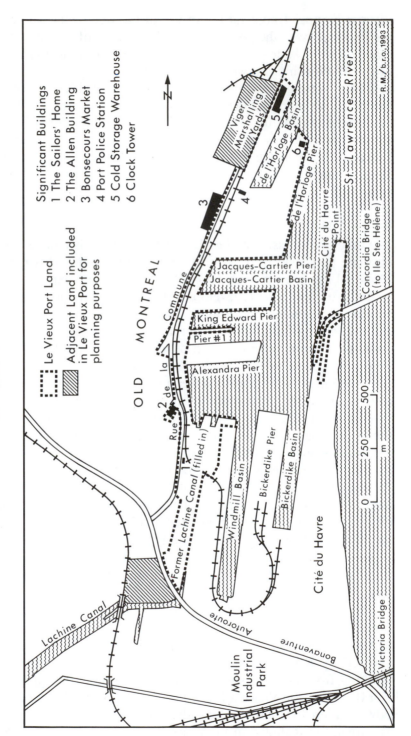

Le Vieux Port Land

Adjacent Land included
in Le Vieux Port for
planning purposes

Significant Buildings
1 The Sailors' Home
2 The Allen Building
3 Bonsecours Market
4 Port Police Station
5 Cold Storage Warehouse
6 Clock Tower

N

OLD MONTREAL

Rue 2 de la Commune

1
Former Lachine Canal (filled in)

Lachine Canal

Moulin Industrial Park

Autoroute Bonaventure

Windmill Basin

Bickerdike Pier

Bickerdike Basin

Alexandra Pier

Pier #1

King Edward Pier

Jacques-Cartier Pier

Jacques-Cartier Basin

3

4

de l'Horloge Basin

Viger
Marshalling
Yards

5

6

de l'Horloge Pier

Cité du Havre Point

Cité du Havre

St. Lawrence River

Concordia Bridge
(to Ile Ste.Hélène)

Victoria Bridge

0   250   500
m

R.M./b.r.o.1993

the eastern entrance to the filled-in Lachine Canal. The tip of Cité du Havre is also included in Le Vieux Port. For planning purposes the site includes, in the north, the Viger Marshalling Yards, currently owned by CP Rail, and, in the south, a portion of the Lachine Canal west of the Bonaventure Autoroute, land that is owned by Parks Canada but leased to Le Vieux Port.

In the context of Montreal proper, the site sits between Old Montreal to the west and St. Helen's Island (the site of Expo 67 and present-day La Ronde) to the east. In the south is the industrial area of Moulin and the working port area of Bickerdike Pier; in the north are industries (the closest being Molson Brewery), railway tracks and piers associated with port and industrial activities. Also, there are a number of significant buildings on or near the site. The cold storage warehouse, the Sailors' Clock Tower, and the Port Police Station are found at its north end and Bonsecours Market building, the city-owned site of a farmers' market and the subject of redevelopment plans itself, is in the area too. In the south is the Allen Building and the Sailors' Home. Along much of the length of Rue de la Commune are the original façades of buildings constructed in the last century that await, or are undergoing, renovation. Warehouses and sheds exist on King Edward and Alexandra Piers, but they are infrequently used for port activity; one exception is the Iberville Terminal on the west side of Alexandra Pier, which is used to handle cruise ships in the summer. In the winter, Great Lakes ships tie up at these piers. Two grain elevators that previously stood at the site have been demolished: Elevator Number 2, near Bonsecours Market and Jacques Cartier Pier, was removed in 1978; and Elevator Number 1 at the base of Jetty Number 1, was removed in 1983. These demolitions, undertaken not without controversy (see London, 1982 and Whittaker, 1983), constituted some of the only changes made to the site prior to the initiatives taken in 1991.

Since these demolitions took place, isolated works have been completed in Le Vieux Port, but not in tandem with a master plan. They were performed to enhance the particular area affected, and could eventually fit into an overall plan, though. Among these unco-ordinated events were the dismantling of the Autostade, a stadium in the western part of the the waterfront near the Bonaventure Autoroute in 1978; renovation of tugboat sheds at the approaches to de l'Horloge Basin (1983–84); development of a park on Cité du Havre Point (1985); the restoration of the Clock Tower (1982); the restoration of the Allen Building at the corner of St. Pierre and Youville Streets (1983); excavation of some of the eastern portion of the

Lachine Canal and the construction of a bridge at Mill Street (begun in 1983); the removal of six of the eight railway tracks (extensively used for access to port facilities both south and north of Le Vieux Port) that run along the waterfront (1981); and the construction of a linear park along Rue de la Commune between McGill Street and Place Jacques-Cartier, with bicycle and pedestrian paths that incorporate the scaled-down railway tracks (begun in 1981 and enhanced in 1984-85). This enhancement widened the previous park and introduced new landscaping into the project.

The site of Le Vieux Port was originally owned by the federal government's National Harbours Board, the past owners and operators of the Port of Montreal. Today, the local Montreal Port Corporation, part of the Canada Ports Corporation, has replaced the National Harbours Board. In 1977, the land was given over to the Federal Ministry of State for Urban Affairs. The Harbours Board abandoned the site when it became clear that it would be controversial and uneconomical to build and operate a container terminal on Jacques Cartier Pier, although $3.2 million had already been spent on infilling the basin in front of Bonsecours Market. The controversy involved the city and citizens who protested that a container pier would create heavy truck and train traffic (London, 1982, 20) that would run counter to the current historical redevelopment and preservation in Old Montreal. In 1978 the Association/Le Vieux Port was created to set up a public participation program to determine what the public wanted done with the waterfront. Also in 1978 the Ministry of State for Urban Affairs was disbanded, and Le Vieux Port project was transferred to the Canadian Mortgage and Housing Corporation, another arm of the federal government. Since 1981 the responsibility of the redevelopment of the Montreal old port waterfront has been held by La Societé du Vieux Port de Montréal, a subsidiary of the Canada Lands Company, which is a crown corporation of the federal government. In 1985 La Societé created The Consultative Committee on the Old Port of Montreal, which was to recommend development proposals to the Board of Directors of La Societé.

Since 1974 numerous plans have been put forward for all or sections of Le Vieux Port. Table 5.3 presents a summary of the plans between 1975 and 1985. It is not necessary to review extensively the details of these plans, but it is important to note that all of them tried to focus the resolve of the Societé; some plans were accepted, some were not. Slowly but surely, the proposals for Le Vieux Port were taking on a mixed-use look, with emphasis on open space for access and recreation rather than on the creation of a commercial office and shopping zone with some scattered parks. Between 1985 and the present, the important planning work was done by the Consultative Committee on the Old Port of Montreal and the Societé du Vieux-Port de Montréal itself. The Committee published its report in 1986, and La Societé issued two important documents, one in November 1988 and the other in April 1991. Details of each of these three documents follow.

i) Report of the Consultative Committee on the Old Port of Montreal (1985–86)

Before the end of 1984 and after the federal election of Mulroney's Progressive Conservatives, a new board of Directors was appointed for Le Vieux Port. In June, 1985 the Board created The Consultative Committee on the Old Port of Montreal. This Committee was charged with organizing a public consultation on "the orientations, development principles, and planning criteria for the Old Port of Montreal" (The Consultative Committee on the Old Port of Montreal, 1986, 15) and with making subsequent recommendations to the Board about the development of the site. This exercise, in modified form, was a repetition of the public consultations undertaken by Association/Le Vieux Port (see Table 5.3) except that individuals and groups, including the Societé du Vieux Port itself, were more aware of Le Vieux Port and the possibilities of its redevelopment the second time around. The exercise was developed from first principles, and was not based on any individual plans already put forward. The consultation process involved printing and distributing over 2,000 copies of a background documentation reviewing the progress of planning for the redevelopment of Le Vieux Port, 18 hours of informations sessions, and two sets of public hearings totalling 60 hours. Close to 75 groups and individuals presented reports at the first public hearing; 60 at the second. In addition, 25 written submissions were received. Like its predecessor, this public consultation exercise was one of the largest ever held in Montreal.

The Committee's final report in 1986 reviewed the consultation process and made recommendations to the Societé. It did not contain a detailed development plan; rather, it attempted "to determine the definitive uses and planning principles that the technical staff hired by the Societé du Vieux-Port should follow when developing the master plan for the site" (The Consultative Committee on the Old Port of Montreal, 1986, 17). The report suggested that the site should be used principally for public leisure and recreational activity; there should be no residential use, nor any intensive commercial or indus-

Table 5.3:
Summary of Plans or Proposals for the Development of Some or All of Le Vieux Port (1975–1985)

Plan/Proposal	Major Recommendations	Importance
Lincourt Plan (1975)	"mix of housing, of up to seven stories, shops, a farmers' market, a hotel and recreation space, and the demolition of grain elevators, passenger terminals and warehouses (Allen, 1982, B6).	the plan was never adopted or implemented; its importance lies in bringing together federal authorities and the people of Montreal to consider more precisely what the best use of the waterfront should be; identified the need for structured public input.
Desnoyers Mercure and Moshe Safdie Options (1979)	identified 4 options for redevelopment: 1. minimum development emphasizing parks and recreational activities; 2. maximum development emphasizing high density residential development; 3. mixed development (a compromise of 1 and 2); 4. Lachine Canal basin plan creating a large protected basin linking the refurbished Lachine Canal to the St. Lawrence River east of Le Vieux Port.	some of the common elements of all four options live on and are found in the current master plan e.g. restoration of the eastern entrance to the Lachine Canal for recreation, maintenance of port and industrial activities in Bickerdike and Windmill basins, and the construction of residences on the site of the current Viger marshalling yards.
A Redevelopment Strategy for Le Vieux-Port de Montréal published by Association/Vieux Port (1979)	many recommendations but its underlying theme was that the area should be a public open space to enhance access to the river and preserve the historic character of the area; there should be no public housing built on the piers, there should be no major landform changes.	the preparation of the strategy was the "most extensive [public] participation program in Montreal history" (Association/Le Vieux Port, 1979, 6). The spirit of the strategy is alive today in the current master plan.
Schoenauer Plan for the	resembled the third option of Desnoyers Mercure	rejected by the federal cabinet, perhaps because ...*/cont'd*

Table 5.3 (cont'd)

Jacques Cartier Sector (1982)	and Safdie with mixed residential, recreational and commercial use in the northern portion of Le Vieux Port.	of the estimated $70 million as part of the federal contribution (Allen, 1982, B6).
Poirier Cardinal Preliminary Conceptual Plan (1983)	conceptual rather than detailed planning envisioning a mixed use type of development.	not accepted by La Societé; detailed planning did not proceed.
Peter Rose Development Plan of Le Vieux Port (1983)	the major contribution of the plan was the proposal of an extensive esplanade integrating the already developed linear park.	the esplanade proposal was accepted by La Societé and work began on it almost immediately.
Societé La Haye et Ouettet Development for a Park at 1992 the Eastern Entrance of the Lachine Canal (1983)	reclamation of the Canal for recreation and pleasure boating, development of a park with pathways and brooks, an amusement park, and the restoration of the Sailors' Home.	much of the proposal lives on in the current Development Plan.
Societé Gendron Lefebvre Preparatory Planning Study for Maisonneuve Basin Park (1983)	confined to Pier 1 and the area of the former Grain Elevator 1 demolished in 1983. Proposed recreational and public use of the pier and a park running parallel to the water.	no action was ever taken on this proposal.
Desnoyers-Safdie Planning and Development Concept for the Eastern Section of Le Vieux Port (1984-85)	a mixed use proposal for the area east of and including King Edward Pier drawing on previous options/plans of Desnoyers and Safdie, Schoenauer and Rose.	although this plan was never formally adopted elements of it are present in the current master plan of Le Vieux Port, particularly the excavation of the area between King Edward and de l'Horloge Piers, housing in Viger marshalling yard, a marina between King Edward and Jacques Cartier Piers, an hotel on King Edward Pier and public open space on de l'Horloge Pier.

trial development. Eight planning principles were set out: Le Vieux
Port must be seen as part of the development of the extended downtown core; there should be easy access to the site; the maritime and
historic nature of the site was to be highlighted; development should
be evolutionary and follow a master plan; the site should remain
under public ownership and control; planning and development must
involve federal, provincial, regional and municipal administrations;
development must reflect real needs particularly suited to the site; and
archaeological findings discovered while developing the site should
be fully examined and incorporated in the development (The
Consultative Committee on the Old Port of Montreal, 1986, 21–28).
In addition, the report made recommendations about the type and
location of development activities that should be undertaken. Many
of the following suggestions had appeared in previous planning documents: that the Lachine Canal area east of the Bonaventure Autoroute
should be a park; that Pier No. 1 should be an observation point; that
King Edward and Jacques Cartier Piers should contain museums and
an exhibition hall, and should support limited commercial activities;
that the filled-in land between Jacques Cartier and de l'Horloge Pier
should be excavated and the resultant basin used for recreational purposes; that de l'Horloge Pier should be a park; that de l'Horloge
Basin should be used for recreational activities and the Esplanade
should be completed; that Alexandra Pier should remain an active
maritime passenger terminal; and that the Viger marshalling yards
should be used as a residential area, if the land were made available
by CP Rail.

ii) Preliminary Master Plan, Societé du Vieux-Port de Montréal
     (released November 1988)

Based on the principles and recommendations of the Consultative
Committee and further work by the Societé du Vieux-Port de Montréal
(including technical and financial feasibility studies produced by
Daniel Arbour et Associés and Gendron Lefebvre Inc.), a preliminary
master plan for Le Vieux Port was completed (Le Vieux Port, 1988). It
was released in November 1988, although an early version was submitted to Ottawa for consideration in January 1987 (Peritz, 1987, A1).
According to newspaper reports, the total cost of the project was set at
$481 million, and was to be shared by governments and the private
sector. The federal government would contribute $150.5 million, the
Quebec and Montreal governments would share $81.3 million, and the
rest, $249.2 million, would be met by the private sector.
    The plan divided the site into three sectors: Eastern, Central and

Western. For the Eastern sector, changes to the street pattern were proposed for the vicinity of Viger marshalling yards; housing was to be developed in the Viger yards and along the north side of de l'Horloge Basin; a marina was to be built in de l'Horloge Basin; and the cold storage warehouse was to be converted into housing units, with some complementary retail activity. In the Central sector, the Esplanade would be completed and extended to the east in front of the Bonsecours Market. This work would involve lowering the railway fence that runs along the two tracks; these will continue to be a part of Le Vieux Port. In addition, much was recommended for the piers in the Central sector. The filled-in area between Jacques Cartier and de l'Horloge Piers would be transformed into Bonsecours Basin for summer and winter water recreation activities, including a speed-skating oval. Below there would be underground parking. Jacques Cartier pier would be a classic formal garden, as would de l'Horloge Pier. The Montreal Aquarium, which had been located at La Ronde on St. Helen's Island, would move to de l'Horloge Gardens. The sheds on King Edward Pier would be renovated to house a Science and Technology Museum, a Maritime Museum, a hotel and some commercial activities. A marina was proposed for the Jacques Cartier Basin, and there would be a ferry terminal built at the bottom of Jacques Cartier Basin to connect this area with St. Lawrence River Islands, Pointe de la Cité du Havre Park and other Le Vieux Port terminals. The unloading tower on Pier No. 1 would be converted to an observation tower. Alexandra Pier would continue to function under the Port of Montreal, though some of the sheds would be recycled to take up commercial functions such as an exhibition hall. The Western sector would see the reopening of the Lachine Canal and the construction of a canal park. In addition, the Canadian Railway Museum would be moved from its present location in St. Constant on the south shore of the St. Lawrence to a site to the west of the Bonaventure Autoroute.

This preliminary master plan takes its ideas from the many studies that preceded it. In spirit, it reflects the consensus of the people as expressed in the public consultations conducted by the Association/Le Vieux Port and The Consultative Committee on the Old Port of Montreal. Le Vieux Port is not to be a major commercial and residential city, isolated from Old Montreal and other cores of downtown Montreal; rather it is to reflect "the spirit of the site" as a public open space with attractions that will bring people to the waterfront. It is to be an extension of the city, and is to fit in with ongoing housing, commerce and industry developments in surrounding areas.

iii) 1992 Development Plan, Societé du Vieux Port de Montréal
(April 1991)

In September 1988 the federal government pledged $110 million for infrastructural projects at Le Vieux Port. The 1992 Development Plan outlined the expenditures planned for $65 million of that total. Finally, the physical development of Le Vieux Port was to be undertaken. The development adheres to the eight planning principles put forward in 1986 by the Consultative Committee on the Old Port of Montreal (see above). By the summer of 1992, work was complete in both the Eastern and the Western sectors of Le Vieux Port. In the East, excavation of the landfill between the former Victoria and current Jacques Cartier Piers has created Bonsecours Basin (in front of Bonsecours Market), and Bonsecours Basin Park, an island and grassy peninsula with walkways and a welcoming centre. In addition, landscaping on Jacques Cartier Pier and the construction of Jacques Cartier Pavillion is complete. In the West, the redevelopment has restored the entrance to the Lachine Canal and incorporated the remains of several industrial buildings within a Promenade area called Parc des Écluses.

The 1992 document does not, by any means, embody the entire Preliminary Master Plan. For, example, the Canadian Railway Museum is not yet part of the Western sector; nor is the Montreal Aquarium planned to be moved to de l'Horloge Gardens. Moreover, much of the private sector funding envisaged in the Preliminary Master Plan has not been forthcoming.

Thus the story of the Montreal old port redevelopment is complicated by politics, recent economic history and the character of Montreal itself. First, all three levels of government—the federal government of Canada, the provincial government of Quebec and the municipal government of Montreal—have been involved in the redevelopment of old Montreal waterfront, and over time there have been elections at each level that have affected the pace and support of the redevelopment. The final decision to develop the waterfront lies with the federal government, its landowner and its greatest revenue resource. However, any action by the federal government in the province of Quebec must consider not only Quebec, but also how that action will be viewed by other provinces. Such is the great responsibility of federal-provincial relations in Canada. In theory, all provinces are equal, but Ontario and Quebec are the most powerful, and therefore grants from the federal government to either one are critically watched not only by the other, but by all remaining provinces, too. It is in this political atmosphere that decisions concerning Montreal's waterfront have been made.

Recent economic history, of course, has dictated that caution be exercised in public spending, and it was during the economic recession of 1981–83 that important decisions about the Montreal waterfront were being made. The upturn in the economy after that time should have made it easier for business to invest in the waterfront, but because of a change in federal government in 1984 and its perceived need for new studies, little action was taken. Recently, the scepter of a rising federal deficit has limited the amount of money available for redevelopment, and depending on how the deficit is handled, this may permanently restrict future prospects.

The character of Montreal itself has posed problems for Le Vieux Port. Montreal is not, and does not wish to be, like Toronto, and this is important to the understanding of why Montreal's Le Vieux Port is still mostly empty. Given the involvement of the federal government in the Toronto Harbourfront redevelopment—a project involving hotels, condominiums, shops and offices, and very little public open space—it was natural that such a scheme should be proposed for Montreal. And it was proposed: in 1974, two years after Harbourfront was announced. However, the plan was rejected by the City of Montreal for its "too much, too soon" quality. The City did not want a sub-city on the waterfront, a city which would be as much a barrier to water access as is the port activity it would replace. Instead, the demand was for open space, for "a window on the river" that would fit in with redeveloped Old Montreal. The plans for waterfront redevelopment were not to be forced on the city by the federal government working in conjunction with business interests. Thus it was essential that an open planning process, with public consultation and participation, be implemented, a process that was not used in Toronto; but such planning demands have increased the time required for redevelopment. There is also one basic geographical difference between Toronto's waterfront and that of Montreal: in Toronto, the waterfront was separated from the city by massive railway yards and an urban expressway; in Montreal, only two tracks of railroad and a city street separate Le Vieux Port from Old Montreal. Le Vieux Port is part of the urban environment of Montreal; it is not cut off from the city geographically, and plans must be unique to this city.

Because the political, economic and geographical factors have operated over time, the redevelopment of Le Vieux Port has been painstakingly slow. The major accomplishment to date has been the development of tentative plans that have involved consultation with the public. In the summer of 1991, large-scale physical changes to Le Vieux Port finally began to take place. The plans, consultations and changes have not come cheaply. Again, it was estimated in 1986 that over $30 million has been paid to at least a dozen engineering firms and urban design consultants to develop plans and estimates for the redevelopment of Le Vieux Port, and that over $50 million has been spent by the federal government in demolition, construction and restoration of Le Vieux Port buildings, roadways and piers (Semanak, 1986, A6). This estimate was confirmed and deemed conservative by the federal minister responsible for Le Vieux Port in a 1988 press release (Canada, Regional Industrial Expansion, 1988, 2). A further $110 million contribution by the federal government to assist with the physical construction on the site was announced in 1988. With this recent funding, it is likely that Le Vieux Port will be developed—at least partially—in the way that the planners envisage.

It has taken an inordinate amount of time and money to come to this consensus of what Le Vieux Port will be, but because of this close scrutiny the site will have distinctive qualities. It will not be like the Historic Properties of Halifax, Market Square of Saint John, Le Vieux Port of Quebec, Harbourfront of Toronto, Canada Place or False Creek of Vancouver, Pier 59 or Fisherman's Market of San Francisco, Jack London Square of Oakland, Harborfront of Baltimore, Quincy Market of Boston, or Canary Wharf of London— all of which have undergone waterfront redevelopment in the past. However, Le Vieux Port of Montreal, as envisaged by the planners, is not yet a reality. Although development work using a portion of the federal government's $110 million is ongoing, much is still to be done. Guarantees that the Province of Quebec and the City of Montreal will contribute what is seen as their "fair" share are not automatic. The private sector, likewise, has not taken the initiative anticipated in 1988. There is no doubt now that requirements for the site are clear. What is not clear is the degree of cooperation that exists between all levels of government, and the commitment of the private sector to see the project to completion.

SUMMARY

The waterfront of a city-port is a dynamic site. It is valuable land and serves a variety of purposes. This discussion of Montreal's waterfront has highlighted two elements of its dynamism: ports need waterfront locations, but existing locations may prove inadequate; and, as water-front land becomes available for redevelopment, it is not always clear what form that new development should take.

For both port expansion and waterfront redevelopment, the decision to change land use is an economic, social and political one. At one time the Port of Montreal was eager to expand into La Promenade Bellerive, but was restricted by public opposition. The early objectives for Le Vieux Port's redevelopment were largely financial; but now, the land will be developed for maximum public benefit. Obviously, the will of the residents was heard by those who made decisions about the future use of waterfront land in Montreal. Extensive public consultation exercises were a feature of Le Vieux Port planning; and now that an environmental review panel has been established to consider Montreal port expansion at Contrecoeur, which has implications for development in La Promenade Bellerive, there will be a public forum for residents of East Montreal to voice their concerns.

In the end, it is likely that the Port of Montreal will expand its operations in Contrecoeur, and Le Vieux Port will be built to approximate what was finally planned for the site. But the process of change is not an easy one. Montreal's waterfront illustrates very well the nature of the challenges faced by ports and their cities as they struggle to come to grips with the changing demands made upon the city-port waterfront.

CHAPTER 6

THE GREAT LAKES/ST. LAWRENCE SEAWAY: SUCCESS OR FAILURE?

The opening of the Seaway in 1959 heralded the arrival of Canada's fourth seacoast. As one of the architects of the Seaway stated, "The ocean has been let into the North American heartland" (Chevrier, 1959, 140). Canadian and American grain would reach tidewater and beyond in maximum-sized lake vessels, with the benefits that economies of scale imply. Iron ore from Northern Quebec and Labrador would be the back haul that would make bulk shipping on the waterway even more economical. The Seaway would be one of Canada's greatest resources. But was the prophecy fulfilled? Has ocean shipping penetrated the continent and prospered on this new "seacoast"? Is it the great bulk shipping waterway all that it was expected to be? What is the Seaway's status today? Particular issues facing the Seaway today include the importance of the grain trade to the waterway, containerization, the extension of the operating season, and finances.

a) **The Seaway**

The term "Seaway" is usually reserved for the system of canals, locks and dredged channels from Lake Erie to Montreal under the control of the St. Lawrence Seaway Authority in Canada and the St. Lawrence Seaway Development Corporation in the United States. The Canadian authority has jurisdiction over and responsibility for the operation of the five Canadian locks and channels in the Montreal-to-Lake Ontario section (M - LO) of the St. Lawrence River, and for the operation and maintenance of the Welland Canal (its eight locks link Lake Erie and Lake Ontario, thereby allowing the bypass of Niagara Falls; see Figure 6.1). The American corporation operates two locks near Massena, New York in the M - LO section and maintains the American portion of the route in the Thousand Islands area of the St. Lawrence River. Very strictly speaking, the term "St. Lawrence Seaway" refers only to that section of waterway between Kingston and Montreal which was altered by dredging, damming, and canalization for the construction of seven locks, all of which was completed by 1959. Loosely speaking, though, the term "Seaway" has come to refer to the entire waterway that encompasses the Great Lakes and its interconnections, and that allows water transportation from the head of navigation in Lake Superior to the Gulf of St. Lawrence and the open Atlantic Ocean. In this study, the entire Lake Superior - Atlantic route will be referred to as the Great Lakes/St. Lawrence Waterway; the term "Seaway" will be reserved for the major constructions in the Welland Canal and in the M - LO section of the St. Lawrence River (this definition is consistent with Sussman, 1978 and Ghonima, 1986).

Two needs were addressed with the construction of the Seaway: transportation and hydroelectricity. The former, of course, interests us here, although the latter is of much interest to the economic development of the Provinces of Ontario and Quebec, and also to the state of New York, since it provided the inexpensive electricity that attracted industry (especially aluminium production) to the region. Without the hydroelectricity component of the project, it is unlikely that the Seaway would have been economically or politically acceptable (Schenker, Mayer and Brockel, 1976, 6). Much of the construction cost of facilities jointly used for hydroelectricity and navigation was attributed to hydroelectricity development, and not to the navigation infrastructure.

The Great Lakes and the St. Lawrence River outlet comprise the largest inland freshwater system in the world, stretching from mid-continent to the Atlantic Ocean (a distance of almost 4,000 kilometres). Some have referred to the area as Canada's fourth seacoast; others recognize it as a great inland waterway but, because of limitations to sea-going vessels, most would refrain from classifying it as a

Figure 6.1
Great Lakes/St. Lawrence Waterway

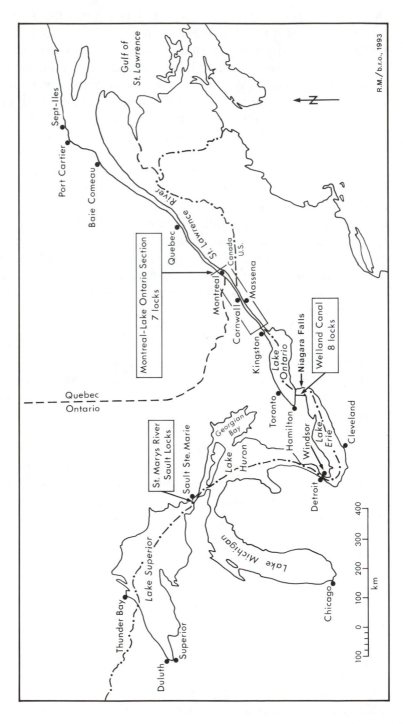

seacoast (Leitch, 1986, 146). Regardless, the system is unique in the world, allowing the marine mode of transportation to reach the heart of the North American continent. The ability of large ocean-going ships and lake carriers to traverse the waterway has been made possible with the construction of canals, locks and dams to control the water level. The Seaway has contributed to the alterations of the natural waterway, as has the channel dredging that takes place in the St. Clair River, Lake St. Clair and the Detroit River linking Lake Huron and Lake Erie; and there have been major alterations in the St. Mary's River, as well, linking Lake Superior and Lake Huron. There, the greatest change has been the construction of parallel locks, four American and one Canadian, the largest of which is the Poe Lock on the American side (it is 365.75 metres long, 33.5 metres wide and 9.75 metres deep, and is larger than the Seaway standard lock of 233.5 m x 24.4 m x 9.1 m). In practice the Seaway is restricted to vessels of 222.5 metre length and 7.7 metre draft, but the Poe Lock will accommodate vessels of approximately 305 metres in length. Such vessels are thus restricted to operations in the Upper Great Lakes west of the Welland Canal (that is, Lakes Erie, Huron, Michigan and Superior).

The construction of the M - LO section of the Seaway was a joint effort of Canada and the United States, but the decision to cooperate was not easily reached (Sussman, 1978, 14–27, and Chevrier, 1959). Both sides were aware of the advantages of constructing a waterway that would allow large ships to use the entire Great Lakes/St. Lawrence waterway. The construction of the Welland Canal in 1932 had allowed large vessels to traverse all five of the Great Lakes, but they could not proceed down the St. Lawrence to tidewater; nor could ocean-going vessels of any substantial size proceed up into the Great Lakes. The obstacle was the M - LO section of the St. Lawrence River, which was restricted to a 4.3 metre canal and took as long as three days to traverse (Schenker, Mayer and Brockel, 1976, 6). Maximum-sized "lakers" (bulk carriers) operating on the Great Lakes through the Welland Canal could carry up to 28,000 tonnes of cargo, but canallers operating in the M - LO section were restricted to 1,600 tonnes carrying capacity (Schenker, Mayer and Brockel, 1976,14). Ocean-going vessels (general cargo carriers) operating above Montreal in pre-Seaway days could carry only about 1,000 tonnes of cargo; but the construction of new locks and channels in the M - LO section, to Welland Canal standards, enabled maximum-sized lakers to proceed directly to tidewater and ocean-going vessels with 9,000 tonne carrying capacities could proceed up into the Great Lakes. By today's standards these are not large vessels, but in the 1950s, when vessels of these sizes were suddenly able to operate in the Great Lakes and to make direct shipments to international markets, a major step forward had been taken in national and international shipping.

Canada and the United States had different plans for the Seaway. The United States looked upon the Seaway as a relatively inexpensive way for American manufactured goods from the industrial heart of the country (Cleveland, Toledo, Detroit, and Chicago) to reach international markets. This intent to change trade routes was opposed by Atlantic coast port cities and the railroads, based on foreseen losses of cargo. Canada, on the other hand, anticipated that the expanded Great Lakes/St. Lawrence Waterway would provide a less expensive and more efficient system for transporting grain from the Prairies to markets throughout the world, particularly to Europe. The Eastern ports and railroads disapproved of these objectives, too; even the Port of Montreal feared some loss of cargo, especially from ocean-going vessels that would bypass Montreal and proceed directly into and from the Great Lakes (as it turned out, this fear was unfounded). The two nations did agree, however, that the Seaway would benefit the iron ore trade and the steel industries of each country.

The discovery of large iron ore deposits in Northern Quebec and Labrador in the post-war period was fortuitous for the proponents of an expanded Great Lakes/St. Lawrence Waterway. Prior to the opening of iron ore mines in those two areas, iron ore for the American steel industry in the Great Lakes area came from depleted mines around Lake Superior, particularly in the Mesabi Range of Minnesota. The new discovery was welcomed, then, and mines were opened, but to take advantage of shipping economies of scale, a larger and deeper St. Lawrence River between Montreal and Lake Ontario was a necessity. As a result of these alterations, the new iron mines would benefit not only the steel industry, but that of grain, too, since the movement of iron ore upbound from the Lower St. Lawrence River to Great Lakes ports (particularly on Lake Erie) provided a back haul for the grain movement downbound from the Lake Superior ports of Thunder Bay, in Canada, and Duluth, in the United States. Thus, the rationale for building the Seaway from the shipping point of view was that lakers could reach tidewater directly and thus bring grain to Lower St. Lawrence ports for trans-shipment to international markets, and that iron ore could be transported from these ports back up into the Great Lakes. It was also expected that ocean-going vesslels would expand direct international trade involving

Figure 6.2
Canadian and United States Grain Passing Through
the M - LO Section of the Seaway

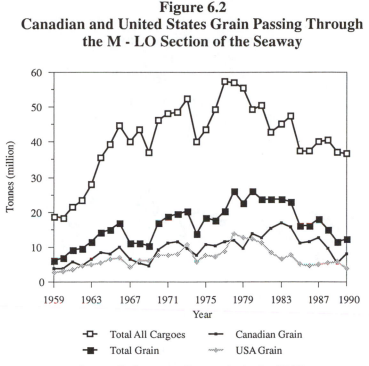

Source: St. Lawrence Seaway Authority (1990)

Great Lakes origins and destinations.

There is little doubt that the grain trade downbound and the iron ore trade upbound have been enhanced because of the Seaway. In 1958, the year before the Seaway opened, grain traffic through the Great Lakes/St. Lawrence Waterway to tidewater—both American and Canadian—was less than 5 million tonnes (Urquart and Buckley, 1965, 544). In 1980, the peak year for grain traffic, 26.0 million tonnes of grain passed through the M - LO section of the Seaway (see Figure 6.2). Usually, more Canadian than American grain passes through the Seaway, but the amount of Canadian and American grain traffic is determined by world and domestic changes in supply and demand, the capacity of the transportation grain-handling systems in both countries, and operational difficulties on the Seaway system itself caused by strikes and accidents (Ghonima, 1986, 8 and 11).[1]

The amount of iron ore moved through the Seaway is second only to the grain trade (Figure 6.3); in isolated years it has even surpassed

---

[1] The grain-handling system capacity is particularly important in the United States, where the Mississippi - Gulf of Mexico route is a major competitor to the Seaway for grain transport from the American mid-West to world markets (especially to Europe).

Figure 6.3
Grain and Iron Ore Traffic in the M - LO
Section of the Seaway

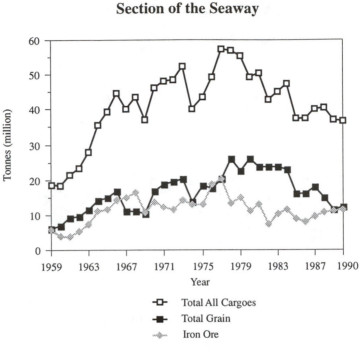

-□-   Total All Cargoes
-■-   Total Grain
··✖··   Iron Ore

Source: See Figure 6.2

the grain traffic. In 1959, iron ore traffic through the M - LO section amounted to 5.6 million tonnes and grew rapidly through the 1960s, to peak at slightly more than 20 million tonnes in 1977. Since then, trade has declined drastically to levels of approximately 10 million tonnes (Ghonima, 1986, 14). The decline is explained by the lower production of steel by American steel producers and, to some extent, by the industry's substitution of Quebec - Labrador iron ore with Lake Superior ore moving to steel producers on Lake Erie (see Chapter 2).

Although the Seaway has benefitted the grain and iron ore trade, it is not clear if ocean-going ships have been increasingly attracted to the Seaway and the Great Lakes beyond. As Figure 6.4 shows, the cargo tonnage handled by ocean-going vessels has increased over the years but its proportion has stayed relatively stable, ranging between 25 and 40 per cent of all cargo tonnes. The average for the period 1959–1990 is 33 per cent.

Bulk commodities are almost exclusively handled by lakers of Canadian registry, whereas general cargo is often handled by ocean-going ships of other countries. Of the approximately 33 million

Figure 6.4
Cargo Tonnes Carried by Class of Vessel
in the M - LO Section

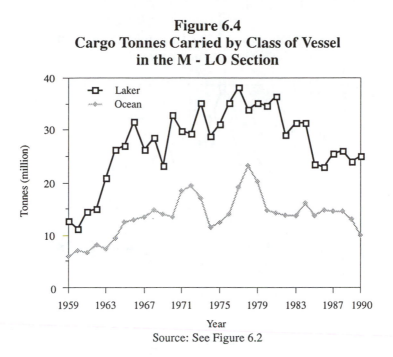

Source: See Figure 6.2

Figure 6.5
Traffic by Origin-Destination in the M - LO
Section of the Seaway

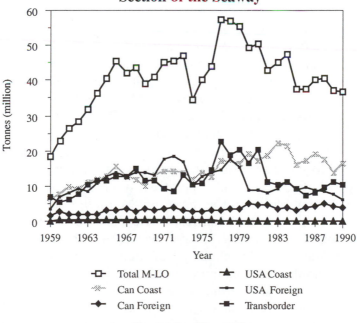

Source: See Figure 6.2

Figure 6.6
Per Cent of Foreign Traffic Tonnage in the M - LO
Section of the Seaway

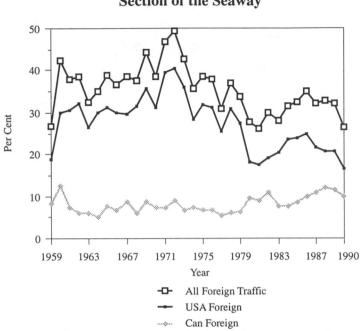

Source: See Figure 6.2

tonnes of bulk and grain cargoes moving through the M - LO section in 1989, about 75 per cent was handled by Canadian- and USA-registered ships, and of this proportion, Canadian ships handled 99.9 per cent. Of the total general cargo and container trade, Canadian and American ships handled only slightly more than 5 per cent. Ships registered in Liberia, Panama, Greece, Norway, Poland and Yugoslavia were the principal carriers of general cargo and containers.

An analysis of the origin and destination of goods passing through the M - LO section of the Seaway shows that, in the first twenty years of the Seaway's operation, three components of the traffic—Canadian coastwise shipping, USA foreign shipping, and Canadian - American transborder traffic—shared approximately equal portions of the trade at 30 per cent each (Figure 6.5). There were wide fluctuations in these proportions for certain years; in 1972, for example, the trans-border traffic (primarily iron ore) was down considerably, and in the same year the USA foreign traffic (primarily iron and steel imports) was unusually high. Since 1971, the proportion of foreign traffic using the Seaway, both Canadian and American, has been in decline (Figure 6.6).

The majority of the foreign traffic continues to be destined for or originate from American ports on the Great Lakes. There is relatively little Canadian traffic using the Seaway that moves directly to or comes directly from overseas destinations or origins (this excludes Canadian grain going to St. Lawrence ports for trans-shipment). Rather, Canadian use of the Seaway is principally for the movement of goods from one Canadian port to another (Canadian coastwise shipping), or for trans-border trade with the United States. The Americans, on the other hand, are much more involved with foreign shipping directly to and from foreign destinations and origins, and make little use of the Seaway for the coastwise shipping trade. That is, almost no American traffic that is destined for or comes from the American Atlantic coast or Gulf coast, and certainly not the Pacific coast, uses the Seaway.

The expected increase in the use of the Seaway by ocean-going ships and for direct international shipping has not occurred. This is particularly true for the Canadian trades and is becoming increasingly true for the American trades, as well, since general cargo imports have declined.

b) The Importance of Grain to the Seaway

Grain is one of the principal commodities handled on the Seaway; a very large proportion of the Great Lakes shipping fleet is dedicated to its transport, and many of the Great Lakes/St. Lawrence River ports depend significantly on its trade (see Chapter 3). There is cause for concern about the future of the grain trade on the waterway, however. A 1990 report commissioned by the Ontario government pinpointed the decline in the grain trade as "the greatest single threat to the Canadian Great Lakes shipping industry" (Lake and Hackson, 1990, 20).

In the early 1980s, close to 50 per cent of cargo tonnage consisted of grain, and in 1982 and 1983 that figure was higher than 50 per cent. With the decline in both trans-border traffic (principally iron ore) and American foreign trade (principally general cargo), the movement of Canadian grain through the Seaway has taken on greater and greater importance. Such a situation must increasingly worry the Seaway authorities at a time when Canadian grain exports, on the whole, are depressed and when competition for handling export grain is increasing on the West coast. The Great Lakes/St. Lawrence Waterway has a greater capacity to handle grain exports than does the West coast: its capacity is in excess of 20 million tonnes, compared to the approximately 15 million tonnes of the coast

(Erickson, 1986, 22). It is necessary that a large proportion of the Great Lakes' capacity be used every year for Canadian grain to reach international markets, as well. Traditionally, more than 50 per cent of all Canadian grain exports pass through the Seaway, but an increasingly greater proportion now passes through Pacific ports. It is likely that capacity will be reached on the Pacific coast, where costs are lower by as much as $20 per tonne (Carter, 1986, 30), leaving the remaining exports to pass through the Seaway. It is anticipated that the Asian market will continue to take more Canadian grain exports.

One study notes that, if Canadian total grain exports were 35 million tonnes with a maximum throughput on the West coast of 16.5 million tonnes, then the Seaway would handle the rest, an amount equal to 53 per cent of the total (Moore, 1986, 117). However, if exports were to fall to 30 million tonnes and the West coast maximum capacity was maintained, then only 45 per cent of exports would pass through the Seaway. Of 25 million exported tonnes, the Seaway would handle only 33 per cent. These projections have been more or less confirmed by actual statistics. In 1986–87, British Columbian ports handled a record 16 million tonnes, or 53.4 per cent, of the 30 million tonne export grain flow. The 1989–90 figures are more impressive for the West coast and dismal for the Seaway: 16.4 million tonnes of grain, or 70 per cent of the 23.5 million tonnes of Canadian grain exports, were handled at Vancouver and Prince Rupert (Canadian Wheat Board, 1989–90). With diminished grain exports through the Seaway, the decline of trans-border trade—especially iron ore, but also USA grain using the Lower St. Lawrence River ports—and with the fall-off in American foreign traffic importing iron and steel products through the Seaway, joint USA - Canadian trade delegations have been sent to Europe and North Africa to promote the use of the Seaway in recent years. The fruits of these efforts remain to be seen.

Based on revenues collected through tolls for various cargoes, grain is not as significant a commodity as the tonnage figures alone would indicate. Figures 6.7 and 6.8 show cargo tonnages and cargo revenues for grains, other bulks and general cargo (including containers) in the M - LO section. The separation of grain tonnages and revenues from those of other bulk goods began in 1978; before that date, there were only two toll categories: bulk and general cargo. As can be seen, since 1978 more revenue has been collected from bulk cargoes than from grain and general cargo (including containers), and general cargo revenues rival those of grain. Thus, although the tonnage of grains is usually the greatest of the three major categories, grain is not the principal revenue generator for the Seaway authorities, because the

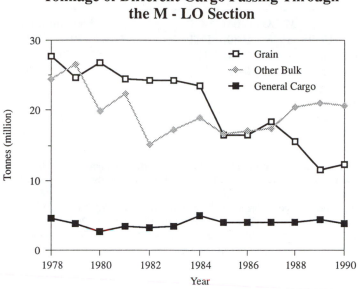

Figure 6.7
Tonnage of Different Cargo Passing Through
the M - LO Section

Source: See Figure 6.2

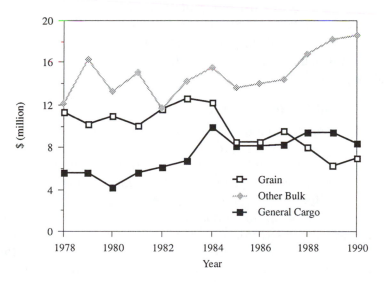

Figure 6.8
Toll Revenues Derived from Different Cargoes
in the M - LO Section

Source: See Figure 6.2

Table 6.1:
Cargo Tolls on the Seaway for Selected Years ($ per tonne)

	M-LO Section				Welland Canal			
	1959[1]	1978	1980	1989	1959[2]	1978	1980	1989
Bulk	0.44	0.50	0.68	0.89	0.055	0.20	0.31	0.44
Grain	n/a	0.41	0.41	0.54	n/a	0.20	0.31	0.44
Gov't Aid Cargoes	n/a	0.41	0.41	0.00	n/a	0.20	0.31	0.00
Containers	n/a	0.68	0.68	0.89	n/a	0.31	0.31	0.44
General	0.99	1.27	1.65	2.15	0.022	0.28	0.50	0.74

[1] The original tolls in $ per short ton have been converted to $ per tonne. The tolls stayed the same on the M - LO section from 1959 to 1978 with only two classes of cargo, bulk and general.

[2] The original tolls in $ per short ton have been converted to $ per tonne. Welland Canal tolls were suspended in 1962 and replaced by lockage fees in 1967. Lockage fees still exist on the Welland Canal (1989 = $355 loaded per lock and $260 in ballast per lock) along with the cargo tolls per tonne as shown.

Source: St. Lawrence Seaway Authority

toll rates for general cargo have been the highest. Even bulks have been charged at a rate higher than that for grains (see Table 6.1).

It is important that the Seaway not lose its share of general cargo trade. For every tonne lost, $2.15 of revenue is given up on the M - LO section and $0.74 is lost on the Welland Canal, whereas only $0.54 and $0.44 are lost per tonne of grain on the M - LO and the Welland, respectively (1989 figures). From the perspective of Seaway toll revenues, then, grain is important and any decline will negatively affect the Seaway, but a much greater loss will be felt if general cargo declines.

c)   The Issue of Containerization

The Seaway is primarily a bulk traffic waterway. Since 1959, close to 90 per cent of goods passing through the M - LO section of the water-way are classed as bulk and/or grains (their proportion in the Welland is even higher, at over 92 per cent). Thus only 10 per cent of the goods are classified as general cargo; in recent years, such cargo has been tallied at 3 to 4 million tonnes (see Figure 6.7), most of which consists of manufactured iron and steel. Finally, the amount of con-tainerized tonnage is very small: less than 0.5 per cent of the total cargo, and between 1 and 5 per cent of general cargo, is container-ized. These figures are summarized in Table 6.2.

Table 6.2:
Cargoes Passing through the Montreal - Lake Ontario
Section of the Seaway (in million tonnes)

Year	Bulk/Grain[1]	General[2]	(Man. Iron/Steel)	(Container)	Total[3]
1959	16.912	1.769	(0.417)	not available	18.681
1960	16.380	2.044	(0.738)	"	18.425
1961	19.362	1.881	(0.532)	"	21.244
1962	20.934	2.283	(0.757)	"	23.218
1963	25.403	2.667	(0.874)	"	28.070
1964	32.325	3.335	(1.233)	"	35.660
1965	34.294	5.061	(2.996)	"	39.356
1966	39.699	4.979	(2.781)	"	44.678
1967	34.532	5.409	(3.179)	"	39.942
1968	36.242	7.260	(4.978)	"	43.502
1969	30.807	6.399	(4.068)	"	37.207
1970	40.481	5.939	(4.032)	"	46.421
1971	40.252	7.816	(5.636)	"	48.069
1972	41.558	7.117	(5.210)	"	48.676
1973	47.000	5.284	(3.958)	"	52.284
1974	35.946	4.102	(3.271)	"	40.048
1975	40.272	3.282	(2.236)	"	43.554
1976	45.231	4.116	(3.026)	"	49.348
1977	51.294	6.161	(4.972)	"	57.456
1978	52.340	4.601	(3.589)	(0.271)	56.942
1979	51.411	3.908	(3.108)	(0.229)	55.332
1980	46.774	2.678	(2.085)	(0.166)	49.454
1981	47.098	3.469	(2.905)	(0.064)	50.569
1982	39.552	3.261	(2.790)	(0.078)	42.815
1983	41.714	3.344	(2.896)	(0.060)	45.060
1984	42.566	4.937	(4.453)	(0.140)	47.505
1985	33.273	4.045	(3.603)	(0.113)	37.321
1986	33.569	4.010	(3.548)	(0.059)	37.581
1987	35.922	4.044	(3.614)	(0.042)	39.968
1988	35.952	4.604	(4.317)	(0.039)	40.558
1989	32.626	4.444	(4.186)	(0.031)	37.070
1990	32.879	3.777	(3.607)	(0.024)	36.656

[1] Includes government aid cargoes after 1977.

[2] Includes manufactured iron and steel and, after 1977, containers.

[3] Bulk/grain plus General may not equal Total because of rounding.

Source: St. Lawrence Seaway Authority (1990)

The fact that less than 30,000 tonnes of containerized cargo passed through the M - LO section of the Seaway in 1989 and 1990 is remarkable compared with the 1989 container figures for other ports: 5.5 million tonnes at Montreal, 3.9 million tonnes at Halifax and 12.5 million tonnes at New York (*Containerization International Yearbook,* 1991). Obviously, the Seaway is not catering to containers. Relatively few container lines serve the Great Lakes (see Table 6.3) and those that do have small container-carrying capacities and carry containers in conjunction with break bulk cargo. There are no specialized container terminals at Canadian ports in the Great Lakes; rather, containers are handled at conventional piers using mobile equipment. In recognition that containers could make up a major proportion of Seaway traffic, the St. Lawrence Seaway Authority introduced a new toll structure in 1978 that recognized containers as a separate traffic. In 1980 containers were to be charged the same amount as bulk cargo—$0.68 per tonne—in contrast to general cargo, which was charged at $1.65 per tonne. However, container traffic remains small and its prospects do not seem much better. Why?

There are at least three reasons why containerized cargo trade on the Seaway has not grown: physical limitations, economic limitations and institutional limitations (Schenker, Mayer and Brockel, 1976, 53–58). First, the size restrictions of the Seaway prevent the movement of medium- to large-sized container vessels. The maximum draft of the Seaway is 7.7 m, but 1,000 teu capacity container vessels draw about 9.5 m; 1,500 teu capacity container vessels draw 11 to 12 m; and vessels larger than this draw 13 m (Beth, Kader and Kappel, 1984, 72). Thus only small container vessels are able to transit the Seaway, but such vessels are very uneconomic on an ocean route where they must compete against 2nd- and 3rd-generation container vessels with 2,000 and even 4,000 teu capacities. Consequently, these small vessels operate most effectively in trades which combine containers and break bulk shipping, to South America or to the Mediterranean, for example; or they operate as feeder services taking small lots of containers to and from a mother port. On the Great Lakes/St. Lawrence Waterway Montreal acts as a mother port due to its strategic location at the entrance to the Seaway; but the mode used to distribute containers throughout the Great Lakes area is not water transport, but rail and truck. At one time a water feeder service was attempted (see Table 6.3), but companies reverted to land transport because of the efficient intermodality of container handling. Road and rail transport take most of the containers from Montreal because of

Table 6.3:
Shipping Lines Operating on the Great Lakes that Offer International Container Services, 1978 and 1989

1978

Line	Ownership	Ports Served
Black Sea Shipping Co.	USSR	Montreal, Toronto and USA Great Lakes ports to/ Black Sea and Mediterranean ports.
Europe Canada Lakes Line	Germany	Northern Europe and Great Lakes ports.
Falline Container Service	Canada	Antwerp, East Canada and Great Lakes ports.
Lyles Line	USA	Great Lakes/St. Lawrence Seaway ports and Mediterranean, Middle East, Pakistan, India and Burma.
Manchester Liners	UK	Based at Montreal providing Great Lakes feeder service to Detroit, Chicago, Milwaukee, Cleveland, Erie and Toledo.
Netumar	Brazil	US Great Lakes/East Coast ports and a range of ports in Brazil, Uruguay and Argentina.
Yugoslav Great Lakes Line	Yugoslavia	Yugoslav and other Mediterranean ports and Canadian Atlantic, St. Lawrence and Great Lakes ports.

1989

Line	Ownership	Ports Served
Armada Lines Ltd	Denmark	Milwaukee, Green Bay, Burns Harbor, Kenosha, Erie, Montreal, to/from West, South and East Africa.
Christensen Canadian African Line	Norway	Toronto, Montreal to/from South Africa.
A/S Dampski-bsselskabet Torm	Denmark	Chicago, Montreal to/from Mediterranean.
Fednav (Belgium) Ltd	Canada	Duluth, Milwaukee, Chicago, Toledo, Detroit, Cleveland, Hamilton, Toronto, Montreal to/from, Northwest Europe.
Jadranska Slobodna Plovidba	Yugoslavia	Chicago, Milwaukee, Detroit, Cleveland, Toronto, Montreal to/from Mediterranean and Adriatic.
Lykes Line	USA	Duluth, Milwaukee, Montreal to/from North Africa.
Netumar S/A	Brazil	Montreal, Toronto to/from Brazilian ports.
Saguenay Shipping Ltd.	Canada	Toronto, Montreal to/from Puerto Rico and Brazil.

Source: *Containerization International Yearbook* (1978 and 1991)

the flexibility of handling by road and the attractive transport rates by rail. The ease of transferring containers from ship to shore, and of the subsequent unloading either at an intermodal transfer station or directly at the door of the destination makes direct transfer to land transport (as opposed to the use of feeder ships) very attractive. A further physical limitation of the Seaway is its closure in the winter season for about three months, and this problem is discussed below.

A fact that affects the economics of container service operations in the Great Lakes/St. Lawrence Waterway is that a round trip through the waterway is very time-consuming. The return time from Montreal to Chicago (with one day allowed for loading and unloading) is nine days, with no port stops along the way. This journey might be made slightly faster or slower than this figure, depending on weather conditions, vessel characteristics and waterway operations. Considering the fact that a vessel can make a trip from Montreal to Continental Europe in nine days, trade operations on the Great Lakes are quite expensive to shipping lines. During the Seaway's season (1 April–15 December), a Continental Europe - Montreal - Continental Europe service with two days for turnaround can make twelve round trips, three more than it could if the ship proceeded into the Great Lakes. Even for a modest sized ship with 600 teu capacity, the extra journeys on the Seaway would be the equivalent of an extra 3,600 teu crossing the Atlantic (1,800 each way). Needless to say, the more cargo a ship carries during the shipping season, the more revenue the ship will generate, so it is little wonder that no fully cellular container ship serves the Great Lakes.

The Montreal service must rely on land transport to link its terminus to Chicago, but this does not seem to be a great problem in logistics, time or cost, since all of the present container services using Montreal already use land transport to distribute and collect containers from hinterland areas. However, if land costs become prohibitive because of increased fuel costs or a lack of competition that would lead to higher rates, then it might be possible for a dedicated container service to come into the Great Lakes. However, at present and in the immediate future, it does not seem likely that direct container services will operate on a large scale on the Great Lakes. As Lake and Hackson also conclude (1990), Montreal will continue to function as the terminal port of such services or, alternatively, containers will continue to find their way to and from tidewater through Atlantic and Pacific coast ports, using existing road or rail (especially double-stack trains).

Institutional limitations of the Seaway include American "cargo preference" legislation, which requires that at least half of all certain cargoes—including government and foreign-aid cargoes—must be shipped in USA flag vessels. However, since there are very few USA carriers serving the Great Lakes, much of the containerized prefer-ence cargoes go out through Atlantic, Gulf of Mexico or even Pacific ports, even though the cargo might originate in the Great Lakes area.

d) Extending the Navigation Season

Because of winter weather in the Great Lakes and the St. Lawrence River region, the Seaway is closed for at least three months each year, and usually longer. On average the M - LO section maintains a 259-day navigation season. The earliest opening was 24 March 1980, while the latest closing recorded for the winter period was 2 January 1984. For the Welland Canal, the navigation season has usually been longer (average 270 days). Opening dates in recent years have been similar, but a few more days have been available for operation before closure. For five of the years since 1959, operations there have continued into January (the latest closing day was 18 January 1974). Periodically, the question is asked: is it feasible to operate the Seaway for even a longer period of time—eventually for the entire year?

The question of season extension was first raised in the 1960s, when traffic through the Seaway was increasing at a rapid rate and fears of reaching capacity were sparked. The first studies, conduct-ed by the the USA Coast Guard and USA Corps of Engineers, con-cluded that it was feasible to extend the navigation season by at least one month, but that the problems posed by wind-blown pack ice that blocks navigation channels constituted a serious obstacle (Schenker, Mayer and Brockel, 1976, 76). The USA Congress approved a Demonstration Program of winter navigation and reports were to be submitted by the end of 1976. This program allowed shipping throughout the winter on the Upper Lakes above the Welland Canal. During the winter, the Poe Lock at Sault Ste. Marie was kept open in order to allow the largest lakers to carry iron ore from American Lake Superior ports to steel-making centres on Lake Michigan and Lake Erie. The success of this program put pressure on Canada to extend the navigation season of the Welland Canal and in the M - LO section.

The Canadian response in 1978 was to commission a benefit-cost study focusing Canadian interests (LBA Consulting Partners, 1978). The results of the study completed for the St. Lawrence Seaway Authority justified an 8 1/2-month operating season, from 1 April to 15 December, but a 9 1/2-month or 11-month season was deemed econom-ically unfeasible. A similar conclusion was drawn in a study for the Marine Administration of Transport Canada in June 1981. The current position of the Seaway Authority is that the canal will operate for 8 1/2 months and that "economical and technically practical works to improve ice conditions throughout the 8 1/2-month season" will be undertaken (St. Lawrence Seaway Authority, 1983, 4). At the beginning and end of the operating season, it is not always possible to operate ships 24 hours a day; navigation aids cannot be placed in the water while there is ice, for instance, since the aids might be moved off-station. In such a situation navigation is possible only during daylight hours when the aids are visible. Because of these limitations, the Seaway Authority supports the development of an electronic navigation system to make navigation in ice-prone times safer and for a continual period. The possibility of a 9 1/2-month season still exists, and could have been achieved at "a relatively modest cost" in 1983 dollars of $42.5 million (St. Lawrence Seaway Authority, 1983, 4), but a lead time of at least five years would be required to implement such a season, and no such lead time has been announced as yet. The Authority has stated that it is "prepared to extend the season [beyond a 9 1/2-month period] when forecasts indicate traffic can no longer be handled effectively within the existing season" (St. Lawrence Seaway Authority, 1983, 4).

It would seem that an extension of the navigation season is not a priority, but in today's economic climate, can anything else be expected? The push for an extended season came when traffic was high and was expected to rise. By the end of the 1980s, that traffic had declined to less than 40 million tonnes, and future prospects were not good. Iron ore shipments were down, grain traffic was uncertain, and therefore there was no guarantee that an extended season would see more traffic. The real benefit of an extended navigation season would be gained by ocean-going vessels carrying general cargo; but even these cargoes are not growing and, after twenty years of operation, containerization trade in the waterway has not developed. Would a guaranteed 9 1/2-month or 11-month operating season bring more general cargo traffic to the Great Lakes? This is doubtful, given that seasonality is only one of the factors that curtail Great Lakes shipping. More pressing is the physical problem of limitations to vessel size due to the size of the locks and channels of the Seaway.

Even during an 8 1/2-month season, the Seaway is not approaching capacity. Thus, season extension is not an issue at present, but if and when traffic rises, one can be sure that there will be talk of canal widening, or of season extension, or both.

e)   The Issue of Finances

The Seaway was built as a self-financing public utility and was to pay for itself within fifty years of its opening. It was boldly claimed that "the seaway will be debt free by 2008" (Chevrier, 1959, 122). Canada's original capital expenditure for the Seaway up to December 31, 1959 was $310.7 million. American expenditure was $131 million (U.S. dollars). In order to pay off its debt and to meet any new capital costs and all operating costs, the St. Lawrence Seaway Authority and the USA Saint Lawrence Seaway Development Corporation were responsible for collecting tolls from the users of the waterway. From 1959 to 1978 these tolls were fixed, on the M - LO section of the waterway, at $0.04 per gross registered ton of the vessel, $0.40 per ton of bulk cargo and $0.90 per ton on general cargo. For the Welland Canal the original tolls were lower, set at $0.02 per gross registered ton, $0.02 per ton of bulk cargo and $0.05 per ton of general cargo; but these rates were suspended in 1962 and replaced in 1967 by a schedule of lockage charges that remained in effect until 1978.

By the middle 1970s, the Seaway was in serious financial trouble. It was not paying for itself on a yearly basis, and very little progress was being made in paying off its outstanding capital investment and accumulated unpaid interest; in fact, its debt was growing at an alarming rate. By March 1978 the Canadian Seaway debt stood at $841.3 million, including the original expenditure ($310.7 million), additional capital expenditures ($314.2 million) for upgrading the waterway (especially the Welland Canal), and accumulated unpaid interest ($216.4 million). In 1976 alone, the St. Lawrence Seaway Authority lost $21.9 million and $30.7 million on the operations of the M - LO section and the Welland Canal, respectively. Many factors account for this dismal situation: projections for traffic use of the Seaway were not realized in the early years; operating and mainte-nance costs grew more quickly than anticipated; and rising interest rates increased the money to be repaid by unanticipated amounts; and, finally, tolls had not increased for eighteen years on the M - LO section, and were artificially low on the Welland Canal (St. Lawrence Seaway Authority, 1975, 2). To complicate matters, any toll increases put into effect required the cooperation and approval of both the Canadian and American governments and, over the years, it proved more and more difficult to achieve such cooperation.

Several initiatives were undertaken in 1977 and 1978 to address the Seaway debt. The outstanding loans to the Seaway Authority were converted to equity effective 1 April 1977. The accumulated, unpaid interest was forgiven. In effect, the entire $841 million of Seaway debt was wiped from the books. Furthermore, new tolls were established to be phased in over a three year period beginning in

Figure 6.9
Seaway Net Income from Operations
(Includes Investment Income)[1]

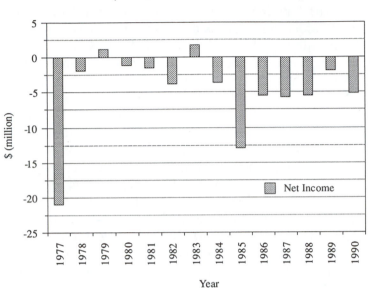

Year

[1]Does not include $1.431 million expense in 1985 and $2.882 million expense on M - LO section in 1987 because of the Valleyfield bridge accident (unusual maintenance expense), nor $10.843 million expense on Welland Canal because of the closure of the Canal due to a lock wall collapse (unusual maintenance expense). Does not include Welland Canal Rehabilitation Project expenses of $13.2 million in 1986, $24.5 million in 1987, $25.4 million in 1988, $26.9 million in 1989 and $27.3 million in 1990.

Source: St. Lawrence Seaway (1977–1990)

1978. These new tolls recognized different cargoes (grains, bulk, general, containers and government aid), whereas the old tolls had been based upon two classes of commodities—bulk and general. Lockage fees on the Welland Canal were replaced by the five cargo tolls charged on a per tonne basis, similar to (though lower than) those imposed on the M - LO section. The new tariffs were expected to double, approximately, the revenue collected from users of the Canadian portion of the Seaway. The Authority confidently predicted that the "implementation of these measures will enable the St. Lawrence Seaway Authority to become the self-supporting corporation it was originally intended to be" (St. Lawrence Seaway Authority, 1977, 5). However, this debt-free status has not yet been, and may never be, reached. Between 1977 and 1990 inclusive, there have been only two years in which operating revenues, including interest gained from investments, have been greater than expenses (see Figure 6.9). Over this twelve year-period, the Seaway has lost, on average, $4.8 million per year (calculated from Annual Reports of the St. Lawrence Seaway Authority, 1977–1990). This figure does not include extraordinary expenses associated with closures of the Seaway: in November, 1984 a bridge failure at Valleyfield in the Beauharnois Canal caused the closure of a section of the M - LO Waterway for nineteen days; and in October, 1985 the Welland Canal was closed when a lock wall collapsed. Further loss was caused by the rehabilitation of the Welland Canal, which began in 1986 and continued for a five year period at a total cost of $175 million (this cost was met by special funding from the Canadian federal government, and not from the working capital of the Seaway Authority).

The Seaway has not met its obligation to pay for itself; it is doubtful if it will even meet operating expenses. Although tolls continue to rise, so also do expenses, the biggest one being maintenance. Of the two sections of the Seaway—the M - LO and the Welland Canal—the latter has consistently lost more money than the former. It is anticipated that the rehabilitation program will cut down on the maintenance expenses, and that increased tolls will generate more revenue. But in order for the tolls to generate this new revenue, there must be at least the same amount of traffic, and preferably more. However, as has been discussed, the traffic forecasts for the future are not good.

SUMMARY

The Seaway was heralded as a North American water transportation accomplishment without equal when it opened in 1959. Bulk trades would be stimulated; general cargo shipping from around the world would have access to the rich heartlands of both the United States and Canada. In a general way, these predictions were realized: grain trade did increase; iron ore trade expanded; general cargo shipping increased; and, although not discussed here, the coal trade on the Great Lakes also grew (see Chapter 2). Why is it then, that the Seaway continues to lose money, even though its capital expenses and debts were forgiven in 1978?

Clearly the Seaway has not met its expectations for trade. Not only has its poor financial performance continued, but tonnage levels have been dropping, not rising, in recent years. Grain trade is expected to be depressed in the future, as overseas markets for grain continue to decline in Europe and grow in Asia, and as European farm subsidies that encourage farmers to grow their own grain continue to be provided. Iron ore tonnages from Quebec - Labrador are a shadow of their former selves, although these may improve as the Canadian and USA steel industry expands its output. However, there are no guarantees that Quebec - Labrador iron ore will be in great demand as the steel industry expands, because Michigan and Minnesota deposits are closer and are of equally high quality.

Though the Seaway may not have lived up to expectations, and though it may be outmoded and not able to cope with modern larger ships, it seems likely that the Seaway will continue to play a vital role in North American trade, especially that of Canada. Traditionally, water transportation has proven to be the least expensive way to transport bulk commodities over long distances. As long as grain, iron ore, coal, limestone, and other lesser bulks need to be transported on the Great Lakes to and from markets beyond, then the Seaway will continue to play a role in Canadian water transportation. As one administrator said, in the middle 1980s, "we want you there, Great Lakes Seaway, although we are not sure that we want to use you [just] now" (Hodgson, 1986, 155). This sentiment lingers, it would seem, today.

CHAPTER 7

VANCOUVER: CRUISE CAPITAL OF CANADA

Vancouver is the largest dry cargo port on the West coast of the Americas, and rivals Los Angeles and Long Beach, California as the largest all-cargo port. There is no doubt that Vancouver is Canada's largest and most important port. Unlike the East coast, where the four major ports of Montreal, Quebec, Saint John and Halifax—as well as ports on the North Shore of the St. Lawrence River—all play important roles in Canada's international waterborne trade, Canada's West coast has only a handful of ports handling international cargo. The dominant port among them is Vancouver; Prince Rupert has developed to take some of the strain from Vancouver, especially in grain exports, and is a major exporter of coal, too, now that Ridley Island coal terminal has been built. Nanaimo, Kitimat, and New Westminster (administratively separate from the Port of Vancouver) handle export cargoes of lumber and pulp, but all pale in importance next to Vancouver.

Vancouver is the gateway through which western Canadian resources reach the world. Grain from the Prairies, coal from Alberta and British Columbia, potash from Saskatchewan, sulphur from Alberta and lumber from British Columbia all pass through

Vancouver. Vancouver is Canada's largest grain port; it handles more coal, potash, sulphur, lumber and sawn timber than any other Canadian port. It is Canada's busiest port with 11,949 vessel movements into and out of the port in 1990; in total, 64.5 million tonnes of cargo were handled by the port of Vancouver that year. As important as Vancouver is in the bulk trades, it is also Canada's premier foreign passenger port. More people use the port of Vancouver than any other in Canada in their travels to and from foreign destinations, primarily Alaska. In the cruising season, cruise ships are as common a sight in Vancouver as container ships or grain vessels.

The handling of people at a port is a demanding business. Over the past twenty-five years there has been a large increase in cruising as a vacation and therefore shipping activity. The cruise ships require modern and special facilities to effect the transfer of their "cargo" from land to sea and vice versa. In this regard, port facilities for cruise ships are no different than those for container ships or oil tankers. However, the cargo of cruise ships is people, and handling them is not as simple as lifting a container or connecting a pipe. Those ports that have specialized in passenger movements have done so only through a lot of hard work and attention to detail. Vancouver is one of those ports.

a)   Cruise Shipping as an International Activity

Before the universal adoption of the jet engine that made intercontinental air travel possible, travel between continents was undertaken largely by ship. This was particularly the case on the busy North Atlantic. All of the major European nations (Britain, France, and Germany) and the United States had large fleets of registered passenger liners. At the end of the 1950s the trans-Atlantic liner fleet reached its zenith. But it was all to change. The airplane replaced the ship as the favoured way to cross the ocean. Speed, as much as price, was the attraction. 1957 was the last year in which more people crossed the Atlantic Ocean by ship than by airplane (Beth, Hader and Kappel, 1984, 100). With the demise of passenger liners, the world's seas were left to charter operators. Cruising, as this chartering of passenger vessels came to be called, had its modern day start in the Aegean Sea at about the same time as the trans-Atlantic liner industry first felt the effects of the jet airplane. "In 1955 the National Tourist Organization of Greece chartered the SEMIRAMIS in order to promote maritime tourism" (Beth, Hader and Kappel, 1984, 103)—especially amongst visiting Americans, but also amongst Germans and the British. In the 1960s the cruise industry spread to the Caribbean, where the emphasis on winter cruising complemented the spring-to-fall season in the Mediterranean. Also, the Caribbean is much closer to the American market, which was attracted by lower fares. By the end of the 1960s and the beginning of the 1970s, Norwegian shipowners saw an opportunity to enter the cruising business on a large scale. The increased demand for cruising holidays allowed Norway to enter the industry competitively: "Between 1969 and 1973 ten Norwegian companies put a total of twelve new vessels into service in the Caribbean" (Beth, Hader and Kappel, 1984, 105). Cruising destinations expanded beyond those of the original Mediterranean and Caribbean to include seasonal operations in Scandinavia, South East Asia, the Far East, Australia and the North American West coast (California to Mexico in the winter, and San Francisco/Seattle/Vancouver to Alaska in the summer).

In 1986 over 2.5 million people took a cruise (Don Ference & Associates, 1988, Table 2.2), and of these, the vast majority (close to 75 per cent) were American. Europeans accounted for the second largest proportion of cruise ship customers (17 per cent), Australians 4 per cent and Canadians 3 per cent. Close to 86 per cent of the world's cruise passengers left from North America. Europe trailed far behind, and of even lesser importance were Australia and the Far East. The most popular destinations for North Americans were, in decreasing order, the Caribbean, Bahamas, Mexico, Alaska and Bermuda (Don Ference & Associates, 1988, Table 2.3).

b) Cruising at Vancouver

As the cruise industry has expanded worldwide, the port of Vancouver has become one of its important centres. For decades British Columbia and Alaska cruising had been a sideline for Canadian coastal steamers. Both Canadian Pacific and Canadian National Railways combined regular passenger cruises and regular freight services. However, modern cruising along the North American Pacific coast began in 1963 when a Seattle businessman, Stan McDonald, successfully promoted a Los Angeles - Mexico cruise with the PRINCESS PATRICIA chartered from the CPR (Montgomery, 1981, 14). The success of this venture prompted him to charter the ITALIA, with which he was able to initiate foreign-flag cruising to Alaska from Vancouver (Stallard, 1986, 27–29). Other foreign operators soon joined the service, and Canadian Pacific refurbished the PRINCESS PATRICIA and entered the British Columbia-Alaska service anew. The PATRICIA continued to operate in the Alaska service until 1981, when it failed to meet American anti-pol-

Figure 7.1
Cruise Vessel Voyages and Passengers at the
Port of Vancouver

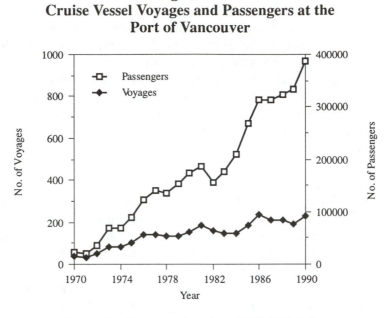

Source: Don Ference & Associates (1988, Table 3.2)
and Port of Vancouver (unpublished data)

lution standards. The CNR continued to operate the PRINCE
GEORGE until 1975 (Montgomery, 1981, 14).

Figure 7.1 shows the growth in the number of cruise ships calling
at the port of Vancouver and in the number of cruise passengers since
1970. From a modest beginning of 38 ships and 22,800 passengers in
1970 the numbers have grown to over 200 voyages and over 388,000
passengers in 1990. The year of Expo 86, which attracted tourists
from around the world and stimulated new cruising interest in
Vancouver, marked a reduction in the rate of growth. Canada Place,
the cruise terminal, was opened that year as well. Since 1986, the
cruise industry has gone on each year to set new records, proving that
cruising to/from Vancouver is an established industry not dependent
on happenings in Vancouver itself. The attraction for tourists is the
scenery of the Inside Passage and ultimately Alaska.

The passenger numbers in Figure 7.1 represent the number of
times a passenger embarks, disembarks or transits. Therefore, round
trip passengers embarking for and disembarking from an Alaskan trip
are counted twice. These numbers show impressive growth over the
years, and are far greater than those of any other Canadian port; however, Vancouver falls short of Miami, with over 2.5 million cruise

passengers (Charlier, 1989), and Port Everglades, with 1.5 million (Thiele, 1989). Such is the attraction of the Caribbean as a cruise destination. On the North American West coast, Vancouver trails Los Angeles as the most popular embarkation/debarkation port for cruise passengers. However, Vancouver handles more cruise passengers than either San Francisco (54,000 in 1987, for example) and Seattle (22,000 in 1987) (Cruise Industry Task Force, 1988, 5). In fact, while cruise passengers have been declining in number at the latter two ports, they have been on the increase at Vancouver.

In 1989 seventeen ships owned by nine cruise lines in the Alaska trade regularly called at Vancouver. Fifteen of these ships used Vancouver as a base of operation. These ships operate to a very precise schedule with an extremely high occupancy (estimated at 95 per cent for 1987) (Ference & Associates, 1988, 29). The cruise season runs from the middle of May to the middle of October, but most vessels have left by the end of September. Like migratory waterfowl, the vessels come north in the spring, either from cruises based in Los Angeles serving the Mexican coast, or from the Caribbean. In the fall, they return to their winter cruising grounds.

The Alaska cruise season is usually organized around a seven-day return trip with Vancouver as base, or a seven-day one-way trip with arrivals/departures at Vancouver every fourteen days. The turnaround ports where Vancouver passengers end their trip or Vancouver-destined passengers begin their trip are either Whittier or Seward, Alaska. Other schedules require that ships call at Vancouver every eleven, twelve or twenty-one days. The seven-day or fourteen-day schedules allow a vessel to be in port on the same weekday throughout the cruise season, usually on the weekend to coincide with tourists who plan their holidays based on week-long vacations anchored by weekends. Eight of the seventeen cruise ships calling at Vancouver in 1989 scheduled either regular Saturday or Sunday departures. Four others departed on Fridays to take advantage of the weekend, as well. Consequently, it is not unusual to see four or five cruise vessels in port at the same time, and this puts strain on the passenger facilities, whereas on other days, especially Wednesday, it is unusual to see a single cruise vessel in port. The location of Vancouver relative to Alaska makes the seven-day return trip possible, and this is one of the reasons that Vancouver has prospered more so than Seattle or San Francisco.

Figure 7.2 shows the travel paths of the cruise ships calling at Vancouver in 1990. A few of these ships made other Canadian port calls, but the majority used Vancouver as their only Canadian stop,

Figure 7.2
The Itineraries of Cruise Ships Calling at the
Port of Vancouver, 1990

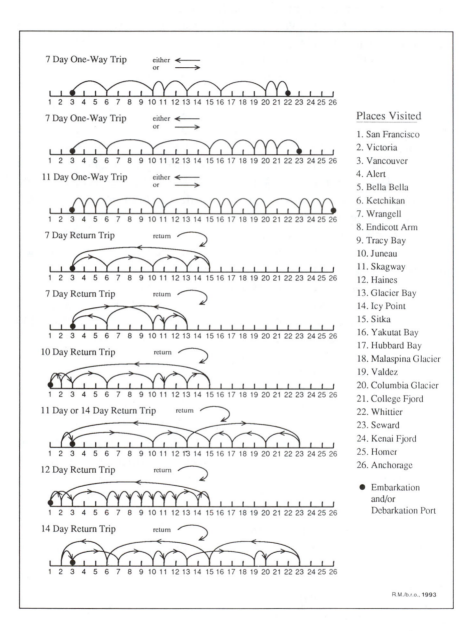

Places Visited

1. San Francisco
2. Victoria
3. Vancouver
4. Alert
5. Bella Bella
6. Ketchikan
7. Wrangell
8. Endicott Arm
9. Tracy Bay
10. Juneau
11. Skagway
12. Haines
13. Glacier Bay
14. Icy Point
15. Sitka
16. Yakutat Bay
17. Hubbard Bay
18. Malaspina Glacier
19. Valdez
20. Columbia Glacier
21. College Fjord
22. Whittier
23. Seward
24. Kenai Fjord
25. Homer
26. Anchorage

● Embarkation
and/or
Debarkation Port

R.M./b.r.o., 1993

Table 7.1:
Projected Direct Economic Benefits Accruing from the
Cruise Ship Industry, British Columbia, 1988

Service Related Benefits	Benefit Estimate ($ million)	
	Low	High
Bunkering	14.60	15.00
Provisioning	8.50	10.50
Pilotage	2.70	2.90
Moorage and Port Charges	2.90	3.40
Repairs and Maintenance	2.00	3.50
Passenger Handling	3.10	3.40
Office and Related Expenses	0.80	1.00
Use of Airports	1.30	1.45
Crew Expenses	0.40	0.60
SubTotal	**36.30**	**41.75**
Passenger Related Benefits		
Use of Canadian Air Carriers	9.00	12.00
Tours and Excursions	1.30	1.70
General Expenditures	8.60	13.80
Hotel Accommodations and Meals	3.90	4.55
Pre- and Post Tours	7.50	11.50
SubTotal	**30.30**	**43.55**
Total Economic Benefits	**66.60**	**85.30**

Source: Gary Duke & Associates (1988, Table XI)

either for embarkation/debarkation or as a port call. In economic terms, British Columbia would benefit from even more calls in Vancouver and other ports in the province. An economic impact study of the cruise industry in British Columbia estimated that in 1988, $13.8 million to $20.05 million was spent by tourists on meals, tours and shopping during port calls (Gary Duke & Associates, 1988). This figure is based on a passenger spending between $25–$40 per day on a port call. Other dimensions of the estimated economic impact in 1988 are shown in Table 7.1.

The benefits that directly affect the port of Vancouver and related shipping services are bunkering, pilotage (the majority takes place in the Inside Passage, on the way to Alaska), moorage, port charges and services, repairs and maintenance, and passenger handling. If the pilotage component is removed and it is assumed that 90 per cent of the port and shipping benefits are felt in Vancouver, as opposed to other British Columbia ports, then the estimated direct economic benefit to the port of Vancouver from the cruise industry was between $20.3 and $22.7 million for 1988.

There are a number of reasons why Vancouver has enjoyed an increase in cruise shipping and the economic benefits of this increase, including the initiative of the port itself, the location of Vancouver relative to Alaska, and the increase in leisure spending. The most significant explanation of its success, however, is "geopolitical" in nature. Strangely enough, events occurring as far away as Washington, D.C., the Mediterranean Sea and the Middle East have had a great influence on the prosperity of Vancouver as a cruise centre.

United States laws for passenger shipping and cabotage[1] explain to a large degree why the port of Vancouver has benefitted from the cruise industry. The USA's *Passenger Service Act* of 1866 prohibits the carriage of passengers between two United States ports on a vessel built in a country other than the United States. This is a significant restriction given that almost all cruise ships are built and registered outside of the United States (and Canada) and that the overwhelming majority of people taking cruises to/from Alaska are American. In effect, this law prohibits foreign-flag ships from taking passengers one way from Seattle or San Francisco to ports in Alaska. The law does allow foreign-flag ships to disembark passengers at the same port at which they were embarked, provided that the voyage includes an international stop. Therefore, foreign-flag cruise ships based in Seattle or San Francisco wishing to participate in the Alaska cruise business can only offer round-trip voyages that either last longer than seven days, or have little Alaskan content—neither of which is very acceptable to those tourists who attempt to organize their holiday on a seven-day schedule, and wish to see as much of Alaska as they can in their limited time. This disadvantage of lengthy travel time and the restrictive American cabotage law is exacerbated by the trend for cruise passengers to take a fly/cruise vacation involving one-way cruise trips. In this way, time is maximized in Alaska, but because such cruise passengers cannot take one-way cruises between American ports in foreign-flag ships, Vancouver has become the point of departure of choice. San Francisco explained its loss (and Vancouver's increase) of cruise passengers in the following way: "In a market where cruises are getting shorter and more affordable, it is more economical for cruise lines to fly passengers to the gateway cities such as Vancouver for the Alaska cruises . . . than incur the

---

[1] Cabotage laws are trade laws that prohibit foreign ships from carrying domestic cargo between a country's ports.

expense of extra sailing days to and from San Francisco" (Cruise Industry Task Force, 1988, 8).

In Vancouver, there is concern that the restrictive American passenger law will be relaxed to enable foreign-flag ships to make one way trips involving American West coast ports to/from Alaska (Chamber of Shipping of British Columbia, 1988). Foreign-flag cruise vessels are allowed to trade between Puerto Rico and mainland United States, so why not between Alaska and the "lower 48"? The State of Alaska has proposed exemption from the cabotage law and the port of San Francisco sees such an exemption as having "a significant effect on San Francisco's ability to achieve quantum gains in passenger vessel activity" (Cruise Industry Task Force, 1988, 9). The Port of Seattle is lobbying the USA Congress to change the passenger law so that Seattle can take over Vancouver's role (Crowley, 1991). It is particularly frustrating for Seattle not to have some of the Alaska cruise trade since the majority of cruise passengers passing through Vancouver use the Seattle - Tacoma Airport on their way to or from Vancouver, and are then bused between Seattle and Vancouver. Given that most of the passengers are American and that air connections are easier and less expensive within the United States, it is advantageous for the cruise lines to fly their passengers to an American airport and bus them to Vancouver rather than fly directly to Vancouver. There is no doubt that changes to the USA's *Passenger Service Act* to accommodate Seattle and San Francisco concerns would adversely affect the port of Vancouver, but it is doubtful that the port would lose many of its cruising passengers; Vancouver is the closest major mainland port to Alaska, and is a major attraction in its own right.

Canada Place and Ballantyne Pier provide two dedicated cruise terminal facilities in Vancouver, and this is an advantage over Seattle. Canada Place was built especially for Expo 86 and serves as more than just a cruise ship terminal. Also on site is a major hotel, World Trade Centre offices and the Vancouver Trade and Convention Centre. Its downtown location is also attractive. Canada Place has five berths and, in the cruising season, is so heavily used that overflow berthing is needed at nearby Ballantyne Pier. Although it was originally built in 1923 and has always served as a general cargo facility, Ballantyne also has been handling cruise vessels since 1980, and in 1990 received a much needed renovation and structural upgrade.

Events world wide also have contributed to the success of Vancouver. Terrorism in the Middle East, which has spilled over into Europe and the Mediterranean Sea, has tempered the enthusiasm for tourists to spend cruise vacations in the Mediterranean. The highjack-

Table 7.2:
Cruise Ships Calling at Selected Eastern Canadian
Ports and Vancouver (for Comparison)

Year	Montreal	Quebec	Halifax	Saint John	Vancouver
1984	50	51	12	0	145
1985	50	47	17	0	184
1986	57	67	34	0	233
1987	76	100	57	12	212
1988	59	79	31	1	209

Source: Tourism Canada (1988), Don Ference & Associates (1988)
and personal communications with the ports

ing of the ACHILLE LAURO in October 1985 in the eastern
Mediterranean Sea probably did more to promote Vancouver and the
Alaska cruise experience than any marketing ploy that the cruise
companies could have invented. Similarly, the events in Iraq in the
winter of 1991 have made North American cruise destinations, on
both West and East coasts, much more attractive. The international
threat of terrorism is felt not only in the cruise business; it hits particularly hard at the airline industry. And, given that virtually all of the
Mediterranean cruising involving Americans is of the fly/cruise type,
fear has had a doubly negative effect on Mediterranean cruising.

c) Cruising in Eastern Canada

The success of cruising at Vancouver, and indeed around the world,
has prompted other Canadian ports to assess cruise shipping as an
activity. For example, in 1987 the Port of Halifax undertook an extensive review of cruising and its potential for promotion in Eastern
Canada. Tourism Canada commissioned a study in 1988 entitled
"Profile of the Eastern Canadian Cruise Industry." The Port of Saint
John initiated a Cruise Ship Committee in 1990, with representatives
from the port, the local tourist promotion agencies, tour companies,
and the New Brunswick Department of Tourism, Recreation and
Culture. Both Quebec and Montreal are involved in promoting their
ports as cruise stops. However, in all cases the actual numbers of
cruise ships and passengers pale in comparison with Vancouver's; it
is unlikely that any of these ports will challenge Vancouver's position
as the cruise capital of Canada.

Table 7.2 gives some statistics about cruise ships calling at
Eastern Canadian ports in the late 1980s. Since these figures were
published there has been further growth in Eastern Canadian ports in

cruise ship activity. For example, 80 cruise ship calls were made at Halifax in 1991.

The large number of ship visits to Quebec and Montreal can be explained by "pocket cruise" ships: those of less than 100-passenger capacity that operate on the St. Lawrence or in and out of the East coast waterways. Both Montreal and Quebec are more attractive than Atlantic coast ports because of the cultural attractions of the former port cities. Montreal, with its size and world-class airport facilities, operates as an embarkation/debarkation port for passengers; consequently, the economic impact of cruise operations is much greater in Montreal than the other ports, which act as ports of call only. It is unlikely that Halifax, Saint John or Quebec will ever achieve a "home port" status or function as bases for cruise ships, since they are not at the beginning or the end of a popular cruise route. Rather, they are only one port along the route.

The cruises operating on the East coast follow three routes: USA New England - Canada (Atlantic coast) - St. Lawrence River; trans-Atlantic; and northern adventure tours (Tourism Canada, 1988, ii). By far, the most important route is the first. Typically, cruise ships operating between the USA East coast and going up the St. Lawrence as far as Montreal do so on seven-day trips, with embarkation at Philadelphia, New York or Boston, stops at ports in New England, the Maritime Provinces and St. Lawrence River, and disembarkation at Montreal. They then return on the same route, but often call at different ports. Some cruises operate solely on the St. Lawrence River between Kingston and Quebec using relatively small vessels. Such pocket cruises also have been operating between Rhode Island in New England to the St. Lawrence.

The main advantage that Eastern Canadian cruising has over that of Western Canada is the very large American cruise market at its doorstep. One end of the journey can begin or end in the heart of that market. In addition, the scenery of the St. Lawrence River, especially in the Saguenay area, is spectacular. The fall foliage adds to the spectacle, and for that reason almost half of the cruises in 1988 between USA East coast and the St. Lawrence were scheduled for September and October. It is easy for the cruise companies to deploy vessels into this area at this time since many of them spend only the winter months in the Caribbean. The East coast is also a "safe" cruising area, free of terrorism and the threat of war. However, there are disadvantages of cruising in Eastern Canada, such as the relatively mundane nature of the physical environment. There are no spectacular Caribbean islands with white sands and clear tropical waters; there is not the huge physical spectacle of glaciers breaking off and crashing into the sea; the weather can be unpredictable, and visibility may be poor due to offshore fog in the summer months. For the most part, the Canadian ports themselves are not geared to handle cruise ships. Only Montreal has a dedicated cruise ship terminal. Also, the Canadian East coast and the St. Lawrence are close enough to large American cities to allow for the critical seven-day cruise schedule to operate from home ports in one of the American cities. Consequently, none of the Canadian East coast ports will take on a home port function as Vancouver has done, and therefore it is unlikely that any of the Canadian East coast ports will derive economic gains that would approach those at Vancouver. Finally, geopolitics are different on the East coast than on the West. Vancouver has benefitted from American laws, which prevent foreign-registered ships from carrying passengers between a USA origin (Seattle or San Francisco) and a US destination (Whittier or Seward, Alaska), but no USA law prohibits foreign-built and -registered ships from taking passengers from a USA origin such as New York or Boston to a foreign destination such as Quebec or Montreal.

SUMMARY

Vancouver is Canada's cruise capital for a variety of reasons. It is strategically placed, able to take advantage of both the physical geography of the North American West coast and the shipping laws of the United States. Over the past ten years, especially, the port has solidified its hold as a home port for the Alaskan cruise trade. As a result, the port and city of Vancouver have benefitted economically from cruise ships visiting the port and cruise passengers beginning, ending or prolonging their trips there.

The Vancouver success has prompted Eastern Canadian ports to assess their status as cruising ports. Although ports such as Saint John, Halifax, Quebec and Montreal fulfill the cruise port function, they do so on a scale that does not compare to Vancouver's. It is likely that these East coast ports, as well as Vancouver, will achieve higher passenger levels in the future, given the increased worldwide interest in cruising as a tourist activity—especially since Canadian waters are seen as safe havens. The only potential threat to the Vancouver scene would be changes made to American passenger shipping laws. If changes were to occur, Vancouver would lose its "home port" status for some of the cruise ships, but it would still be a port of call on most Alaskan cruise operations, since it is a major international tourist attraction in its own right.

The Vancouver experience with cruising illustrates that ports do not only handle the raw materials, the semi-processed and processed goods demanded by industry and consumer alike. Handling people— the most fragile and demanding "commodity" of all—is also an important port function, one at which Vancouver has achieved great success to date.

CHAPTER 8

SOVEREIGNTY AND SHIPPING IN THE CANADIAN ARCTIC ARCHIPELAGO

In the international context, the Arctic Ocean is not generally perceived to be a vital shipping area. It has been the scene of adventure and international attention when explorers in the distant and more recent past have searched for, discovered and proceeded through the Northwest Passage; but as an international shipping link, the Arctic Ocean is of little importance. Its status, however, may change, as resources (such as hydrocarbons) are developed, and as ships are built to operate in one of the harshest marine environments in the world. In the Canadian context, though, shipping in the Arctic is of major importance, and plays a life-supporting role for many communities. It also transports resources to domestic and international markets, albeit on a limited scale. Although the tonnages are small, compared to those on the Great Lakes or on the Atlantic or Pacific coasts, the fact that they exist at all is significant not only to the economic and social conditions of Arctic communities and to the economics of resource exploration, but also to Canada's sovereignty claim on the Arctic archipelago and its waters. Shipping has played a large role in defining that claim and in giving the claim substance.

a) Shipping, Canadian Sovereignty and the Arctic

The use of the Arctic Ocean by and for Canadian shipping interests reinforces Canada's claim that the waters lying within the Canadian Arctic archipelago are, in fact, Canadian and not international waters. The claim that the islands of the archipelago are Canadian, based on the acquisition of the land from the Hudson Bay Company (HBC) in 1870 when its lands were transferred to the government, has met with no serious challenge. All other territorial rights to the lands of the archipelago held by Britain were transferred to Canada in 1880, although neither Britain nor Canada had a firm idea about the limits of the territories being transferred (Reid, 1974, 113). The only disputes which have arisen on the land claims have been with Denmark over Ellesmere Island in the 1920s and Norway over the Sverdrup Islands in 1930—both of which were decided in Canada's favour through bilateral agreement. The so-called "sector theory" supports Canada's claim,[1] but the Canadian government has never taken a formal stand to adopt the idea (Gilmour, 1982, 163; Reid, 1974; and Head, 1963) preferring instead to argue the issue based on discovery, acquisition and use.

The claim to the waters of the archipelago are not so clear cut. Canada's claim to the waters is based on traditional use and on the argument that the Canadian Arctic is a special place, environmentally, and deserves special status. The passage of two ships, the MANHATTEN in 1969 and the POLAR SEA in 1985, forced Canada to take a position on the sovereignty of the Canadian Arctic archipelago waters. Prior to 1969 there was not much concern about the control and jurisdiction of Arctic waters. There was limited interest in the waters, the population of the area was small, and the resource potential, although known in vague terms, was not seen as vital to Canadian or world interests. The discovery of commercial quantities of oil at Prudhoe Bay, Alaska in 1968 and the question of its transport south to American markets stirred a series of events and elicited political initiatives on the part of Canada, in order to establish that the waters are Canadian and, as such, are under the firm control of Canada. Any operation of any vessel, foreign or Canadian, must abide by Canadian laws and regulations. This claim to all of the waters of the Canadian archipelago extends to include the waters that make up the Northwest Passage, that long-sought for link between East and West which fired the imagination of governments

---

[1] The sector theory determines the claim to lands of the northern latitudes; each country with a continental coastline on the Arctic Ocean automatically falls heir to the territory lying between its coastline and the North Pole.

and explorers for over two centuries. According to Canada, the Northwest Passage is Canadian and not an international strait open to the free passage of any ship.

The ship that first drew attention to the waters of the Arctic archipelago was the MANHATTEN, an ice-strengthened tanker of 145,200 dwt which, in 1969, was sent north from the American Eastern seaboard by Humble Oil company. This ship was to transit the Northwest Passage from east to west (to Prudhoe Bay) and to return on the same route to the East coast. A follow-up voyage was made in 1970, but the ship went only as far west as Resolute to test the operation of the vessel in existing winter ice. The journeys were part of an experiment to test the efficiency of tanker transport in moving the Alaskan North slope oil to southern markets. The conclusions of the project were: Arctic icebreaking tankers are technically feasible for year-round transport of Alaskan crude to the USA East and West coasts; feasibility designs for the icebreaking tanker demonstrate that the technology for construction and operation of the marine system does exist; and the Arctic marine transportation system is economically competitive with alternate systems such as pipelines (Arctec Incorporated, 1979, 7–8). However, it was decided that the trans-Alaskan pipeline was preferable because "it had an economic advantage at the time and was judged to have a greater probability of success" (Arctec Incorporated, 1979, 8).

The MANHATTEN tests brought to Canada's attention the possibility that the Northwest Passage could become a major commercial shipping route. Although Humble Oil showed a willingness to cooperate by notifying Canada of its intentions and asking Ottawa for information on ice conditions, the official position of the United States government was to cooperate with Canada as much as possible, but not to act in any way which could be construed as support for Canada's jurisdictional claims (Kirton and Munton, 1987, 71). For example, the USA did not respond to Canada's informal suggestion that permission for a American icebreaker to accompany the MANHATTEN be sought. Such a request by the USA government would have been the equivalent of an admission that Canada did have sovereign rights to the waters that the MANHATTEN and its accompanying ships would be traversing. Canada, for its part, volunteered the services of the powerful Canadian Coast Guard icebreaker JOHN A. MACDONALD to accompany the MANHATTEN and to lend assistance, if necessary. Thus, the MANHATTEN voyage of the Northwest Passage was really the voyage of three ships: the MAN-

HATTEN, the JOHN A. MACDONALD and the USA Coast Guard icebreaker NORTHWIND. The route followed by the trio was to be more than 12 nautical miles from land, in waters that were recognized by all nations as international waters. However, the inability of the MANHATTEN to transit the M'Clure Strait between Melville and Banks Islands forced the trio to proceed through Prince of Wales Strait, a waterway of less than 24 nautical miles width to the south of Banks Island. The MACDONALD was a much more powerful icebreaker than any the Americans possessed at the time, and was called on frequently to assist the MANHATTEN and the NORTH-WIND. Thus American operations in these waters were possible only with Canada's support.

As a result of the MANHATTEN voyages, a great deal of political intrigue was wrought within the Canadian government departments, between Canada and the United States, and between Canada and international agencies such as the United Nations and the International Marine Consultative Organization (see Kirton and Munton, 1987, 79–93). The *Arctic Waters Pollution Prevention Act* (Canada. Revised Statutes of Canada, 1970 1st Supplement) was soon introduced and passed by Parliament in April 1970. This *Act* "enabled Canada to enforce certain pollution prevention standards of construction, manning and equipment against all ships navigating in the waters of the Archipelago north of the 60th parallel and up to a distance of 100 miles outside the Archipelago" (Pharand, 1988, 124). Although the *Act* and subsequent regulations adopted in 1972 made no claims to Canada's sovereignty over the waters of the archipelago, it did introduce regulations and controls over those waters which address the "purpose-specific jurisdiction" of pollution by ships at sea (Kirton and Munton, 1987, 91). Canada was able to control the nature of ships and shipping in Arctic waters for the sole purpose of preventing and controlling pollution in those waters.

Sixteen shipping safety control zones were established in the subsequent regulations (Canada. Consolidated Regulations of Canada, 1978) and shipping seasons were determined according to the class of vessel. For example in Zone 13, which applies to Lancaster Sound and adjacent waters, a vessel of Class 10 (able to transit ice 10 feet thick while maintaining a forward speed of 3 knots) could operate year round, but a Class 1 vessel could operate only from 15 July to 15 October. When the *Arctic Waters Pollution Prevention Act* was introduced, the Canadian government also extended the territorial limit of Canada's waters from 3 miles to 12 miles, the standard that fifty-six other countries maintained (Kirton

and Munton, 1987, 92). The effect of this extension was to place the
waters of Prince of Wales Strait and Barrow Strait (west of Lancaster
Sound) under the jurisdiction and control of Canada. In effect,
Canada had taken steps to control shipping within the Canadian
Arctic archipelago, and especially through the Northwest Passage.

The ship that next precipitated Canada's concern about its control
of the Arctic waters was the POLAR SEA, a USA Coast Guard icebreaker that passed through the Northwest Passage in August 1985
without first seeking the permission of the Canadian government. The
POLAR SEA and its sister ship, the POLAR STAR, are the world's
second most powerful icebreakers, with 60,000 shaft horsepower.
The world's most powerful icebreakers are the Russian ARTIKA and
SIBIR, both of which are nuclear powered, at 75,000 shaft horsepower. In comparison, Canada's most powerful icebreaker is the LOUIS
S. ST-LAURENT at 24,000 shaft horsepower. The JOHN A. MAC-
DONALD, decommissioned in late 1991, had a shaft horsepower of
only 11,200. The POLAR STAR and the POLAR SEA were built in
direct response to the American's inability to assist the MANHAT-
TEN in her voyages of 1969 and 1970, and were to end reliance on
the Canadian JOHN A. MACDONALD.

The journey of the POLAR SEA in 1985 through the Northwest
Passage began in Thule, Greenland and ended in Point Barrow,
Alaska. The route was taken to save time and fuel in repositioning the
ship from the Eastern Arctic to the Western Arctic without going
through the Panama Canal—a journey that would have taken 20 to 30
days longer (*Toronto Star*, 2 August 1985). The journey was not perceived by the Americans to be a threat to Canadian jurisdictional
claims in Arctic waters. The Americans claimed that the Northwest
Passage is an international strait, open for the innocent passage of any
ship. This is an important issue for American global naval mobility,
since the Navy needs to be able to move ships freely around the
world. For this reason the United States has not endorsed Canada's
position on the Northwest Passage, nor has it signed the Law of the
Sea Convention of 1982 which contains an "Arctic clause":

Coastal States have the right to adopt and enforce non-discriminating laws
and regulations for the prevention, reduction and control of marine pollution from vessels in ice-covered areas within the limits of the exclusive
economic zone, where particularly severe climatic conditions and the presence of ice covering such areas for most of the year create obstructions or
exceptional hazards to navigation, and pollution of the marine environment
would cause major harm to or irreversible disturbance of the ecological

balance. Such laws and regulations shall have due regard to navigation and the protection and reservation of the marine environment based on the best available scientific evidence. (as quoted from Pharand, 1988, 237 in reference to 1982 Convention, Art. 234)

Although the POLAR SEA did not seek Canada's permission to make the passage, it did receive permission from Canada to do so. Also, three Canadian observers were on board the icebreaker; it was accompanied on part of its journey by the JOHN A. MACDONALD, and monitored by Canadian military aircraft. The United States agreed in writing to clean up any pollution damage caused by the passage of the POLAR SEA.

As a direct result of the passage of the POLAR SEA, Canada announced several measures in September 1985 to further strengthen its claim to Arctic waters. Among them was the establishment of straight baselines around the perimeter of the Canadian Arctic archipelago. These baselines are drawn across the many straits passing between the islands on the outer edge of the archipelago. For example, there are lines across the Amudsen Gulf, M'Clure Strait, and other waterways in the Queen Elizabeth Islands on the western edge of the archipelago, and lines across Jones Sound, Lancaster Sound and Hudson Strait on the eastern side. In effect, these lines define the "outer limit of Canada's historic internal waters" (Pharand, 1988, 155, quoting Secretary for External Affairs Joe Clark, 10 Sept. 1985). In drawing these lines and making the claim that the waters are Canadian internal waters, Canada is following the lead of at least sixty other coastal states (Pharand, 1988, 147).

The claim that these waters are internal, and not part of the territorial sea, challenges the status of the Northwest Passage as an "international strait with the right of innocent passage," as claimed by the United States. Under customary international law and supported by the Fisheries Case decision of 1951 (in which the International Court of Justice ruled in favour of Norway and against the United Kingdom), all waters enclosed by straight baselines have the status of internal waters, and the right of innocent passage does not exist within a nation's internal waters. However, the right of innocent passage does exist within territorial seas or waters. By drawing straight baselines, Canada has, in effect, closed the right of innocent passage through the Northwest Passage. It is still possible, however, that the Northwest Passage could become an international strait with the right of transit passage recognized in the 1982 Law of the Sea Convention. The status of any strait depends upon the degree of its use for international shipping, and upon the measures taken by the host nation to control such shipping through the strait (Pharand, 1988, 230). If extensive use of the Northwest Passage by non-Canadian commercial vessels for the shipment of hydrocarbons from the North slope of Alaska to the East coast of North America were to become common place, for example, and if Canada took no action to control this shipping by attempting to inspect the vessels according to Canadian *Arctic Waters Pollution Prevention* regulations—or by not providing assistance to vessels that become distressed while operating in the passage—then it is highly likely that Canada's sovereignty claim to the waters would not be honoured, and the strait would be seen as an international one with the right of transit passage.

The transit passage clause allows for "the freedom of navigation and overflight solely for the purpose of continuous and expeditious transit of the strait between one part of the high seas or an exclusive economic zone and another part of the high seas or an exclusive economic zone" (Pharand, 1988, 231, quoting the 1982 Law of the Sea Convention, Art. 38, para. 2). Thus, in order for Canada to support its claim that the waters of the Canadian Arctic archipelago, especially the Northwest Passage, are Canadian internal waters and not subject to transit passage, Canada must be prepared to enforce its position year-round. The construction of ships capable of operating throughout the Arctic in all seasons would seem to be essential for Canada's case. When Canada announced the enclosure of the Canadian Arctic Archipelago by straight baselines, plans indeed were made to reinforce Canada's position. These plans were: to construct an Arctic Class 8 icebreaker; to increase surveillance overflights of Arctic waters; to conduct naval activity in Eastern Arctic waters; and to negotiate with the United States for an agreement on Canadian sovereignty claims and United States' desired use of the waters. It is the icebreaker that is of interest here.

Canada's largest icebreaker, the LOUIS S. ST-LAURENT, has a rating of Arctic Class 3.5 (the vessel is able to continually move forward through solid ice 3.5 feet thick). The ST-LAURENT is incapable of operating anywhere in the Arctic throughout the winter months and, according to *Arctic Waters Pollution Prevention* regulations, it cannot operate anywhere in the Arctic before June 1. A Class 8 vessel, on the other hand, can proceed continually through solid ice 8 feet thick, and is allowed to operate all year in fifteen of the sixteen shipping safety control zones established under the *Arctic Waters Pollution Prevention* regulations. The only zone from which it is excluded for the period of 16 October to 1 July is Zone 1, in the

Queen Elizabeth Islands area on the west side of the Canadian Arctic archipelago. This zone includes M'Clure Strait through which the MANHATTEN tried to pass in 1969 without success.

A third ship, the POLAR 8, might have had a great impact on whether or not those claims stand up to international scrutiny, but given that the ship's construction was cancelled in February 1990 by the Canadian government, we may never know its impact. The cancellation was a result of federal government cost-cutting measures. This cancellation should not be surprising given the record of the Canadian government on this issue. Since the voyages of the MANHATTEN, the Cabinet has considered three different plans for acquiring a polar icebreaker (Nossal, 1987, 228); proposals have included a Polar 7 vessel, a Polar 10 and finally a Polar 8. Originally, the Polar 7 was to be conventionally powered, but then consideration was given to nuclear propulsion as a possible technology. The POLAR 8 was to have been conventionally powered.

The cancellation of the POLAR 8 threatens Canada's future ability to monitor and assist shipping in the Arctic. The program to construct nuclear-powered submarines that could have performed some of the monitoring function of ships was cancelled in May 1989, so it was even more important that the POLAR 8 be built, and be built quickly. Without the means to enforce the regulations of the *Arctic Waters Pollution Prevention Act* and to monitor ships using the Northwest Passage, Canada's claim to these waters is dubious. Presently, Canada does have the capability to monitor shipping in the summer months in the Arctic (see below), but there are no vessels of any kind which can operate during the winter months on the surface of the Arctic Ocean; not even the large American and Russian icebreakers are capable of this. The construction of the POLAR 8, the most powerful and largest icebreaking ship in the world, would have sent a clear message to all parties that Canada was serious in its sovereignty claims in the waters of the Canadian Arctic archipelago, and was prepared to enforce them. However, given Canada's recent history of responding to threats of shipping in the Arctic with after-the-fact legislation, it may be that another international foray into the Arctic by the Americans, the Russians, the Japanese, or any other nation will be necessary before the POLAR 8 is considered again. Presently, the possibility of a commercial or test case by international shipping seems unlikely but, in time, international shipping in the Northwest Passage will be a reality. If Canada wishes to hold onto these waters as her own, she best be prepared to defend them. An icebreaker with the capabilities of the POLAR 8 will be required.

Diplomatic discussions in 1988 aimed to smooth over the differences between Canada and the United States regarding the use of Arctic waters, and in January 1988 Canada and the United States signed an agreement on Arctic cooperation in which "each and every transit of a United States government-owned or government-operated icebreaker through the waters of the Canadian Arctic archipelago, including the Northwest Passage, will be subject to the prior consent of Canada" (Clark, 1988). This is the type of agreement that Canada had hoped would come out of its initiatives announced in September 1985. However, the agreement is limited in that it applies only to USA icebreakers such as the POLAR SEA and POLAR STAR, and not to commercial shipping or to military vessels such as submarines. The first test of the bilateral agreement on USA icebreakers entering Canadian waters occurred in October 1988 when the United States sought and was granted permission for the POLAR STAR to transit the Northwest Passage from west to east. The ship had been damaged by ice and was running low on fuel (Koring, 1988).

Despite the agreement, the United States still does not recognize Canada's claim to sovereignty in Arctic waters. The two countries have taken a very practical step at solving a problem about icebreakers operating in the waters. The Americans will not recognize Canada's sovereignty in these waters because to do so would be to limit the American right of transit passage through the waters. If the United States were to recognize Canada's claim in the Arctic, it might be forced to acknowledge sovereignty claims over other straits by other nations, as well, including those of Indonesia, Greece and the former Soviet Union. Then the USA right of transit passage would be challenged worldwide. It would appear that the United States will honour Canadian claims in the Arctic, but only on an issue-by-issue basis, and not with a blanket endorsement that would have ramifications for other disputed claims by other nations.

Canada's claim that the waters of the Canadian archipelago are internal waters rests on historical arguments, political initiatives, and legal precedents. It also depends upon demonstrated use and control of the waters by Canadian ships, or by ships acting for and with permission of Canadian interests. Canadian commercial shipping in the north has been a long-standing activity, and its importance is likely to increase in the future. If so, Canada's claim to the waters will become entrenched in practice.

b)   Use of the Arctic for Commercial Shipping

Commercial shipping in the Arctic can be divided into two main categories: resupply and resource shipping. The former involves the shipment north of general cargo, encompassing a broad range of goods such as foodstuffs, clothing, transportation equipment, building materials, recreational equipment and consumer goods of various kinds for the residents of Arctic communities. General cargo also includes materials used by resource companies for the exploration of resources, especially hydrocarbons in the Beaufort Sea. Also included in resupply activity is the transport of bulk fuels, gasoline and fuel oil in tankers. "Resource shipping" is the movement of minerals, hydrocarbons and grain through Arctic waters. Minerals originate from two sources: the Nanisivik mine on the north coast of Baffin Island, and Polaris mine on Little Cornwallis Island. Prior to 1984, asbestos was exported from Deception Bay in northern Quebec on Hudson Strait. Crude oil, in very limited amounts, is taken from Cameron Island. Grain, originating in the Canadian Prairies, passes through Churchill and is shipped through Hudson Bay and Hudson Strait to world markets primarily in Europe, the Mediterranean and Latin America. All of these activities, resupply and resources, are a summer only operation; there is no year-round shipping in the Arctic, yet.

i) Resupply

Eastern Arctic: Arctic resupply is organized into three geographical areas: the Eastern Arctic, the Keewatin and the Mackenzie River including the Western Arctic. Each area's resupply activity is distinctive. It has been the responsibility of the Canadian Coast Guard to organize an Eastern Arctic Sealift—a yearly maritime resupply of communities and military bases throughout the Eastern Arctic, an area that stretches from southern Hudson Bay in Quebec north to Eureka on Ellesmere Island, and from Resolute Bay east to Greenland. Although the Canadian government began regular annual patrols to the Arctic in 1922 (with the dispatch of the original ARCTIC under the command of Captain Bernier) and has regularly taken goods north to supply communities, the entire responsibility for the maritime resupply of joint USA - Canada facilities and government needs in northern communities has been assumed gradually since World War 2, with the establishment of weather stations in the Arctic archipelago, the construction of the DEW line in the mid-1950s, and the development of government services for the native population (Canadian Coast Guard, 1979).

In recent years, this responsibility has been met by eight to twelve dry cargo vessels and four or five tankers working under Coast Guard contracts. Tonnages carried are around 50,000 tonnes (see Figure 8.1), of which about two-thirds to three-quarters consists of

Figure 8.1
Cargo Tonnages in the Eastern Arctic Sealift Resupply

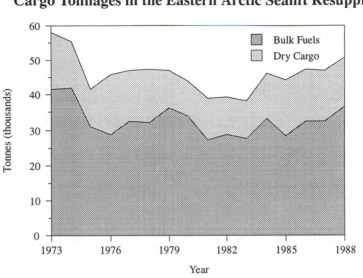

Source: Canadian Coast Guard, Coast Guard Northern, unpublished data

bulk petroleum. The higher tonnages in the early 1970s included Sealift cargo destined for the Keewatin area from Montreal. In 1975 the Keewatin resupply was reorganized, and the Northern Transportation Company Limited was given the responsibility to supply the Keewatin area from Churchill (see below). For organizational and administrative purposes, the Coast Guard has divided the Eastern Arctic including the coast of Labrador into seven areas (Figure 8.2): Area A, Arctic Quebec; Area B, Foxe Basin; Area C, South Baffin; Area E, East Baffin; Area F, Mid/High Arctic; Area G, Greenland (Thule); and Area Z, Labrador. Table 8.1 gives a breakdown of the dry cargo tonnages destined for the various areas, on average, for 1984–1988. In those years, the main shippers in the Eastern Arctic Sealift have been the Government of the Northwest Territories (40 to 50 per cent of all cargoes) and the USA Air Force (20 to 30 per cent). The latter cargo originates from Ogdensburg, New York on the St. Lawrence River, while the rest is loaded at Montreal.

The Sealift does not move all resupply cargoes in the Eastern Arctic, but to determine the proportion it serves would be difficult. Other cargoes are carried for other major shippers under private contracts; for example, Northern Stores Inc. operates its own vessel and another on a bare boat charter basis, and has carried cargo for

Figure 8.2
Eastern Arctic Resupply Areas

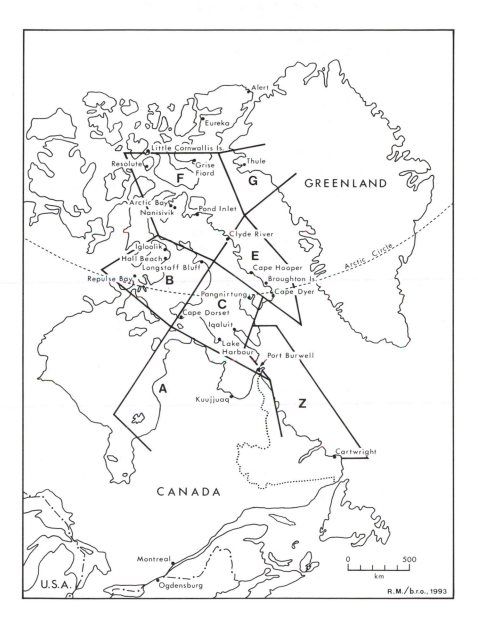

Source: Canadian Coast Guard (1988)

Table 8.1:
Eastern Arctic Sealift Operations, Average
Dry Cargo Tonnages, 1984–1988

Area of Operation	Average Tonnage
A - Arctic Quebec	561
B - Foxe Basin	344*
	1,479
C - South Baffin	6,463
E - East Baffin	221*
	763
F - Mid/High Arctic	3,058
G - Greenland (Thule)	543
Z - Labrador	150* (1987 only)
	340 (1987–88 average)

*Exit Ogdensburg, N.Y.; otherwise exit Montreal.

Source: Canadian Coast Guard (1988)

the Hudson Bay Co. since 1982. In 1988, 7,800 revenue tonnes (approximately 5,200 cargo tonnes) were transported (Boudreau, 1989). There are large quantities of bulk petroleum brought to Iqaluit and Resolute outside of the terms of the Eastern Arctic Sealift, as well. For example, Shell Canada ships fuel oil and gasoline to Iqaluit, which is subsequently sold to local users for automobiles, aircraft, and for heating private housing and buildings. A comparison between Eastern Arctic Sealift data supplied by the Canadian Coast Guard and information collected by Statistics Canada shows that the Sealift cargo represents about 10 per cent of all cargoes by weight at Iqaluit since 1978. As is shown in Table 8.2, visits by Sealift vessels to Iqaluit and Resolute made up only a small proportion of the ships calling at these ports. There are also cargoes moving outside of the Sealift to Nanisivik and Polaris mines to resupply their operations.

Keewatin: The District of Keewatin encompasses that area of the Northwest Territories on the west side of Hudson Bay that lies between the District of Mackenzie in the west, and the District of Franklin in the north and east. The communities that are served by marine resupply are Eskimo Point, Whale Cove, Rankin Inlet, Chesterfield Inlet, Baker Lake and Coral Harbour. Gjoa Haven and Spence Bay, in the northern part of Keewatin but not on Hudson Bay, are served by the Mackenzie River and Western Arctic resup-

Table 8.2:
Commercial Vessels Calling at Iqaluit and Resolute during the Shipping Season, 1988

Iqaluit

Date	Name of Vessel	Remarks
29–31 July	ARCTIC VIKING	Sealift cargo
1– 3 Aug	HANCOCK TRADER	Private cargo
1– 4 Aug	FORT LAUZON	Hudson Bay Co. cargo
5–15 Aug	SOODOC	Sealift cargo
12–17 Aug	TERRA NORDICA	Sealift cargo
16–17 Aug	HUBERT GAUCHER	Bulk petroleum
23–23 Aug	POLARIS	Cruise
24–24 Aug	TERRA NORDICA	Discharge equipment
28–30 Aug	FORT LAUZON	Hudson Bay Co. cargo
1–10 Sept	EASTERN SHELL	Bulk petroleum
6– 7 Sept	CECILIA DESGAGNÉS	Discharge equipment
12–14 Sept	HANCOCK TRADER	Private cargo
12–14 Sept	SOODOC	Sealift cargo
13–14 Sept	HUBERT GAUCHER	Bulk petroleum
14–14 Sept	FORT LAUZON	Private cargo
19–21 Sept	ARCTIC VIKING	Private cargo
2– 6 Oct	KANGUK	Hudson Bay Co. cargo
2– 3 Oct	FORT LAUZON	Hudson Bay Co. cargo
2– 4 Oct	HUBERT GAUCHER	Bulk petroleum
12–14 Oct	HANCOCK TRADER	Private cargo
13–14 Oct	ARCTIC VIKING	Private cargo
15–17 Oct	LE BRAVE	Bulk petroleum

Resolute

Date	Name of Vessel	Remarks
20–25 Aug	CECILIA DESGAGNÉS	Sealift cargo
25–26 Aug	IMPERIAL BEDFORD	Bulk petroleum
1– 2 Sept	IRVING OURS POLAIRE	Bent Horn crude petroleum
3– 4 Sept	KANGUK	Hudson Bay Co. cargo
12–13 Sept	SOCIETY EXPLORER	Cruise
15–16 Sept	IMPERIAL BEDFORD	Bulk petroleum

Source: Canadian Coast Guard (1988, 38 and 46)

ply (see below).

This resupply area is entirely on the west shore of Hudson Bay, and since there is little dispute that Hudson Bay is an internal water of Canada, commercial shipping in this area is weak evidence of Canadian use and control of Arctic waters. However, northern water

Figure 8.3
Cargo Tonnages in Keewatin Resupply

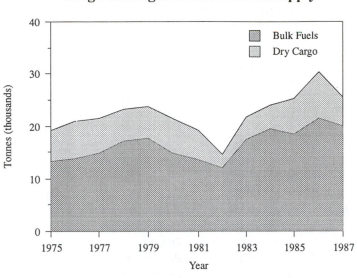

Source: 1975–1982 Canadian Transportation Commission (1983)
1983–1987 Transport Canada (1988)

transportation is important to the Canadian economy. Since 1975 resupply to these communities has been handled exclusively from Churchill by the Northern Transportation Company Limited (NTCL) under the jurisdiction of the Coast Guard Northern division of Transport Canada. Freight rates are subject to government imposed tariff ceilings. Prior to 1975, government-organized resupply was coordinated out of Montreal and the materials reached the area in ships operating under the Eastern Arctic Sealift. The decision to switch to a Churchill-based operation was made at the insistence of the governments of Manitoba, Saskatchewan, and to a lesser extent, Alberta, which argued that small businesses in the West were at a disadvantage when bidding on contracts to resupply the Keewatin communities (Western Economic Opportunities Conference, 1977, 60).

The tonnes carried in the resupply since 1975 have fluctuated between 14,600 in 1982 and 30,400 in 1986 (Figure 8.3). Bulk fuels make up between 66 and 80 per cent of the cargoes transported and, in recent years, its share has increased. The relative increase in bulk fuels can be attributed to the relative decline in dry cargo. This decline, in turn, can be attributed to a shift of dry cargo transport from the water to the air mode. Air transport is preferred for a number of reasons. Since NTCL charges uniform prices for delivery throughout the entire area and does not base its rates on distance and weight (volume) transported, those areas close to Churchill (Eskimo Point and Whale Cove) pay freight rates that are comparable to air transport rates (which are based on weight, volume and distance). There are also customers who would rather pay the extra cost associated with air transport, but save costs associated with storage and inventory. Finally, air transport is available all year, whereas water transport is restricted to the summer months only. For activities such as construction, for example, it is preferable to use air transport to bring materials for immediate use, thus reducing expenses associated with weather damage and pilferage of materials that might be brought in by water one year, but not used until the next (Transport Canada, 1988, 34 and Canadian Transport Commission, 1983, 62–63).

Mackenzie River including the Western Arctic: This area is divided into four areas: the River itself from Hay River to Tuktoyaktuk, a distance of 1,800 km; the Western Arctic shore from the Yukon/Alaska boundary in the west to the west side of the Boothia Peninsula in the east, a distance of about 2,000 km; Great Slave Lake; and the Laird River and Fort Nelson River, linking Fort Nelson, B.C. in the south to Fort Simpson, N.W.T. in the north. Almost all of the cargoes moved on these rivers and lakes are carried by barge and tug; the traffic along the Arctic coast is transferred from barge to ocean-going vessels at Tuktoyaktuk.[2] A limited amount of cargo enters the Western Arctic by way of Vancouver, the Bering Strait and the Beaufort Sea, in what is called the "Western Arctic Summer Sealift Operation."

The Mackenzie River has been a highway for freight and people since its discovery in 1789. The major player on the river was the Hudson Bay Company, both as a common carrier and a carrier of its own freight; but since 1947, with the discontinuance of the Hudson Bay Company as a common carrier, the principal carrier on the river has been NTCL. NTCL began as a private company called Northern Waterways Ltd. in 1931, and took on its present name in 1934, just two years before it was acquired by Eldorado Gold Mines to assure water transportation services to its mine at Port Radium on Great Bear Lake. NTCL became a Crown Corporation when its parent, Eldorado Mining and Refining, was expropriated by the Government of Canada in 1944 (Northern Transportation Company Limited,

---

[2] From the perspective of water claims, the activity along the Arctic coast is most important; but since it is difficult to separate the activity on the river from that of along the coast, the area will be treated as one in this discussion.

Figure 8.4
Cargo Tonnages on the Mackenzie River and Western Arctic

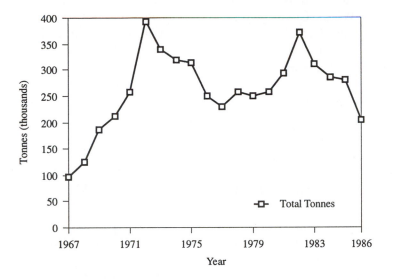

Source: National Transportation Agency of Canada (unpublished data)

1971). In 1985, NTCL was sold to two private, native-owned companies—the Inuvialuit Development Corporation and the Nunasi
Group—both established to pursue business opportunities for native
people in the Arctic and Mackenzie Delta. The company now operates as a private carrier. Over the years, the proportion of water cargo
in the Mackenzie area that is handled by NTCL has grown as it has
taken over other carriers (including the Yellowknife Transportation
Company Ltd in 1965, and the river operations of Arctic
Transportation Limited in 1988) and as other carriers have dropped
out of the market (the Hudson Bay Company dropped its Arctic
freight service in 1963). It was estimated that NTCL carried about 78
per cent of the freight on the Mackenzie in 1976 (Canadian Transport
Commission, 1978, 34–46); in 1986 it handled about 80 per cent of
the cargo (Transport Canada, 1988, 37); and in 1988, it was likely to
have handled over 95 per cent of cargoes.

The tonnages of cargo which move on the Mackenzie and into the
Western Arctic have fluctuated over time (see Figure 8.4). While the
resupply function has remained rather stable, and even increased slowly, the cargoes associated with exploration for resources—primarily
hydrocarbons—have varied along with the intensity of drilling activity; this, in turn, is affected by government policies, the rate of discov-

ery and the estimated price and market for hydrocarbons in the future.

Up until the mid-1960s, traffic on the Mackenzie was largely associated with community resupply, and only to a limited extent with resource exploration and development. In the 1950s increased tonnages were attributed to the development of the DEW Line system, and periodic fluctuations before that time were associated with mining at Port Radium on Great Bear Lake. However, with the discovery of commercial quantities of oil at Prudhoe Bay in Alaska in 1968 and increased interest and activity in oil and gas exploration in the Mackenzie Delta and the Beaufort Sea, the demand for transportation increased and higher levels of freight were moved on the river in the late 1960s and the early 1970s (see Figure 8.4). In 1972, for example, close to 60 per cent of the freight originating at Hay River and Norman Wells was associated with exploration activities (Canadian Transport Commission, 1978, 56). However, the 1970s were uncertain times for oil and gas exploration in the Delta and Beaufort Sea, and the pace of exploration and discovery declined which, in turn, reflected on traffic levels of the river. NTCL handled 170,000 tonnes of freight in support of exploration activity in 1972, but only handled 26,000 tonnes in 1976 (Canadian Transport Commission, 1978, 63).

Three main causes have been suggested to explain the decrease in exploration activity: the lack of continued exploration success in the Delta region; uncertainty regarding the construction of a Mackenzie Valley gas pipeline; and some uncertainty with regards to government regulations, especially with respect to oil and gas tenure regulations (Canadian Transport Commission, 1978, 63). The moratorium on construction of a Mackenzie Valley pipeline, recommended by the Justice Berger in 1977, made concrete the worst fears of the oil and gas companies. However, the introduction of the National Energy Policy in 1980, with its Petroleum Incentive Program (PIP) grants to encourage the search for oil and gas in remote areas, exploration activity and associated cargoes improved again and peaked in 1982. In that year it was estimated that 148,000 tonnes of exploration cargo were moved north by NTCL and Arctic Transportation Limited (Acres International Ltd., 1987, Table 10-2), in contrast to only 113,000 tonnes moved for resupply. Since 1982 exploration tonnages have again declined, while resupply tonnages have remained stable, producing an overall decline of tonnages on the Mackenzie and the Western Arctic. Again, the explanation rests on a decline in the search for hydrocarbons due to declining prices for oil and gas and the withdrawal of PIP grants. If and when approval is obtained for either a natural gas pipeline or oil pipeline, or both, then traffic carried on the Mackenzie is anticipated to increase substantially. Offshore production facilities will need to be built, as will pipelines linking these facilities with the Mackenzie Valley pipeline, and increased activity to discover further reserves of oil and gas will also lead to more freight moving north. A large proportion of this freight will be carried via the Mackenzie barge and tug operations.

It is also likely that the Western Arctic Summer Sealift operations, by way of Vancouver, Point Barrow, Alaska and the Beaufort Sea, will also increase with pipeline construction. This method of moving cargo to the Beaufort and the Mackenzie Delta has been in operation, to a limited and varied extent, since the 1970s. While only 1,200 tonnes of cargo were carried in 1980, almost 110,000 tonnes were transported in 1983 (Transport Canada, 1988, Table 4.5; derived from Acres International, 1987, Table 10.4). The amount of cargo which can be transported in this sealift is constrained by the the lack of unloading facilities and the short shipping season of about six weeks, from late July to early September. Tugs and barges must pass through the Bering Strait, the Chukchi and Beaufort Seas and return to safety at Point Barrow before freeze-up. In 1985 plans were announced to build a large unloading and loading facility at King Port, Yukon, about half way between Prudhoe Bay and Tuktoyaktuk, to cater to ships of up to 35,000 tonnes. Such facilities would encourage exploration and offshore development equipment and consumable goods would require transportation (Martin, 1985). The port did not proceed, however, because of the decline in interest in Beaufort and Mackenzie Delta gas when oil and gas prices fell and when PIP grants were withdrawn. However, the possibility remains that such a port might be developed and, with icebreaker support, substantial tonnages could be brought to the area, all of which would reduce the amount of cargo moving on the Mackenzie River.

ii) Resource Shipping

The transportation of resources in the Arctic has been confined in recent years to grain (moving through the port of Churchill), lead and zinc (exported from Nanisivik mine on northern Baffin Island and Polaris mine from Little Cornwallis Island near Resolute), and a small amount of crude petroleum (from Bent Horn on Cameron Island). The potential to transport hydrocarbons from the Sverdrup Basin and the Beaufort Sea to eastern North America and Europe has been the subject of much speculation and intense study. Most studies and authors conclude that it is feasible to transport oil and gas by very large icebreaking tankers and Liquid National Gas (LNG) carriers operating year-round through the Northwest Passage, and that it is only a matter of time before this type of shipping will be a reality (Pullen, 1983, 588; Pharand, 1988, 230; Griffiths, 1987, 5; Senate of Canada, 1983).

Grain from Churchill: Grain has been shipped through Churchill since 1931. The great advantage of using Churchill's port is its close proximity to the grain-growing areas of the Prairies. The distance from the northeast corner of this area to tidewater at Churchill is less than 900 km (Robusky,1988), compared to the over 1,000 km from the western edge of the Prairies to the West coast ports of Prince Rupert and Vancouver. The distance from the eastern edge of the grain-growing area to Thunder Bay is about 700 km, but another 2,000 km must be travelled via the Great Lakes and the St. Lawrence River to reach grain export terminals on the North shore of the St. Lawrence. The disadvantages of Churchill, however, outweigh the advantage of proximity. The rail link to Churchill, completed in 1929 but upgraded since then, still cannot handle modern efficient hopper cars. The discontinuous permafrost creates an unstable rail bed, and grain must therefore be moved in smaller and less efficient boxcars. The shipping season is a short one, too, from the end of July to the end of October, and although the harbour at Churchill is free of ice before the end of July, ships that are not ice-strengthened must await the thaw in Hudson Strait if they want to save the substantially increased insurance costs of operating in ice infested waters. In the fall, too, ice is a problem in the harbour itself, where, because of the fresh water from the Churchill River, freeze-up commences before that of Hudson Bay or Hudson Strait. Churchill also faces the problem of shifting markets for Canadian grains. The developing markets have been in Asia, not Europe or the Mediterranean area or even Africa—all of which Churchill is better able to serve than Asia, sitting as it does on Hudson Bay and connected to the Atlantic Ocean by Hudson Strait .

Figure 8.5 shows the tonnages of grain exported from Churchill since 1960 in absolute and relative amounts. The wide fluctuations in the amount moved are indicative of changing overseas grain yields and markets. The worst year for exports was 1988 when they dropped to about 50,000 tonnes. In relative terms, Churchill has been losing out to other Canadian ports, particularly on the West coast, as international markets change from Europe to Asia. The number of ships calling at Churchill to load exports has declined from over 40 in the

Figure 8.5
Churchill Grain Exports, 1960–1990

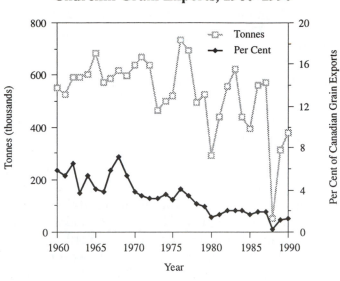

Source: Canadian Wheat Board, Annual Reports

1960s (48 in 1960; 49 in 1963; 46 in 1965) to numbers in the teens in the 1980s (12 in 1980; 18 in 1982; 13 in 1985). Only 8 ships called there in 1989. This decline in numbers is a reflection of growing ship size more than a decline in grain being handled, since the total net tonnage of shipping from the port has remained relatively steady (Statistics Canada, 54–203, 54–205, 54–209, 54–211). All of these ships must use Hudson Strait and Hudson Bay to arrive at Churchill, and then must retrace their paths on exiting.

Mineral Shipments: Two mines ship lead and zinc from the Arctic using ice-strengthened ships. Nanisivik began shipments in 1977, Polaris in 1982. Both mines send their mineral concentrates to Europe for processing. On average, since 1982, the Nanisivik mine has shipped about 128,000 tonnes each year; Polaris has shipped, on average, 248,000 tonnes annually (Zwann, 1989). Usually five or six shipments leave Nanisivik and upwards to eleven leave Polaris. One of the ships involved in the shipments is the M.V. ARCTIC, an Arctic Class 4 icebreaking OBO especially built to operate in the Arctic from mid-May to mid-November (see Chapter 3). The ARCTIC entered service in June 1978, and has served not only as a means to transport minerals from the Arctic, but also as an experimental vessel that aims to increase Canadian knowledge of Arctic ice conditions and of the operation of a large vessel in ice. In its latter role it serves as a prototype for the operation of the much larger icebreaking bulk carriers and tankers that may be used in the future. As pointed out in Chapter 3, the ARCTIC has been used once or twice a year to carry crude petroleum from Panarctic's Bent Horn field on Cameron Island, as well.

In addition to the actual shipments of lead and zinc from the two existing mine sites, there have been shipments of asbestos from Deception Bay in Northern Quebec on the south west side of Hudson Strait. These shipments stopped in 1983, but during the 1970s and early 1980s they consisted of up to 275,000 tonnes a year. The potential exists for increased shipments of other minerals that have been discovered in the Arctic, but such development has been halted because of unfavourable world prices of minerals, high transportation costs or the existence of more accessible deposits elsewhere (Beauchamp, 1985, 15). The most probable mineral production sites exist at Melville Peninsula (iron ore), Mary River, Baffin Island (iron ore), and Bathurst Inlet in the Western Arctic (lead, zinc and silver) (Beauchamp, 1985, 17–18). All are close to tidewater.

c) The Potential to Transport Hydrocarbons by Ship

Two main hydrocarbon resource areas exist in the Canadian Arctic archipelago: the Beaufort Sea, including the Mackenzie Delta, and the Sverdrup Basin in the western High Arctic. A large hydrocarbon area is located on the North slope of Alaska, as well. Estimates of the quantities of hydrocarbons to be found in these areas vary by year and by the agency or company making the estimate; but in the Canadian context alone, there has been sufficient discovery of the resource to prompt the oil companies to apply again in 1989 to the Canadian government for the construction of a Mackenzie Valley pipeline. The Arctic Pilot Project, proposed in the early 1980s to bring gas from the Sverdrup Basin, argued that there was sufficient gas reserves to make the project feasible. Oil is currently transported from Bent Horn with plans to increase that activity to 50,000 barrels a day using large icebreaking tankers (Pharand, 1988, 211). So the hydrocarbons are there—perhaps not at the threshold levels the oil companies need at existing world oil prices, but in time those thresholds will be reached, and decisions will be made to proceed with development and transportation of the hydrocarbons to southern markets. It is possible that the marine mode will be the transport method of choice.

A summary of the various proposals put forward for the transport of oil and gas from the Arctic can be found in Table 8.3. None of the

Table 8.3:

Suggested Marine Mode Operations to Bring Arctic Oil and Gas to Southern Markets

Proponent	Type of Ship	Details of Operation
CANADIAN		
Dome Petroleum (oil)	Arctic Class 10 tankers	Transportation of Beaufort Sea oil through the Northwest Passage in 200,000 dwt tankers, 390 m long and 52 m wide in a year round operation
Arctic Pilot Project (gas)	Arctic Class 7 LNG carriers	Transportation of natural gas from Melville Island to a Canadian East coast location in two 140,000 cu m capacity LNG carriers, 372 m long and 43 m wide, year round operation. The proposal was the subject of a favourable environmental assessment review in 1980 but the project was withdrawn a year later because of changes in gas prices, uncertain markets and the high cost of borrowing money.
TransCanada Pipe-lines (gas)	Arctic Class 10 LNG carriers	Transportation of natural gas from King Christian Island to Europe in three 75,000 dwt LNG carriers in a year round operation.
AMERICAN		
U.S. Maritime Administration (oil)	Arctic Class 10 tankers	Transportation of Prudhoe Bay crude oil to US East coast in twenty-one to thirty-three 245,000 dwt tankers in a year-round operation. First put forward in 1973 with a follow-up confirmation of feasibility in 1978.
Seatrain Lines (oil)	Class B tankers	Transportation of Prudhoe Bay crude oil to US East coast in three 225,000 dwt tankers in a year round operation.

.../cont'd

Table 8.3 (cont'd)

Proponent	Type of Ship	Details of Operation
Globtik Tankers (oil)	Arctic Class 10 tankers	Transportation of Alaskan crude oil to US East coast with a trans-shipment terminal in Newfoundland in one to twenty-four 350,000 dwt tankers in a year round operation. The number of ships would depend on the amount of daily production and was based on the assumption of 12 round trips per year for each ship.
Globtik Tankers (gas)	Arctic Class 10 LNG carriers	Similar to previous proposal, but involving transportation of Alaskan and Canadian Arctic Islands gas to East coast using between four and twenty 125,000 to 165,000 cu m capacity LNG carriers.
General Dynamics	Submarine (gas) Tankers	Transportation of Alaskan gas in either 17 non-nuclear or 14 nuclear powered 140,000 cu m capacity submarines. The advantages of such a vessels would be that they are relatively unaffected by surface ice and weather conditions, and there would be relatively little social and environmental impact. Arguments against their use focus on their sheer size which would be prohibitive to their operation in confined and shallow channels. For example, their estimated safe operating depth is 150 m, whereas depths in Barrow Strait are as shallow as 22 m.

Source: Pharand (1984, 74–79)

proposals has gone very far beyond the study stage, although the Arctic Pilot Project proposal did provide an environmental impact assessment and received qualified approval (Federal Environmental Assessment Review Office, 1980). With the uncertainty of world oil and gas prices, instability in markets and the high cost of the projects, though, the development of Arctic oil and gas has been delayed, and the use of tankers and LNG carriers has been postponed. However, such vessels may be used eventually, and the Arctic water may be used for the year-round shipment of oil and gas in the future. Transport Canada projected in 1982 that, if Arctic oil and gas development and production were to proceed immediately based on figures assumed as of 10 September 1980, then by 1995 as many as 510 one-way ship transits through the Northwest Passage would be needed for its transport: 168 trips to move oil from the Beaufort Sea; 60 to move oil and 210 to move gas from the Arctic Islands; and 72 to move gas from Alaska. Clearly these levels of activity will not be reached by 1995, but they may be achieved by 2005, or beyond, depending on the pace of Arctic development.

The most recent official review of the transportation of oil and gas from the Arctic was undertaken by The Special Committee of the Senate on the Northern Pipeline in 1982. Its recommendation was "that transport of hydrocarbons from the Arctic region commence by tanker on a small scale and that consideration be given to various combinations of tanker and/or pipeline systems as other factors warrant" (Senate of Canada, 1983, 4). This positive, yet cautious, endorsement of tanker transport of oil has been recently tempered by a review of tanker safety (see Chapter 3) which has recommended to the Canadian government that "overland pipelines be the preferred transportation option for Arctic crude oil from the Beaufort Sea - Mackenzie Delta region and that the Government of Canada establish policy to this effect" (Public Review Panel on Tanker Safety and Marine Spills Response Capability, 1990, 174). When, or if, the transportation of oil and gas from the Arctic by ship becomes a reality, Canada must be ready to control its movement under the jurisdiction of Canadian laws and regulations that apply to shipping. It also must be able to support the movement of ships through an established infrastructure of icebreakers that are able to operate year-round (as could the POLAR 8), navigational aids, charts, sailing directions, tide tables and ice information (Pullen, 1984, 596).

d) Canadian Coast Guard Activity in the Arctic

Although Canadian Coast Guard activity is not commercial itself, it does support such activity and, by its very presence, it reinforces Canadian claims to the waters of the Canadian Arctic archipelago. The Canadian Coast Guard assists shipping by providing icebreaking assistance; by deploying and removing navigational aids; by reporting on ice conditions; and by supplying general aid when required. It also supports research, conducts hydrographic surveys, and undertakes limited resupply activity. In recent years the Canadian Coast Guard has operated eight or nine icebreakers in the Arctic. For example in 1988, of the nine ships operating, six vessels made their way North from bases on the East coast, two from Victoria on the West coast, and one from Hay River on the Mackenzie River. The earliest date of departure for the North was 31 May; the last icebreaker returned on 24 November. A complete summary of icebreaker operations is found in Table 8.4. Figure 8.6 shows the 1988 operations of Canadian Coast Guard icebreakers in the waters of the Canadian Arctic archipelago.

SUMMARY

The Canadian claim to the Northwest Passage is founded mainly upon historical use of the waterway. The actions of the MANHATTEN and the POLAR SEA have forced Canada to take a stand on these waters for all the world, and especially the United States, to see. Presently, there is not a great deal of controversy surrounding Canada's claims to the islands and waters of the archipelago. However, in order for Canada's claim to the waters to be recognized further, the country must be prepared to monitor, control and provide assistance to shipping in the waters. The construction of an icebreaker capable of operating year-round (such as the POLAR 8) would have been a significant step towards that goal. Its cancellation delays the international recognition of Canada's ability to back its claim with substance. This delay will prove critical if the Northwest Passage and surrounding waters become used more heavily for international shipping in the near future.

Currently, the Canadian presence in the waters has been for resupply shipping to Arctic communities and military sites, for resource shipping and for Coast Guard support of shipping. There is little "international shipping" in the Arctic. This may change very quickly, though, if demand for oil and gas—which is in large supply in the Western Arctic and the Beaufort Sea—increases, and it becomes necessary to move the hydrocarbons out to markets. Since shipping is a viable alternative to pipelines, much research and design have been

Table 8.4:
Canadian Coast Guard Icebreaker Operations in the Canadian Arctic, 1988

Icebreaker	Sailing Date, from	Return Date, to	Mission
CCGS NAHIDIK	17 June, Hay River	17 Oct, Hay River	Western Arctic navigational aids patrol servicing the Mackenzie River and the area from Tuktoyaktuk to Spence Bay. Conducted scientific research on the history of the Beaufort Continental Shelf.
CCGS HENRY LARSEN	27 July, Victoria	9 Sept, Dartmouth	Maiden voyage from Victoria, B.C. to Dartmouth, N.S. through the Northwest Passage.
CCGS MARTHA L. BLACK	5 July, Victoria	20 Oct, Dartmouth	Navigational aids program from Cambridge Bay to Spence Bay and icebreaker escort to shipping in Western Canadian Arctic. Because of propeller damage in heavy ice off Pt. Barrow, Alaska forced to transit the Northwest Passage to Dartmouth, N.S. for repair, and then proceed to Victoria via the Panama Canal.
CCGS DES GROSEILLIERS	31 May, Quebec City; 11 July, Quebec City	23 June, Quebec City; 20 Sept, Quebec City	1. Icebreaker support to M/V ARCTIC at Nanisivik 2. Icebreaker support to shipping in Hudson Strait - Lancaster Sound - Little Cornwallis Island
CCGS NORMAN MCLEOD RODGERS	4 July, Quebec City	27 Sept, Quebec City	Navigational aids Hudson Strait; icebreaker support to shipping in Hudson Strait and Bay and Foxe Basin

.../cont'd

Table 8.4 (cont'd)

Icebreaker	Sailing Date,	Return Date,	Mission
CCGS NARWHAL	21 July, Charlottetown	1 Oct, Charlottetown	Dedicated hydrographic survey in Eastern Hudson Bay
CCGS SIR JOHN FRANKLIN	12 Aug, St. John's	28 Oct, St. John's	Icebreaker support to shipping along East Baffin Island coast and aids deactivation program, Hudson Strait
CCGS PIERRE RADISSON	19 July, Quebec City	20 Oct, Quebec City	Icebreaker support to shipping in Hudson Strait - Barrow Strait - Cameron Island (Bent Horn)
CCGS JOHN A. MACDONALD	4 July, Dartmouth	24 Nov, Dartmouth	Icebreaker support to shipping in Lancaster Sound and resupply of weather station at Eureka. In Oct. accompanied USCGS POLAR STAR from Demarcation Point to Resolute.

Source: Canadian Coast Guard (1989)

Figure 8.6
Canadian Coast Guard Activity in the Arctic, 1988

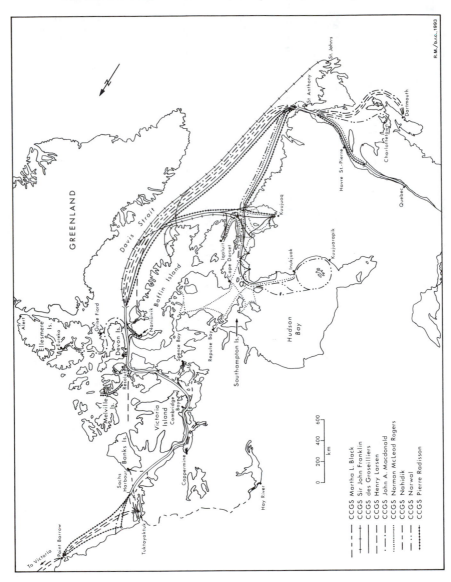

Source: Canadian Coast Guard (1989)

invested in the creation of very large ships that could operate year-round in the Arctic. None have been built, yet, but if and when they are constructed and put into operation, the Northwest Passage will indeed become an international shipping route. Canada will still claim that these waters belong to her, but with the projected increase in shipping, she had best be prepared to enforce these claims.

CONCLUSION

The objective of this book has been to illustrate the geography of change associated with Canadian water transportation and to suggest where these changes might lead. The changes have taken place in the activity of shipping to Canada; in the exports, imports and coastwise trading of the commodities themselves; and in the infrastructure associated with shipping—the waterways, the ships and the ports. Some specific changes are evident in those ports and regions presented here as "case studies."

Can all of these changes be summarized? Are there clues to the future of Canadian waterborne trade in the trends noted here? In what follows, the retrospective changes as discussed throughout the book are summarized, and prospective changes are suggested for Canadian water trade during years to come.

a) The Importance of Water Transportation and Waterborne Trade

i) Retrospect

- The water mode has lost ground relative to other modes in handling Canadian trade, especially exports. The loss has been to road transport in the USA trade, and air transport in the deep-sea trade. Still, though, about 80 per cent of all exports by value to the deep-sea trade go by water; but in the USA trade less than 4 per cent of exports are handled by water.

- International waterborne trade has grown at a faster rate than coastwise trade. Exports dominate imports; and the deep-sea trade has taken over from the USA trade as the most important component of international waterborne trade.

- Waterborne exports are dominated by dry bulk cargoes. This has not changed; what has changed is the destination of these exports. No longer are the markets dominated by the USA, or by Europe, or by Asia; rather Canadian exports are sent to all corners of the globe, much more so today than ever before.

- Waterborne imports also come from everywhere, but there is a pattern to their type depending on where they are destined in Canada. Atlantic coast and the Lower St. Lawrence region are dominated by crude oil, fuel oil, bauxite and alumina; the Great Lakes specialize in iron ore and coal imports; the Pacific coast receives no one single dominant import.

- Coastwise trading concentrates on bulk goods. The Atlantic coast and Lower St. Lawrence River, the Great Lakes and the Pacific coast contribute about equally to the total coasting trade, but different commodities dominate in each region.

Canada's prosperity depends on its ability to trade. As explained in Chapter 1, the value of exports and imports as a proportion of the Gross Domestic Product has increased over time. For this trade to proceed there must be an elaborate infrastructure of transportation and beyond the water mode. In fact, in the cross-border trade with the USA, the water mode has lost ground to the land-based transport, particularly road transport, because of the changing nature of the trade between Canada and the United States and vice versa. Water transport is best suited to the carriage of bulk goods, either wet or dry, that are not time-constrained; it does not cater well to high-priced manufactured goods, or goods that have time constraints upon their delivery. The increasing Canadian - American trade in semi-processed and processed consumer goods has not been handled by the water mode. Trucking has taken on enormous importance in this regard, mostly to the detriment of the railroads that traditionally handled automobile parts, clothing, electronic goods, and the myriad of manufactured goods passing across the border. Water transport in the cross-border trade continues to perform in its traditional capacity: it moves iron ore, coal, grains, fuel oil, chemicals, scrap metal, and all of the other raw or partially-processed resources that industry demands.

The deep-sea trade is the most significant to Canada's water trade success. There is little modal competition for moving goods across oceans and between continents. Air transport can cut into the market for moving highly valued, low-bulk and time-sensitive, or very fragile goods, and it has done so in a limited way; but the air mode is restricted in terms of what it can carry. For most trans-ocean, intercontinental trade, there really is very little alternative to the ship. Consequently, in the Canadian context, about 80 per cent of deep-sea exports (by value) go by ship. Again, the ship is best at carrying the bulky, low-value commodities, without time constraints, and it is these goods that Canada has in abundance, and is able to offer the world. Canadian deep-sea exports are dominated by grains, ores, coal and forest products. And since airplane competition is limited, most highly valued manufactured goods move by water also. Here is where containerization comes to the fore. Containerization has transformed the carriage of manufactured goods into a bulk operation. All containers, ships, port and land equipment needed to move the containers are standardized, designed to handle the contained goods as if they were bulk cargoes.

Canadian waterborne imports from overseas are also dominated by the bulk goods, as is the coastwise trade. Import and coastwise goods are not the same on all coasts, of course, but depend on the indigenous resources of the area and on the structure of the land-based transport system that competes with the water mode. For example, the import of crude petroleum is an East coast phenomenon; imports of coal and coastwise shipping of coal are concentrated on the Great Lakes; and the coastwise movement of logs is highly practiced on the Pacific coast.

ii) Prospect

The water mode will continue to play an essential role in Canada's deep-sea trade, but it is likely that the use of water transport will decline in the USA trade. Exports will continue to outperform imports, and container ports will survive. International waterborne commerce will continue to overshadow coastwise shipping, but the latter will remain essential to serve the needs of coastal communities and activities where there is no alternative.

In the deep-sea trade there is really no alternative to shipping. As long as Canada participates in an expanding world trade economy, then shipping will be in demand. It is difficult to foresee a time when Canadian world trade will be in decline; therefore, it is difficult to see a decline in the importance of Canada's water transportation industry. What is more difficult to surmise is the exact dimension of its trade with the world. What will be in demand? Where will the markets be? It is not feasible to undertake a detailed commodity analysis here in order to forecast future demand and markets for Canadian exports; but tradition dictates that Canada has always offered the world its raw materials, and as it continues to do so, water transportation will service this need. The fact that markets for Canadian exports have been internationalized over time means that Canada is not dependent on any one world region to absorb its exports. This augers well for the future. As the developed nations change from manufacturing-based to serviced-based economies, and as manufacturing is taken up by the developing nations, it is likely that the latter will increase their demand for resources used in the manufacturing process. Commodities such as iron ore, metal ores, coal, forest products will find their way to these newly industrializing nations; consequently, Canada's trade with these nations will increase. And, as these nations develop their industries, their products will be exported to countries around the world, including Canada.

There are, of course, a number of questions about future trade in Canada. What impact will the sustainable development concept have on the demand for Canadian resources? For example, will Canada continue to develop its natural resources in the same manner as in the past? Does it have that luxury? Will the discovery of raw material sources elsewhere in the world, new production processes, substitution of resources, or recycling of materials affect the traditional demand for Canadian resources? Will the developing nations be able to restructure their heavy debt load and so be able to undertake the massive investments necessary for the import of raw materials?

In the USA trade, water transportation will continue to be of little significance to Canada and it will continue to decline in importance when measured in terms of value of commodities carried. The foundation of Canadian - American cross-border waterborne trade is dry bulk goods, such as iron ore, coal and grains. The iron ore and coal trade depends on the health of the steel industry. No one foresees this industry expanding and demanding increased raw materials to feed it, which will become particularly damaging to the iron ore trade. Furthermore in the coal trade, Canadian coal is being substituted for American coal. The grain trade involves a trans-shipment and is confined to the Great Lakes and St. Lawrence River, where American grain passes through Canadian ports on its way to world markets. There will be little expansion of this trade because markets for such grain are not best reached through the East coast; the Mississippi waterway provides a better alternative to reach the markets. Even if these bulk trades expand more than is expected, or if other bulk trades develop (Canadian Arctic oil and gas to the USA, for example), their value is low when compared to processed consumer goods passing across the border via the other modes. There is little chance that the water mode will handle any increased trade in manufactured goods, either, because land-based transport has become specialized.

It is likely that Canadian waterborne trade, as measured by weight, will continue to be dominated by exports as opposed to imports; decline in exports of heavy bulk goods is unlikely, as is a significant increase in high weight imports. Consequently, the 2:1 ratio of exports to imports will be maintained or increased, according to the trends of the past thirty years.

It is worthwhile as well to speculate about the container trade passing through Canadian ports. Given the standardized and inter-modal nature of containers, the Canadian container trade is not limited to the Canadian transport infrastructure. The use of American ports and land-based transport is a viable alternative to using an entirely Canadian-based system of transportation. Consequently, Seattle and Tacoma are serious rivals to Vancouver; New York and Baltimore are competitive with Halifax and Montreal. Even Los Angeles and Oakland can be considered rivals to Vancouver and Halifax in the Central Canada - Asian trade. The future of Canadian ports maintaining, and attracting new, container business is not really in the hands of the ports, however, but lies instead with the shipping lines and their individual decisions about the number of ports of call needed to serve the vast North American market. The land-based transport system, with its ability to serve the inland markets, will also affect the container trade in Canada. The ports must be diligent in their level of service and competitive in their pricing, but these factors alone will not assure their success. Overall, then, it seems reasonable to expect that container traffic to and from Canadian destinations and origins will increase, but the benefit to Canadian ports is not guaranteed. Halifax, Montreal and Vancouver have been container ports of long standing, and "geographical inertia" may ensure their continued success. They have demonstrated their ability to handle the needs of their customers and, as long as they remain competitive, they will be able to keep these customers and attract new ones. Some loss is inevitable as customers rationalize their services or are attracted elsewhere by competitive pricing or service, but the demise of Canadian container ports is not anticipated. There is too much vested interest in the Canadian transport infrastructure, which goes beyond the ports themselves, to allow for this to happen.

Finally, little change is forecast for coastwise shipping. It will always place second to international shipping in terms of tonnage of commodities handled. The Canadian market is not large enough to generate a huge domestic transportation demand; nor is water transport the sole means by which Canadian transportation requirements are satisfied. However, for those existing demands in areas where water transport has the advantage over other modes of transport, it seems reasonable to suggest that coastwise shipping will continue to perform its essential role. Arctic shipping could take on a higher profile than it presently enjoys, depending on the market for oil and gas, and on whether water transport will be chosen as the mode by which these products reach southern markets.

b) Water Transportation Infrastructure (Waterways, Ships and Ports)

i) Retrospect

- Canada has an enormous coastal area available for commercial shipping. Due to navigation assistance, the monitoring of ship traffic, and regulations now in force, the navigation of ships in Canadian waters is gradually shifting away from ship's masters.

- The Canadian-registered merchant fleet is insignificant in world terms, as measured by tonnage, and is destined to remain so.

- Waterborne cargoes have become concentrated in fewer ports; ports on the Pacific coast outperform those in the East, especially those on the Great Lakes.

An elaborate transportation infrastructure, both land and water-based, serves the international and domestic needs of Canadian shippers and consumers. In the water trade context this infrastructure consists of waterways, ships and ports. Physically and geographically, the waterways today are much as they have been for centuries—notwithstanding the construction of the Seaway, harbour improvements (such as dredging), or the expansion of the actual size of the Canadian waterway, accomplished by the change of territorial sea limits from three to twelve miles. But the navigation infrastructure has changed greatly, as have the regulations overseeing this infrastructure; they are much more concerned with safe navigation and ship operations now, in order to prevent accidents and resultant environmental damage, than ever before.

As for ships, the Canadian merchant marine is geared to serve all domestic and international shipping demands on the Great Lakes, in the provision of passenger transport on the coasts, and in limited coastwise shipping (particularly in the Arctic); but in the deep-sea trade, Canadian shipping needs rest in the hands of the competitive marketplace.

Canada's ports are many, and they are diverse in the goods they handle; some are multi-functional, some are one dimensional. They may handle millions of tonnes of cargo, or they may handle less than one hundred. Chapter 3 has shown that there is an increasingly high concentration of cargoes in a handful of ports, and that the Pacific coast ports have outperformed those in the East, since the international focus of Canadian trade has shifted to the Pacific Ocean away from the Atlantic and as coastwise shipping of logs has become increasingly important.

ii) Prospect

The waterways themselves will not change; the Seaway, for example, will not be reconstructed to handle larger ships. But shipping regulations will be tightened even more, and the navigation infrastructure will be improved when funding is available. Ship traffic control will approach air traffic control in its style of operation, with ships proceeding where they are told to go. The Canadian merchant marine will remain insignificant in the world; it is unlikely that there will be construction of new Great Lakes vessels, since the demand for shipping in the Great Lakes would not justify them. There may be a need for Arctic class ships in the future, but to forecast when they might appear is impossible to do. Ports will continue to fulfil their many functions, and the concentration of cargoes in few ports will be a continuing and even increasing trend. Vancouver will continue as Canada's premier port; Prince Rupert will continue to take on an increasing role as a gateway for Western Canadian resources to reach world, and Asian markets in particular. Competition amongst and between ports will continue as shippers attempt to get the best service and price possible. New port construction is unlikely; existing ports will improve their facilities as the demand warrants, instead.

Of these prospects, those of with the greatest "import" are the tightened regulations for ship operations and the related attempt of officials to better control where ships go. Such developments will help to prevent ship accidents and environmental damage. No one wants an EXXON VALDEZ to occur in Canadian waters. But in order to prevent such an incident, better ships should be built, more competent people should operate them and, ultimately, strict control of their passage should be in place. The greatest risk of shipping accidents exists in ice conditions; thus, shipping in the Gulf of St. Lawrence during the winter season will come under increasing scrutiny, and if ships do operate in the Arctic on a regular basis, they will do so under very strict control. Because of heightened public awareness of marine accidents and their environmental impact, very strong recommendation was made by the Public Review Panel on Tanker Safety urging that crude oil tanker traffic in the Arctic be prohibited. Of course, the best way to minimize environmental damage from a marine accident is to prevent the ship from operating in the first place. Barring this drastic measure, which would extinguish the Canadian water transport industry and severely damage, if not destroy, the national economy, ships should be under greater control than they are at present.

c) The Functioning of the Infrastructure (The Case Studies)

i) Retrospect

- Containerization has been a challenge for Saint John and Halifax, and the latter has been the more successful port; but containerization at Halifax must still contend with competition from other ports, notably New York, Montreal and even Los Angeles.

- The Montreal waterfront epitomizes the challenges faced by ports and their cities, as they struggle to come to grips with the changing demands on the city-port waterfront.

- The Seaway is outmoded and not able to cope with modern larger vessels, and maintenance costs are rising. Its future is uncertain.

- Cruise shipping is a recent development in the industry that has placed new demands on ports. Vancouver has succeeded because of geopolitics; it is doubtful if other Canadian ports will have the same success.

• Shipping in the Arctic is carried out for commercial purposes, and has a long-standing history; its monitoring supports Canada's claim to the waters of the archipelago.

The case studies illustrate that the operation of water transportation in Canada has far reaching implications that must be studied in a number of ways. In all cases, the operation's relation to geography has been established. In the Halifax and Saint John comparison, geography plays a role in accounting for Halifax's relative success. In the Montreal case, the development of the port is actually changing the geography of the city-port waterfront. The construction of the Seaway implemented major changes to the geography of the St. Lawrence River, and the use of the Seaway has brought about changing trade patterns. The cruise industry in Vancouver has developed as a result of geography; the port's proximity to Alaska, and geopolitics that have forced non-American cruise lines to use a Canadian port have been contributing factors. Finally, the use of the Arctic archipelago waterways for and by commercial shipping is one of the main reasons Canada is able to claim these waters as its own, and thereby define the geography of Canadian territory.

The case studies also display the various challenges that the shipping industry faces in its operation. Competition between ports, conflict in land use, changing trade patterns, the development of new port activity and economic and political objectives of shipping have been exemplified in these studies.

ii) Prospect

The geography of Canadian water transportation will continue to evolve and challenges to the industry will continue to arise. Nothing is ever static in the shipping world.

The relationship between water transportation and geography is symbiotic. On the one hand, water transportation has an impact on the physical and human environment, but that environment also affects water transportation. For example, on the physical side, waterways are altered to accommodate shipping; the construction of elaborate port facilities changes forever the natural landscape; and pollution from a tanker accident has devastating effects on bird and fish population. Water transportation affects the human environment, too: ports attract certain types of industry that may drive down land values in their immediate vicinity, for example. The reverse effect, that of the environment on water transportation, includes disruptions in ship operations caused by fog or ice; but it also determines where port facilities are located, since deep water and room for expansion are criteria for such sites.

This relationship between water transportation and the environment is dynamic. Geography has much to study in this regard: the changing infrastructure associated with water transportation, the changing trading patterns, and the changing impacts of water transportation on its environs will require continual analysis. This book has attempted to outline some of the overlapping considerations of geography, water transportation and change. What is fascinating about a study of this sort is that it is continually evolving; the changes discussed here have occurred, but they are not final. There will always be a new geography to study as the future unfolds.

BIBLIOGRAPHY

Abbott R. and Z. Mockus (1986) *The Coasting Trade of Eastern Canada.* Ottawa: Canadian Transport Commission, WP20–86–09.

Acres International Ltd. (1987) *Mackenzie River Economic Study.* Vancouver: Acres International Ltd. for Canadian Coast Guard.

Allen, G. (1982) "Finally, Montrealers get their waterfront back." *Montreal Gazette*, 28 August: B6.

Anon (1969) "An inquiry into traffic separation at sea." *The Journal of the Institute of Navigation* 22.3, 342–349.

Archambault, M. (1986) *Recent Trends in Canadian and American Trade through Each Other's Ports.* Ottawa: Canadian Transportation Commission, Research Branch, Transport Industries Analysis, WP 20–86–15.

Arctec Incorporated (1979) *Executive Summary: SS Manhatten Arctic Marine Project.* Columbia, Md.: Arctec Inc.

Association/Le Vieux Port (1979) *A Redevelopment Stategy for Le Vieux-Port de Montréal.* Montreal: Association/Le Vieux Port.

Atlantic Provinces Transportation Commission (1972–1990) *Directory of Ocean Shipping Services between the Ports of Saint John-Halifax and World Ports* (published intermittently since 1972). Moncton: Atlantic Provinces Transportation Commission.

_____ (1991) "CP purchase of the Delaware and Hudson." *Tips and Topics* 31 (1), 2.

Beauchamp, K. (1985) *Port Policy for the Canadian Arctic Coast.* Ottawa: Canadian Arctic Resources Committee, Policy Paper 1.

Beth, H., A. Kader and R. Kappel (1984) *25 Years of World Shipping.* London: Fairplay Publications.

Boudreau, M. (1989) Personnal telephone communication with General Manager, Northern Stores Inc. 2 May 1989.

British Columbia Ferry Corporation (n.d.) "A Little Bit of our History." Victoria: British Columbia Ferry Corporation.

Brown M. and M. Brooks (n.d.) "Changing hinterlands for Eastern Canadian ports: 1978–1981" (mimeograph). Halifax: Canadian Marine Transportation Centre.

Canada Ports Corporation (1989) *Competitive Strategies for Canada's Transportation System*. Ottawa: Canada Ports Corporation, Corporate Services.

_____ (1991a) *The Economic Impact of the Ports Canada System*. Ottawa: Canada Ports Corporation, Corporate Services.

_____ (1991b) *Towards a Canadian Intermodal System: Recommendations for Change*. Ottawa: Canada Ports Corporation.

Canada. Consolidated Regulations of Canada (1978) Shipping Safety Control Zone Order. *Arctic Waters Pollution Prevention Act.*, Chapter 356, 2283–2289.

Canada. Regional Industrial Expansion (1988) "Ottawa confirms its participation to the development of the Vieux-Port de Montréal." News release, 30 September.

Canada. Revised Statutes of Canada (1970 1st Supplement) *Arctic Waters Pollution Prevention Act*, Chapter 2, 3–25.

Canada Yearbook (1990) Ottawa: Statistics Canada.

Canadian Coast Guard (1979) "Chronology of Marine Operations in the Canadian Arctic" (mimeo). Ottawa: CCG, Public Affairs Branch.

_____ (1988) *Report of Eastern Arctic Sealift Including Pacer Basin/DEW, 1988*. Ottawa: Coast Guard Northern, TP 2506 (1988).

_____ (1989a) *Notices to Mariners, 1 to 43* (Annual). Ottawa: Minister of Supply and Services Canada, T1–5/1989E.

_____ (1989b) Unpublished material on icebreaker operations available from Coast Guard Northern, Arctic Operations, Ottawa.

_____ (1990) *Canada Shipping Act*. Ottawa: Minister of Supply and Services Canada, YX76–S9/1990.

_____ (1991) International Regulations for Preventing Collisions at Sea, 1972, with Canadian Modifications, in *Collision Regulations*. Ottawa: Minister of Supply and Services, 1991.

Canadian Encyclopedia, 2nd edition (1988) Edmonton: Hurtig.

Canadian Hydrographic Service (1985) *Sailing Directions, Gulf and River St. Lawrence*, 6th edition. Ottawa: Minister of Supply and Services Canada, FS 72–16/1985E.

_____ (1986) Sailing Directions, Great Lakes, Volume 1, 10th edition. Ottawa: Minister of Supply and Services Canada, 10th Edition, Fs 72–3/1986–1E.

Canadian Minerals Yearbook (1969) Ottawa: Energy, Mines and Resources Canada.

_____ (1974) Ottawa: Energy, Mines and Resources Canada.

_____ (1981) Ottawa: Energy, Mines and Resources Canada.

_____ (1985) Ottawa: Energy, Mines and Resources Canada.

_____ (1990) Ottawa: Energy, Mines and Resources Canada.

Canadian Ports and Seaway Directory (1986) Don Mills, Ontario: Southam.

Canadian Sailings (1988) "New $12 million container terminal for Port of Quebec." 28 November.

Canadian Shipowners Association (1988) *Annual Report.* Ottawa: Canadian Shipowners Association.

Canadian Transport Commission (1978) *The Transport Act: Regulation of the Mackenzie River.* Ottawa: Water Transport Committee.

_____ (1983) *The Role of Churchill in the Transportation System for Northern Canada.* Ottawa: Research Branch, 1983/03E.

_____ (1984) *Canadian Exports of General Cargo and Port Activity in Eastern Canada.* Ottawa: Canadian Transport Commission, Research Branch, No. 1984/05E.

_____ (1987) "Commercial Water Transportation on the Mackenzie River and in the Western Arctic." Unpublished draft report. Ottawa: Water Transport Committee.

Canadian Wheat Board (1967–68) *Annual Report.* Winnipeg: Canadian Wheat Board.

_____ (1974–75) *Annual Report.* Winnipeg: Canadian Wheat Board.

_____ (1989–90) *Annual Report.* Winnipeg: Canadian Wheat Board.

Canarctic Shipping Co. (1990) Personal letter from A. R. Sneyd, General Manager, Business Development, Canarctic Shipping Co. Ltd., Ottawa, 6 June 1990.

Carey, B. (1987) "Life is good at the port of Montreal." *American Shipper* (January), 28, 30.

Carter, C. (1986) "Projecting Future Grain Flows," in *The Future of the Great Lakes-St. Lawrence Seaway System,* D.A. Leitch, ed., 27–30. Winnipeg: University of Manitoba Transport Institute, Occasional Paper No. 2.

Chamber of Shipping of British Columbia (1988) "Submission to the Senate Standing Committee on Transport and Communication re: Bill C–52 Coasting Trade and Commercial Marine Activities Act." With letter signed by Richard C. Stevens, Executive Director, Chamber of Shipping of British Columbia, dated 24 May 1988.

Charlier, J. (1989) "Miami, capitale mondiale des croisièrs." *Transports,* 337 (Septembre—Octobre).

Chevrier, L. (1959) *The St. Lawrence Seaway.* Toronto: Macmillan.

Clark, J. (1988) "Government committed to Arctic sovereignty." *Calgary Herald,* 15 January: A5.

Containerization International Yearbook (1978) London: National Magazine

Co. Ltd.

_____ (1991) London: National Magazine Co. Ltd.

Côté, M-Y (1987) "Port de Montréal Plan Directeur." Présentation à l'Honorable Marc-Yvan Côté, Ministre des Transports du Québec, le 30 Novembre 1987 (présenté par la direction de la planification et développement).

Couper, A. (1983) *The Times Atlas of the Oceans*. London: Van Nostrand Reinhold Co.

Crowley, W. (1991) "Putting cruise ships in Seattle." *Tradelines (Port of Seattle U.S.A.)* (Winter), 6–7.

Cruise Industry Task Force (1988) *Cruise Industry Marketing Plan*, San Francisco: San Francisco Port Authority.

Dagenais, M. and Martin F. (1985) *Forecasting Containerized Traffic for the Port of Montreal (1981–1995)*. Montréal: Département de Science Économique et Centre de Recherche et Développement en Économique, Cahier 8504, Université de Montréal.

de Silva, K.E.A. (1988) "An Economic Analysis of the Shipbuilding Industry Assistance Program." *Discussion Paper No. 351*. Ottawa: Economic Council of Canada.

Dominion Marine Association (1968) *Annual Report*. Ottawa: Dominion Marine Association.

Don Ference & Associates (1988) *B.C. Cruise Industry Development Strategy*. Victoria and Ottawa: Canada - British Columbia Tourist Industry Development Subsidiary Agreement.

Erickson, P. (1986) "Outlook on Canadian Grain Exports through the St. Lawrence River," in *The Future of the Great Lakes-St. Lawrence Seaway System*, D.A. Leitch, ed., 19–26. Winnipeg: University of Manitoba Transport Institute, Occasional Paper No. 2.

Federal Environmental Assessment Review Office (1980) *Arctic Pilot Project (Northern Component) Report of the Environmental Assessment Panel*. Ottawa: FEARO.

_____ (1989) "Terms of Reference for the Montreal Port Expansion Project Environmental Assessment Panel." Ottawa: Environment Canada, FEARO.

Financial Post (1967) "For Halifax, not a bird, not a plane but superfreighter." 24 June: M2.

_____ (1968a) "Port fights back for winter trade." 20 April: J7 (microfiche).

_____ (1968b) "Crown Corporation to push Halifax as container port." 23 November: 43 (microfiche).

_____ (1969) "Rivalry prompts Saint John to drop out of Port Day." 15 February: 2 (microfiche).

Fleming, D.K. (1989) "On the beaten track: a view of West Coast container port competition." *Maritime Policy and Management* 16(2), 93–107.

Fraser River Estuary Management Program (1991) *Log Management in the Fraser River Estuary*. Vancouver: Report of the Log Management Activity Workgroup.

Gary Duke & Associates (1988) *Economic Benefits to Canada from Alaska Cruise Industry*. Vancouver.

Ghonima, H. (1986) "The future of the Seaway Traffic," in *The Future of the Great Lakes-St. Lawrence Seaway System*, D.A. Leitch, ed., 1–18. Winnipeg: University of Manitoba Transport Institute, Occasional Paper No. 2.

Gilmour, J. (1982) "Jurisdiction in Canadian Waters - Unresolved Issues," in *The Challenge of the Eighties*, Proceedings of the Northern Transportation Conference, Whitehorse, Yukon, 5–7 October, 163–168.

Globe and Mail (1991) "Foreign shipowners to receive tax break." 22 February: B6

Griffiths, F. (1987) *Politics of the Northwest Passage*. Kingston and Montreal: McGill-Queen's University Press.

Halifax-Dartmouth Port Development Commission (1986) *Port of Halifax Directory*. Halifax: Halifax-Dartmouth Port Development Commission.

Harris, L. (1983) "White elephant feared if port expanded to Contrecoeur." *Montreal Gazette*, 14 December: C3.

Hodgson, R. (1986) "A Canadian Government Perspective," in *The Future of the Great Lakes-St. Lawrence Seaway System*, D.A. Leitch, ed., 155–159. Winnipeg: University of Manitoba Transport Institute, Occasional Paper No. 2.

Hoyle, B. et al (1988) *Revitalizing the Waterfront. International Dimensions of Dockland Redevelopment*. London: Belhaven Press.

Hoyle, B. (1988) "Development dynamics at the port-city interface," in *Revitalizing the waterfront: International Dimensions of Dockland Redevelopment*, B. Hoyle, D. Pinder and M. Husain, eds., 3–19. London: Belhaven Press.

International Maritime Organization (1984) *Ships' Routeings*, 5th edition. London: IMO.

Japan Statistical Yearbook (1990) Tokyo: Statistics Bureau, Management and Coordination Agency.

Kirton, J. and Munton, D. (1987) "The MANHATTEN Voyages and Their Aftermath," in *Politics of the Northwest Passage*, F. Griffiths, ed., 67–97. Kingston and Montreal: McGill-Queen's University Press.

Koring, P. (1988) "Canada grants permission for entry of US icebreaker." *Globe and Mail*, 7 October: A10.

_____(1989) "Bouchard delays plans for Polar 8 as cost rises." *Globe and Mail*, 8 May: A1, A6.

_____(1990) "POLAR 8 founders on shoals of Tory cuts." *Globe and Mail*, 21 February: A10.

Kucharsky, D. (1988) "Keep port expansion in Montreal: executive." *This Week in Business,* 14 May: 25.

Lake, R. and D. Hackston (1990) *The Great Lakes/Seaway Enters the Nineties.* Toronto: The Research and Traffic Group for Marine Office, (Ontario) Ministry of Transportation.

LBA Consulting Partners (1978) *The Seaway in Winter: A Benefit-Cost Study.* Ottawa.

Le Comité de la Promenade Bellerive (1988) "Expansion du Port: Manque de Transparence de l'Administration Portuaire." Press release, 30 Août.

Lecours, L. (1988a) "Le Port n'insisterait pas pour s'emparer de la Promenade Bellerive!" *Flambeau de l'Est,* 30 Août: 2, 3.

_____ (1988b) "La Ville de Montréal maintient sa position: 'Cet espace vert est une chose réglée pour la Ville'", *Flambeau de l'Est,* 30 Août: 3.

Leitch, D., ed. (1986) *The Future of the Great Lakes-St. Lawrence Seaway System.* Winnipeg: University of Manitoba Transport Institute, Occasional Paper No. 2.

Le Vieux-Port de Montréal (1988) *Preliminary Master Plan.* Montreal: Societé de Vieux-Port de Montréal.

Lloyd's Ports of the World (1989) Colchester, England: Lloyd's of London Press.

London, M. (1982) "On the waterfront: The fight for Montreal's Vieux-Port." *Canadian Heritage* 38 (December), 20–21, 23.

Lotz, J. (1974) "The container box on the East coast." *Canadian Business* (October), 25–28, 30.

Luce, M.P. (1985) "The M.V. ARCTIC operational perspective." *Seaports and the Shipping World* (November), 24–25.

The Mail-Star (1967) "Promotes welfare of the Port of Halifax." 5 December: 15–16 (microfiche).

_____ (1982) "Port's problems may spell good news for Halifax." 13 September: 6–P (microfiche).

_____ (1986a) "Saint John to lose two more shipping lines." 25 January: 26 (microfiche).

_____ (1986b) "Halterm's business is up 60 per cent." 5 September: 50 (microfiche).

Marcus, H. (1987) *Marine Transportation Management.* London: Croom Helm.

Marine Atlantic (1991) Personal interview with, and letter from, Ted Bartlett, Manager, Public Relations, 3 July and 16 July, respectively.

Martin, D. (1985) "Arctic Port waits in wings." *Calgary Herald,* 21 August: D1.

Mason, J. (1990) "Waves from Halifax." *Seaports and the Shipping World* (September), 25.

McCalla, R. (1982) "Canadian Port Administration: its future structure." *Maritime Policy and Management,* 9 (4), 279–293.

Misener Shipping Co. (1990) Personal communication with David K. Gardiner, President, Misener Shipping, St. Catharines, Ont. 16 May.

Montgomery, G. (1981) *An Evaluation of the Tourism Potential of the Cruise Ship Industry of British Columbia.* Victoria and Ottawa: Canada - British Columbia Travel Industry Development Subsidiary Agreement.

Moore, G. (1986) "The Economics of Using West Coast Terminals for Moving Grain to Export," in *The Future of the Great Lakes-St. Lawrence Seaway System*, D.A. Leitch, ed., 114–128. Winnipeg: University of Manitoba Transport Institute, Occasional Paper No. 2.

National Transportation Agency of Canada (1992) *Annual Review 1991.* Ottawa: NTA.

National Transportation Agency and Canadian Transport Commission (1968–1988) *Canadian Merchant Fleet*, List A. Ottawa: NTA and CTC.

Northern Transportation Company Limited (1971) *Annual Report.* Edmonton.

Nossal, K. (1987) "Polar Icebreakers: The Politics of Inertia," in *Politics of the Northwest Passage*, F. Griffiths, ed., 216–240. Kingston and Montreal: McGill-Queen's University Press.

OECD (1989) *Maritime Transport, 1988.* Paris: Organization for Economic Cooperation and Development.

_____ (1993) *Maritime Transport, 1991.* Paris: Organization for Economic Cooperation and Development.

Official Airline Guides (1990) *Worldwide Cruise and Shipline Guide, March–April 1990.* Oak Brook, Illinois: OAG.

Oland, P. (1969) "Container Port: Saint John." *Atlantic Advocate* (December), 21–23.

Oudet, L. (1979) "Routeing at Sea." *The Journal of Navigation* 32 (1), 53–74.

Peritz, I. (1987) "Old Port plan would cost $481 million." *Montreal Gazette,* 6 April: A1, A2.

Peters, T. (1991) "CN to double-stack rail container cars." *The Chronicle-Herald,* 17 August: A1, A2.

Pharand, D. (1984) *The Northwest Passage: Arctic Straits.* Dordrecht: Martinus Nijoff Publishers, in association with L. Legault.

_____ (1988) *Canada's Arctic Waters in International Law.* Cambridge: Cambridge University Press.

Public Review Panel on Tanker Safety and Marine Spills Response Capability (1990) *Protecting our Waters.* Ottawa: Minister of Supply and Services Canada, EN21–91/1990E.

Pullen, T. (1983) "Arctic Marine Transportation: A View from the Bridge," in National and Regional Interests in the North, Canadian Arctic Resources Committee (Proceedings of the Third National Workshop on People,

Resources and the Environment North of 60°, Yellowknife, NWT, 1–3 June), 587–597. Ottawa: CARC

Port of Montreal (1988a) "The transformation of the port of Montreal since its entry into the containerized shipping market." Unpublished. Montreal: Port of Montreal.

_____ (1988b) Unpublished Speech by Mr. Ronald Corey, Chairman of the Board, Montreal Port Corporation, at the Press Conference on the Development Strategy Horizon 2010, 24 August. Montreal: Port of Montreal.

_____ (1988c) Unpublished Speech by Mr. Dominic J. Taddeo, General Manager and Chief Executive Officer, Montreal Port Corporation, at the Press Conference on the Development Strategy, Horizon 2010, 24 August. Montreal: Port of Montreal.

Port of Saint John (1990) Personal interview with P. Clark, Director of Marketing, Port of Saint John, 9 July.

Reid, R. (1974) "The Canadian Claim to Sovereignty Over the Waters of the Arctic." *The Canadian Yearbook of International Law* 12, 111–136.

Report of the Royal Commission on Pilotage (1968–1970a) Part IV (1970) Ottawa: Queen's Printer, Gulf and St. Lawrence.

_____ (1968–1970b) Part III (1969). Ottawa: Queen's Printer, Atlantic Provinces.

Rimmer, P. (1966) "The Status of Ports – a method of comparative evaluation." *The Dock and Harbour Authority*, xlvii (547), 2–7.

Robertson, R. (1988) "US ports step up efforts to gain Canadian traffic." *Canadian Transportation and Distribution Management* (June), 41.

Robusky, R. C. (1988) "Churchill: The Port on Canada's Other Ocean." *Portus* (Summer), 34–35.

Ryan, Leo (1989) "Shipping is Canada's forgotten industry: CSL chief." *This Week in Business,* 24 June: 11.

Sadler, C. (1991a) "Port of Halifax's weak link rail service – shipping exec." *The Daily News,* 14 February: 22.

_____ (1991b) "Port losing to Montreal in cargo shift." *The Daily News,* 18 May: 3.

St. Lawrence Seaway Authority (1975) *Annual Report.* Ottawa: St. Lawrence Seaway Authority.

_____ (1977) *The Seaway: Operations, Outlook and Statistics.* Ottawa: St. Lawrence Seaway Authority.

_____ (1983) "Position paper on navigation season extension,"4 August (mimeo). Ottawa: St. Lawerence Seaway Authority, Planning and Development Division.

_____ (1977–1990) *Annual Reports.* Ottawa: St. Lawrence Seaway Authority.

_____ (1990) *The Seaway Traffic Report.* Ottawa: St. Lawrence Seaway

Authority.

Schenker, E., H. Mayer and H. Brockel (1976) *The Great Lakes Transportation System*. University of Wisconsin Sea Grant College Program, Technical Report 230.

Seaports and the Shipping World (1984) "Large Topping-Off of Coal a Big Success" (March), 34.

Semanak, S. (1986) "Turn Old Port into public haven by 1992: report." *Montreal Gazette,* 9 May: A1, A6.

Senate of Canada (1982) "The Department of Transport Brief to The Special Committee of the Senate on the Northern Pipeline," Vol 30A. Ottawa: June 1982.

_____ (1983) *Marching to the Beat of the Same Drum: Transportation of Petroleum and Natural Gas North of 60°*. Ottawa: Queen's Printer.

Shaw, Gordon C. (1978) "Changes in Canadian Great Lakes Shipping Since the Opening of the St. Lawrence Seaway in 1959," in the Proceedings of the 19th Annual Meeting, Transportation Research Forum, 571–591. Oxford, Indiana: Richard B. Cross Co.

Slack, B. (1989) "Gateway or Cul-de-Sac? The St. Lawrence River and Eastern Canadian Container Traffic." *Etudes Canadiennes* 26, 49–55.

Stallard, G. (1986) "West Coast report: good news and bad," in *Fairplay Cruise Review*, 27–29. London: Fairplay Publications.

Statistical Abstract of the United States (1990) Washington: U.S. Bureau of the Census.

Statistics Canada (13–210) *National Income and Expenditures Accounts* (annual). Ottawa: Statistics Canada.

_____ (54–202) *Shipping Report, Part 1, International Seaborne Shipping (by country)* (annual, ceased in 1977). Ottawa: Statistics Canada

_____ (54–203) *Shipping Report, Part II, International Seaborne Shipping (by port)* (annual, ceased in 1977).Ottawa: Statistics Canada

_____ (54–204) *Shipping Report, Part III, Coastwise Shipping* (annual, ceased in 1977) Ottawa: Statistics Canada .

_____ (54–205) *Shipping in Canada* (annual beginning in 1986) Ottawa: Statistics Canada

_____(54–209) *International Seaborne Shipping Statistics* (annual, 1980–1985) Ottawa: Statistics Canada.

_____ (54–210) *Coastwise Shipping Statistics* (annual, 1978–1985) Ottawa: Statistics Canada .

_____ (54–211) *International Seaborne Shipping Port Statistics* (annual 1980–1983) Ottawa: Statistics Canada.

_____ (65–202) *Exports, Merchandise Trade* (annual) Ottawa: Statistics Canada.

_____ (65–203) *Imports, Merchandise Trade* (annual) Ottawa: Statistics

Canada.

_____(1989) Special ranking of ports handling international and coastwise cargo for 1989, Unpublished.

Sussman, G. (1978) *The St. Lawrence Seaway: History and Analysis of a Joint Waterway Highway.* Montreal: C.D. Howe Institute and Washington: National Planning Association.

Temple, Barker & Sloane (1988) *Port of Halifax Double-Stack Train Feasibility Study* (Final Report prepared for the Port of Halifax). Lexington, Ma.: Temple, Barker & Sloane, Inc.

The Consultative Committee on the Old Port of Montreal (1985) *The Old Port of Montreal Public Consultation: Background Information Summary.* Montreal: The Consultative Committee on the Old Port of Montreal.

_____ (1986) *The Old Port of Montreal Public Consultation: Final Report 1986.* Montreal: The Consultative Committee on the Old Port of Montreal.

Thiele, J. (1989) "US cruise ports reach for the top." *Marine Log* (February), 43, 45.

Toronto Star (1985) "Arctic Straits not for Soviets, US Envoy States." 2 August: A1, A4.

Tourism Canada (1988) *Profile of Eastern Canadian Cruise Industry.* Ottawa: Gary Duke & Associates and Don Ference & Associates.

Transport Canada (1979) *A Shipping Policy for Canada.* Ottawa: Minister of Supply and Services Canada, TP 1676.

_____ (1985) *Task Force on Deep-Sea Shipping. Report to the Minister of Transport.* Ottawa: Minister of Supply and Services Canada, T22–68/1985E.

_____ (1988) *Transportation Survey of Northern Canada. Revised Summary Report.* Ottawa: Policy and Coordination, Economic Research.

Tunbridge, J. (1988) "Policy convergence on the waterfront? A comparative assessment of North American revitalisation strategies," in *Revitalising the Waterfront: International Dimensions of Dockland Redevelopment*, B.S. Hoyle, D.A. Pinder and M.S. Husain, eds., 67–91. London: Belhaven Press.

ULS Marbulk Inc. (1990) Personal letter from R. Abraham, Manager, Marketing, ULS Marbulk Inc., Salem, MA, 26 July.

Urquart, M. and K. Buckley (1965) *Historical Statistics of Canada.* Cambridge: Cambridge University Press.

Verbatim Record and Documents (1977) Proceedings of the Western Economic Opportunities Conference, Calgary, Alberta, July 24–26, 1973. Ottawa: Supply and Services Canada.

Wallace, I. (1975) "Containerization at Canadian Ports." *Annals of the Association of American Geographers* 65 (3), 433–48.

Webb, K. (1978) "A ship for all seasons." *North/Nord* (May/June), 20–27.

Whittaker, S.(1983) "How to give waterfront back to people." *Montreal Gazette,* 11 June: B1.

Zwann, J. (1989) Personal letter from J. Zwann, for Superintendent, Cargoes and Containers, Canadian Coast Guard, Ottawa. 18 May.

INDEX

SUBJECTS

SHIPS